COMMUNICATING ANTHROPOSOPHY

RUDOLF STEINER (1915)

COMMUNICATING ANTHROPOSOPHY

The Course for Speakers to Promote the Idea of Threefolding

Twelve lectures and a question-and-answer session
held in Stuttgart
January 1–2, and February 12–17, 1921

TRANSLATED BY RORY BRADLEY

INTRODUCTION BY CHRISTOPHER BAMFORD

RUDOLF STEINER

SteinerBooks

CW 338

SteinerBooks
Anthropsophic Press

610 Main Street
Great Barrington, Massachusetts 01230
www.steinerbooks.org

Original translation from the German by Rory Bradley.

This book is volume 338 in the Collected Works (CW) of Rudolf Steiner, published by SteinerBooks, 2015. It is a translation of the German edition *Wie wirkt man für den Impuls der Dreigliederung des sozialen Organismus?* published by Rudolf Steiner Verlag, Dornach, Switzerland, 1986.

ISBN: 978-1-62148-125-6
eBook ISBN: 978-1-62148-045-7

On the publication of Rudolf Steiner's lectures

The written works of Rudolf Steiner are the foundation of anthroposophical spiritual science. In addition to the books he wrote, Steiner also offered numerous lectures and courses, both public and private, between 1900 and 1924, intended specifically for members of the Theosophical (later Anthroposophical) Society. Initially he did not want his lectures to be set down in writing, since they were intended as "verbal communications not meant for print." But after an increasing number of incomplete and erroneous transcripts of these lectures were printed and distributed by attendees, it became clear that he needed to regulate the publication process. He entrusted this task to Marie Steiner-von Sivers. It was incumbent upon her to arrange for the stenographers and to oversee the entire process. Since there was never enough time for Rudolf Steiner to correct the transcripts himself, except in a very few instances, his disclaimer must be taken into consideration in regard to all of his published lectures: "It must simply be accepted that errors are to be found in the drafts, which I have not looked through myself." After the death of Marie Steiner in 1948, work on a collected edition of all of Rudolf Steiner's writings and lectures began, in keeping with her guidelines. This volume is part of these collected works. Notes on the training course for speakers from Notebook, Archive No. 50 and "An Appeal for the Rescue of Upper Silesia," which was published in *The Coming Day,* are also included.

CONTENTS

II
Training Course for Upper Silesians

Lecture 1

STUTTGART, JANUARY 1, 1921

The necessity for activists to not cling to old categories of public life; substance and true content rather than slogans. Knowledge of the threefold downfall as demonstrated by examples from spiritual-cultural and political life. On the problem of whether Upper Silesians should be Polish or German. Poland as the area of conflict between influences from the East and West, taking into account the historical changes in social structure in Germany, Russia, and Austria. The three streams that form the Polish element. Reasons for dividing Poland between Prussia, Austria, and Russia. The spiritual influence of Russia, the rights-political influence of Austria, and the economic influence of Prussia on Poland. Poland's fate from the perspective of this threefold division. From Europe's threefold downfall to its threefold rise.

Lecture 2

STUTTGART, JANUARY 2, 1921

Illusions about Europe's future. The necessity of enlightenment in regard to all world relationships. The illusion of an accord between Middle and Eastern Europe with the West on the basis of old relationships as the stumbling block for the vote in Upper Silesia. Critical remarks on three suggestions for the modernization of economic relationships in Europe: further expansion of American credit, credit from individuals, a global economic organization connected to the League of Nations. Results of the annexation of Silesia by Prussian Germany. On the illusionary imagination of J. M. Keynes and N. Angell that the American economy is dependent upon the European economy. The possibility of leaving Europe to its fate. The absurdity of a vote in Upper Silesia. The "threefold" evolution of the Polish lower class. The transformation of the labor movement in Central Europe into a middle-class movement. On the living conditions of Bolshevism and their impact on the West. Reasons for a second World War: economic relationships and the defense against Bolshevism. On the increasing conflicts between Asia and America. The necessity of having sufficient clarity about the threefold social organism, and the development of spiritual leadership as the task of Central Europe. The task of the Germans as

INTRODUCTION

From time to time, reading Rudolf Steiner's Collected Works, one encounters a previously unknown set of lectures with a stated theme (that one might not have thought of as being of particular interest), but then one discovers various sub-themes that unexpectedly spark new insights not only into anthroposophy but also Rudolf Steiner, who suddenly stands before one in a new light. In such cases, in the course of reading, we come across a passage or a lecture that illuminates, challenges, and ultimately transforms what we think we know, changing our perspective. Often, the most powerful examples of these moments come about not through the presentation of any new or startling piece of esoteric "information," but rather through something quite simple, even obvious. Once we see it, it forces us to rethink or reframe everything we thought we knew. At the same time, without anticipating it, we also sense in a new way Rudolf Steiner's presence, his humanity, as well as the extraordinary depth of subtlety, insight and prodigious learning with which he was able to permeate and illumine in a living, accessible way the findings of his spiritual research. Our view of who he was, and what anthroposophy is, becomes different. The richness of what he said, and the tone and depth of feeling implicit in how he did so, acts to transform what otherwise might merely reinforce what we think we know. Our habitual understanding falls away and we grasp that what we are reading is not information or description, but a call to act differently. Thereby we become no longer simply readers, but participants in the adventure of anthroposophy. We feel that a far-seeing friend is addressing us out of a deep well of realism, experience, and practical wisdom that significantly transforms and amplifies our understanding of anthroposophy and ourselves.

All this despite the fact that, as in this case, the description of the occasion and origin of the lectures seems to promise no more than a rather specialized content, of interest primarily to those concerned with its apparent theme—here a preparatory course for those about to embark on a speaking tour to promote the "threefolding" of society. At first glance, such a description cannot but appear dry, and perhaps even dated, to those whose interests lie elsewhere. Appearances, however, are often deceptive, and at least to contemporary eyes, this volume presents readers with something quite different.

Factually, the background is as follows. *Chronologically first*, but printed second, there are two lectures given in Stuttgart (January 1-2, 1921), where the Union for Social Threefolding was headquartered, at the request of, and to, some anthroposophists from Breslau in Upper Silesia, who had written seeking guidance in a last-ditch attempt to interject threefold ideas into the political discussions surrounding the upcoming referendum—as mandated by the Treaty of Versailles—to determine whether Upper Silesia would remain part of Germany or revert to Poland. Upper Silesia is one of those boundary or threshold regions of Central Europe where East and West meet. In the ninth century, the region had constituted part of the Slavic state of Great Moravia; it then became part of Poland, and thereafter, sequentially, of Bohemia and Austria; and finally, in 1742, it became part of Prussia. Just over two months after Steiner gave his lectures, the border referendum took place in March 1921, preceded and marked by violence on both sides, German and Polish. The result gave two thirds of Upper Silesia to Germany and one third, including the industrial region, to Poland. In 1945, Upper Silesia returned to Polish rule. *Chronologically second*, but printed first, are ten lectures given a month or so later and similarly aimed to prepare speakers to travel around Germany to promote threefold ideas: in other words, a "training course for speakers."

Filling out this exoteric picture, Christoph Lindenberg in his biography of Rudolf Steiner provides a few more details:

> Beginning in the summer of 1919, political life had perhaps not become more stable, but it was definitely less mobile. It was difficult if not impossible, with the limited resources available for the threefold movement, to find a point of leverage. There was

naturally a whole range of questions, which one could address, but no one was paying attention. In November 1921, a last possibility opened up to gain an audience. Moritz Bartsch wrote a letter to the office of the Threefold Association in Stuttgart on behalf of a group of Silesian anthroposophists in Breslau. He asked if it would be possible for threefold ideas to play a role in the upcoming vote on the national status of Upper Silesia. A vote was planned in March to determine whether the region would henceforth belong to Poland or to Germany. Either way would bring tension to the area and leave an ethnic minority dominated by the ruling majority.

Rudolf Steiner was at the office of the Threefold Association when the letter arrived and Bartsch's request was passed on to him. Karl Heyer recalled his response: "Dr. Steiner was extremely positive about the initiative of the threefold group in Breslau. He was strongly supportive. I remember how he then, and also later, explained that it was our task to take a stand on social threefolding where decisions were pending that would provide solutions to contemporary issues. If we could bring threefolding into the discussion in places upon which the eyes of the world were focused, the world would see the threefold impulse."

In spite of all the negative experiences, and in spite of the minimal chances of success, Steiner embraced this new possibility without hesitation. He focused on the task and the goal, not on possible objections and reasons to hesitate. He immediately asked Karl Heyer and Guenther Wachsmuth to draft an appeal for a threefold campaign in Upper Silesia. He stressed, however, that only people living in Silesia should be involved in the campaign.

Next day, Steiner returned to the office to read through the draft. He was not satisfied with it and proceeded to draft the appeal that he had envisioned. His draft ended with a concrete proposal rejecting either a German or a Polish outcome: "Upper Silesia rejects the connection with either of the boundary countries until such time as an understanding for social threefolding has been awakened. The region will organize itself with self-governing economic concerns and self-governing spiritual-cultural endeavors. Unity between the two will be found through a local, provisory, legal and policing organization with powers limited to the region. It will remain in this form until the entire European situation has been clarified."

...The campaign began in January, after Steiner had given an overview of the historical situation to the handful of Upper Silesians who were designated as speakers. The "threefolders," who travelled from city to city and into the villages in pairs, spoke enthusiastically and courageously about their ideas. They did not have an easy time. The situation had already become poisoned by ethnic tensions. A number of newspapers took up their ideas, and they would have perhaps been able to achieve some success if they had begun earlier. By this time, however, they found themselves in a witch's kettle, battling the bitter resistance of both ethnic groups and the Catholic Church, which—as was reported—reacted with a wave of hate, especially in response to a series of articles by Roman Boos entitled "Jesuitica" that appeared in our journal for threefolding.

In the end, the Upper Silesian campaign became the source for bad feeling throughout Germany. On March 4, 1921, an article, "Traitors against Germany," appeared in the *Frankfurter Zeitung*. It accused the Threefold Association of supporting Polish interests: "Whoever does not vote for Germany, even if he merely abstains, works for Poland. The situation is clear; everyone must decide. Thus Steiner and his people are in fact propagating Polish propaganda, just as though they were being paid by Poland to do so."

.... Independently of the campaign in Upper Silesia, there had been discussions a year earlier, in the spring of 1920, about how, given the lack of success of the first threefold campaign, it might be possible to reawaken interest in social threefolding. Repeatedly the idea came up that Rudolf Steiner should give a special training course for speakers. At first, neither funds nor the people seemed to be at hand. In early 1921, Steiner's *Kernpunkte der sozialen Frage* (*Towards Social Renewal*) appeared in a large new edition with a new foreword by the author. In the foreword, he addressed the misunderstandings that he had encountered concerning social threefolding, in a straightforward, clear manner.

> Following this preparation, Steiner finally gave a course for speakers from February 12-17, 1921. The number of participants is not documented, according to one account there were about fifty people there. Immediately following the course, they were to speak throughout Germany about anthroposophy and social threefolding. Unfortunately there is nothing documenting this undertaking. There is no mention of it at all in the journal for threefolding! However, there is an indication in a lecture from Steiner on March 11, 1921, that the campaign did take place. He seemed to have placed a good deal of hope in this "strong foray" and said: "The goal of the lectures was, on the one hand, to show how anthroposophical spiritual science could address the great cultural tasks of our civilization and then, out of this, to show how an anthroposophical conviction would affect social life."
>
> At the time he had undoubtedly received only a few positive reports of the campaign. Later, in 1923, after he experienced the effects of the campaign in Germany, he arrived at a devastating verdict: "There was this speakers' course I gave before a horde was turned loose on the German public. Look at the echo that this invasion caused! Some of the things that were concocted out there surpass everything in their grotesqueness."
>
> Even if one takes into account that the sharpness of this remark may to some extent be colored by the difficulties of 1923, its meaning cannot be overlooked: the last attempt at a widespread campaign to further understanding of the threefold impulse caused a good deal of damage. Although there were no doubt excellent lectures given by some of the speakers, the general response was completely negative.

Given this account, a reader would not be led to expect much—at best a course about threefolding or, more specifically, "a course for speakers," as the first publication (1933) was named. The lectures do indeed speak to these questions. But they do so largely implicitly. Explicit recommendations for speakers and material relating to threefolding are also given, for the most part embodied in all kinds of other and fascinating material. This—in some sense the actual subject matter—is magisterially and subtly presented in such a way that one gradually realizes that what one is reading is itself a demonstration of what Rudolf Steiner is hoping to convey. As we read with growing excitement we begin to understand that "threefolding," for instance, which is technically a primary content, depends for its understanding and communication on anthroposophy itself *as a living reality*, a way of life and of thinking, feeling, and acting. In this sense, the lectures uniquely communicate the living reality of anthroposophy as it can be manifested in life and words. Put another way, unless anthroposophy is fully understood, practiced, and made wholly one's own as a living reality, one cannot successfully communicate threefolding or any other aspect of anthroposophy. To become a true communicator of any aspect of anthroposophy one must have so absorbed and embodied anthroposophy in one's own being that one's speaking, like all one's activities, has become a free, living, spontaneous, natural expression of it.

Thus these lectures constitute more than a "course for speakers." As a course for speakers, practically speaking, they failed. Realizing that something much more basic was needed, later in the year (October 11-16, 1921), Steiner would address a similar group about to undertake the same work in Switzerland. That course (CW 339) is tightly and explicitly focused on the technical minutiae of "the art of lecturing," and does not have the broad and deep scope of the present lectures. As such, the present lectures can hardly be called a failure.

*

The tone is intimate, personal, direct, and focused. One can feel Rudolf Steiner reaching out to the participants, who are about to go out into the world to speak on behalf of the threefold social organism. He knows that theirs is not an easy task; that what they will be attempting is risky, even dangerous. He does not know them very well or how prepared they are—how deep their anthroposophy goes. Nevertheless, speaking to them as equals, able to understand what he is telling them, and holding nothing back, he paints the "big picture"—or the "deep ground"—against and out of which they are called to make their case.

Reading these lectures, we very soon realize that, since "threefolding" is but one manifestation of anthroposophy, all that Rudolf Steiner enjoins here, and how he does so, applies to a much greater field than that which he is explicitly addressing. In a word, the participants, who will be going out to speak of the threefolding of the social order will be doing so as representatives of anthroposophy. Therefore, when they speak of threefolding it will be as simply one manifestation of what living anthroposophy is. As such, they must themselves become living manifestations of anthroposophy. Thus, from this point of view, this course could be called, or at least subtitled: *How To Be an Anthroposophist.*

*

This realization dawns slowly. Although we might have suspected it, and in hindsight can see clearly that it is implicit throughout, the full force and challenge of what this means in practice—the revelatory moment—does not arrive until just over half way through the lectures, in the sixth lecture. The five previous lectures have dealt (as we shall see) with general guidelines for prospective speakers, the historical and spiritual backgrounds to our present condition, the importance of threefolding, and so on. The sixth lecture begins by Steiner telling the participants that, in the end:

> It will all come down to the fact that the whole approach to the lectures that you are to offer the public is different than what lies behind almost all of the usual discussions out there currently. The approach that you will need take up will be determined above all by the fact that you always must point out the significance of the human being itself in the whole of social life.

In other words, as he goes on explain, it is the centrality of the human being that distinguishes the anthroposophical approach. Anthroposophy always begins with the human being, whereas most contemporary approaches to any question begin abstractly, with anything but the human being concretely in its essence. Social-economic thinking, for instance, thinks about capital, labor, and commodity theoretically and abstractly, without reference either to the "essence of the human" or actual human beings as they live—with what these terms might actually mean in regard to living human spiritual beings—in their real, lived relations. Science likewise "never starts by looking at the human being as such." It has no feeling whatsoever for the human. Indeed, it considers the human as an epiphenomenon of quite other, non-human processes. If science had such a feeling for what is human it could not "treat the human being as merely the conclusion of animal evolution."

Steiner says that in our modern worldview, the human being has everywhere been quite excised from the picture, removed from consideration. This means that in our social institutions—none of which arise from us or speak to our human essence—our humanity is "disabled." We are bound by regulations, and tossed about by economic forces, that have nothing to do with who we truly are. We speak of "the collective," and we are enjoined abstractly to "sacrifice ourselves" to it, but it is forgotten that we can do so only as actual, living "I" beings, and that unless we develop as individuals our sacrifice is worthless. Though individualism, when it is misunderstood as an abstraction of "the external rights-political and economic order" can, and indeed inevitably does, lead to egotism, true individualism—as the development of our true human essence, spiritually understood—leads naturally to selflessness in service to the collective. *Spiritually*, human beings according to their natural disposition are not greedy; what they have spiritually they *wish* to give. Materially, the case is the opposite: what we have we want to keep. But this "selfish" urge does not come from within us, but from without, from the collective, which teaches it. A truly social art, therefore, "would consist in taking everything that surrounds us externally and gradually transforming it in such a way that we could treat other human beings in the way that we treat those things that belong to us inwardly—that flow from our individualities."

In contrast then to other approaches, anthroposophy "places the human being in the absolute center of all its considerations." Indeed, all Steiner's teachings depend on our realizing that as human beings we are infinite beings, one with the evolving infinitude of the universe itself. In order to see that this is the case, one need only consider the many teachings relating to reincarnation, to life between death and rebirth, to life before birth ("unbornness")—not to mention our ongoing relationships with the so-called dead. *An Outline of Esoteric Science*, for instance, presents the evolutionary metamorphosis of the Earth through the Saturn, Sun, Moon, and Earth stages as actually and simultaneously the evolutionary development of the human: the human is present from the beginning (and by implication from before the beginning). All this means that, "for anthroposophy, the human being is never excluded." Divine-cosmic and earthly human evolution are one and the same. In the words of St. Paul, "For he chose us in him before the creation of the world..." (Ephesians 1.4) It is in this light that the Foundation Stone Meditation should be read.

But this is only one side of the mystery that "nothing in the cosmos is considered without simultaneously considering the position of the human being within it." Whatever anthroposophy approaches, then, it must do so from the perspective of the human being. Whatever aspect great or small of existence, the world, or life that anthroposophy considers must always be based on (and lead back to) the essence of the human being. What this might mean is illuminated by a personal account of his own experience that Steiner recounts in his *Autobiography* (Chapter 51). He writes how in the late 1890s, approaching his fortieth year, he was feeling a profound urge to move beyond "theory."

> To find a true relationship to the world through meditation, I had repeatedly placed before my soul this thought: The world is full of mysteries. I can approach them with the power of cognition, but that leads one to a thought content as a solution to a mystery. But (I told myself) mysteries are not solved by thoughts. Thoughts bring one to the path of a solution, but do not contain the solution. A mystery arises within the real world as a phenomenon; the solution arises equally in that reality. Something appears as being or process and solves the mystery.
>
> I also thought: The whole world except for the human being is a mystery—the actual world mystery. And human beings themselves are the solution... but they can never say more of the answer than they have learned about themselves as human beings.

> Thus cognition becomes a process in reality. Questions reveal themselves in the world; answers reveal themselves as realities; knowledge is human participation in what is revealed by the beings and processes of the spiritual and physical worlds.

Since, in the case of these lectures, it is the social process that is being considered, the first task for prospective speakers is to face the reality of the social world and "to shift the human being" into the center of the social process. When they speak, the human being, rather than remaining "a kind of luxury object for knowledge," must become central to all they say. As Steiner admits, in a sense, major thinkers from Adam Smith to Karl Marx already take human reality as their starting-point when they speak of "economic freedom" and "private property." But they do so without actually recognizing the true essence of the human being. After all, economic freedom is not something you can have without owning something; but property is not a given, it must be acquired "whether through theft or conquest or inheritance, or what have you..." But no one speaks of the human processes whereby this comes about: no one thinks it through. As a result, it becomes automatic, abstract, and, in that sense, non-human. *The ability to see connectivity is lacking.*

Connectivity or relation, if anything, is fundamental to the essence—the being—of what it is to be human. The human being is what connects—lives in connections and relations. Thus, in anthroposophy, from beginning to end, the human being as conscious connectivity is the center to which everything is related. From this point of view, the essence of the human being is clearly related to two other realities that also stand under the sign of connectivity: namely, *Life* and *Spirit.* Therefore, the call is to "replace the theoretical perspectives brought into humanity in recent years with a view toward life." In a word, to replace abstract theory with the living inner connectivity of human beings, which (as he put it elsewhere) is in "a kind of synchronous vibration with spiritual existence." That is, to think, feel, and act out of that place of connectivity, the truly human place—where the living essence of the human and the true, as well as actual, reality of life intersect. To this end, Rudolf Steiner is always urging (and admonishing) anthroposophists to make anthroposophy *living*: to cultivate living ideas, living experience, living thinking: to live their anthroposophy, to make it alive.

This is not, as Steiner stresses, a matter of using anthroposophical jargon or terminology, which will only alienate people. Rather, it is a question of communicating and acting out of an anthroposophical understanding of the human being's relationship to the world and life. That is to say, it is a matter of thinking and speaking out of an anthroposophical grasp of the evolving nature of humanity—the human as an infinite, evolving being of absolute value—and the world, co-imbricated with the human being in Life and in Spirit, and hence of equally absolute, evolving, infinite value.

Such issues radiate through these lectures.

*

Steiner begins by stressing certain basic necessities, starting with the need for what he calls conviction—above all, the conviction that "in our current historical moment" the work that the participants in the course are about to undertake is "of the most eminent necessity," "an absolute requirement for the life of present-day civilization." All doubt or skepticism concerning the validity and value of what they are about to do must be excluded from their hearts. Only this inner state of clarity and certainty will be effective in communicating what they have to say.

Right away, then, we are faced with a critical question: what kind of conviction is required? Clearly, the "conviction" meant is different to the kind of ideological conviction manifested, for instance, by "fundamentalists" of any persuasions, whether Marxist, Bolshevik, or National Socialist. Nor can it be any kind of ideologized religious conviction or "faith" in that sense. We know all too well the dangers of such kinds of certainty. What then is it? Though Steiner never returns to this question, in some sense the entire lecture course is intended to demonstrate the path to the kind of conviction he means. Certainly, we may say, it is a conviction that believes in the future: an orientation of confidence, not fear, toward the future. In other words: a questioning, experimental conviction based on love of the world and humanity, one that has done the hard work of both self-knowledge and world-knowledge, and on that basis one that has realistically faced and sought to penetrate the ever-evolving infinite spirit immanent in the cosmos and in human history as the field and the symptomatic manifestation of the evolution of consciousness—including the religious, artistic, scientific, and social realities leading up to and following upon the Christ event, the Mystery of Golgotha.

At the same time, as if to amplify what kind conviction is needed, he adds a dose of reality: the task of those going out on behalf of threefolding will not be easy. They will face fierce opposition. To be prepared for this, thoroughly penetrated understanding—perhaps itself synonymous with *conviction*—provides the only sure way. They must see clearly that "old forces of civilization" are in decline and will resist them with all their might. To inject the anthroposophical approach and anthroposophical insight into the situation will be a struggle. This will have to be done delicately and without a shred of dogmatism.

To such conviction and "realism," Steiner then adds certain "psychological starting points" or "functional foundations for the work." Though these might seem overly general, as he puts it, if thought through concretely, they will prove of "exceptional importance." The first is to develop a genuine *love for the subject* or cause, coupled with real insight into it. The second rule is to develop a *love for humanity*, equally filled with insight.

Here again, Steiner touches on profound issues. What does "love" in this sense mean? How does one "develop" love for humanity or one's subject? This, too, will become clearer as the course progresses. Since it is the *sine qua non* of being able to communicate successfully, like the previous question of conviction, it must constitute a central theme of the whole course. The spiritual path leading to the development of such soul qualities or capacities must also be implicit. As to "insight," this in fact is the theme of the course, which is intended to demonstrate the kind of insight living anthroposophy provides. On the more practical side, as Steiner points out, it is clear that while ambition or vanity may impress one's audience, "egotism" will convince no one and achieve nothing. This is not surprising. Love, whatever else it may mean, always implies selflessness—and service ("washing one another's feet" to one degree or another). From this point of view, the whole of anthroposophy exists to convince us of the divine-cosmic-spiritual value of service;

of the central importance of earthly life which forever calls us to serve its development—through doing the truth "in minute particulars" in whatever capacity we can.

Love in this sense is the ground; and must therefore be related to the conviction. Indeed, it must lead to it. Without love there cannot be conviction. Implicitly, then, Steiner seems to suggest a kind of circle of conditions: that love of anthroposophy (here, in its "threefolding" manifestation) must lead to love of humanity, human beings, and the world—in a word, love of life—that in turn leads back to a love of anthroposophy, which provides concrete content, with "full" insight into it, for one's words and deeds. But the "circle" of anthroposophy and content and love must always remain intact. It must never be broken. For, even the most sophisticated content, if it is without real love for one's fellows and love for what one is doing, will not convince.

All of which is to say that speakers for anthroposophy should avoid generalities and theoretical statements and focus with love on living details, anecdotes, and particular examples. Steiner himself always follows this rule. Although, in general, he is often misread as propounding a "system," in fact in his lectures and books he presents only details, particular points of spiritual research, phenomenologically and lovingly presented, which, though they may illuminate a/the whole to some degree, by no means seek to encompass it. In the words of William Blake: "To Generalize is to be an Idiot. To Particularize is the Alone Distinction of Merit" and:

> He who would do good to another must do it in minute particulars.
> General good is the plea of the scoundrel, hypocrite, and flatterer:
> For art and science cannot exist but in minute particulars,
> And not in generalizing demonstrations of the rational power:
> The infinite alone exists in definite and determinate identity...

Next, and perhaps above all, Steiner insists on the conviction—not just the theoretical understanding—that if humanity is in a more desperate situation than ever before, it is not because of nature, physical changes, or outer forces, but because of the spiritual state of human beings today: that is, *how they think*. The crisis—then as still today—is the result of "a false spirit, a false way of thinking" in all fields: social, economic, political, religious, and scientific. It is a crisis of thinking. No "unknown power has brought about this crisis." The path is clear: we must "replace false thinking with proper thinking." Poverty, starvation, economic turmoil, geopolitical conflict—human pain and suffering—are caused not by nature (nature will always provide) but by the human spirit: by a false way of thinking. We must learn to think differently—which is a difficult message to convey because people are too conventional, too fixed in their habitual, automatic responses. They fear what is new.

Essentially this means that if we wish to speak to others about anthroposophy (or become true anthroposophists) what we are up against is, first of all, that most people today have no awareness or understanding of "the productivity (or creativity) of spiritual life." By this Steiner means our true, free, creative human potential: the creative freedom of the "I" to make something new, to create, to invent, to act outside the bounds of convention, of fixed representations. Because of this, people think "competence is all you need," but end up valuing incompetence above all else, fearing anything that would impel them to think differently. The result is a kind of "crippled intellectuality." People may love thoughts, but they fear thinking and are terrified if you suggest that thoughts should become deeds. In a sense, all this is simply a fear of the spirit. One must give people some idea of the productive potential of the spirit—of the creative spirit, of the spirit's power—in human life.

The second obstacle is that, as Steiner puts it, "because of the particular form of the social life that has appeared in the last few decades, any awareness of the needs of others has been fundamentally lost." In other words, selfishness, or egotism, rules. Interest groups, lobbyists dominate public life. However, "without this awareness of the needs of others, there can be no true form of economic life." In other words: "In economic life, decisions can be made only when we are able to distance ourselves from our own individual interests and be aware of other's interests." That is, again, we must love our fellow human beings. Everything follows from that. For love is always creative of the future, of the new; love is always of the "not-yet." Thus a deep symptom of the lack of this love—Steiner instances Lenin and Trotsky, as well as the Catholic Church—is the tendency to not trust in the new, in beginning again, which requires facing present reality without preconceptions or judgments, and drawing whatever conclusions we must, irrespective of how uncomfortable they are. But, unfortunately, no one trusts enough to truly start from the ground up, present reality, without inherited abstractions. What is needed, therefore, to "heal present-day civilization" is "a new historical impulse," communicated not in logically ordered abstractions, but open-endedly, without dogmatism, based in independent thinking growing out of experience and expressed in pliable, artistic form.

Having introduced these basic themes, Steiner takes a step back, as it were, to present the fundamental historical background or context against and in which, the participants, potential speakers, will be working. A sense of history is vital to understanding one's present condition. Here, again, because of the way civilization has developed and consciousness has been increasingly captured by egotism, we have lost the feeling for historical experiences. We must regain it. We must learn to think and act out of actual historical reality, symptomatically understood. Otherwise, we will simply build structures in the air: our acts will be based in fantasy wishes and dreams, not reality. As Steiner puts it: "You must set aside the theoretical self; you must attempt to speak out of reality. Your work will sometimes succeed, sometimes not—that part does not matter. What matters is that you speak on a foundation of reality." And that foundation of reality requires a clear understanding of internal relations.

With this, we are now given an astonishing dose of reality: a history lesson, demonstrating how deeply incarnated and well read Rudolf Steiner was. He points to two seminal treaties: the Treaty of Nystad (1721) and the Treaty of Paris (1763). The first treaty marked the end of the Great Northern War between the Swedish Empire and a coalition led by Russia. As a result, Russia became a new spiritual and economic power in Europe, and the Swedish Empire and Polish-Lithuanian Commonwealth declined. In the second, among other things, France ceded its North American territories (including Nova Scotia and the Louisiana territory east of the Mississippi) to Great Britain, while its territories in India remained under British control. In other words, Britain became the undisputed sea and colonial power, and Central

Europe was squeezed between the pincers of East and West: in Steiner's terms "Asian" Russia and Anglo-America. These two treaties determined and still determine what followed, including the "great catastrophe" of the First World War. As Steiner says: "These two occurrences are actually, in the world of factual reality, very much part of the life of European civilization; you can see their effects everywhere.... Every morning at breakfast, the way we eat has come about as a result of these events." In a sense, it still does.

Rudolf Steiner, of course, speaks as a Central European. As such, his focus is on Russia, which seemed to many at the time to pose, economically at least, a lesser threat—Anglo-American capitalism was too powerful and would tend to dominate and "enslave." Yet, as a tendency, Russia, too, presented profound ambiguities for Steiner. Internally divided between Europe and Asia (essentially, we might say, between "Europeanizers" and "Slavophiles"), largely agrarian, tending to theocracy, close to nature and the earth, it had no understanding of economic life in the modern sense. America, on the other hand, had equally little sense of economics in the communal sense of "association." Rather, everything was economics: a highly individualistic, willful kind of economic "Darwinism," based on the premise of "inexhaustibility" and, its corollary, infinite growth. Where Russia therefore tended toward Absolutism, America tended toward Anarchism. Neither East nor West thus showed a viable way toward the future for the Central European impulse for a new foundation for civilization based on the creative freedom of the I. To describe the situation, he uses Friedrich Schiller's polarity of barbarism and savagery:

> Now a human being can be opposed to himself or herself in a twofold manner; either as a savage, when feelings rule over principles; or as a barbarian, when principles destroy feelings. Savages despise art, and acknowledge nature as their despotic ruler; barbarians laugh at nature, and dishonor it, but they often proceed in a more contemptible way than the savage to be the slave of their senses. A cultivated person makes of nature his or her friend, and honors its friendship, while only bridling its caprice. *(Letters on the Aesthetic Education of Man)*

In other words, Steiner saw Eastern, "Oriental," Russia as "barbaric," and Anglo-American (but more particularly American) civilization as "savage." "The barbarian tyrannizes the heart and feelings with the head; the savage tyrannizes the head with all that comes from the rest of the human organism, with the life of instincts." In neither is economics actually discussed: "In the East, the collective social structure ... becomes absolutist. In the West, it becomes anarchistic." True economics, assuming its rightful role in society with a free spiritual life and an autonomous but separate life of rights—in other words through the "threefolding of the social organism"—is thus Central Europe's task.

From the point of view of Central Europe, then, its social and economic future was squeezed between the "Russian" East and the "Anglo-American" West. The "West" threatened to overwhelm Europe—to "force Europe into slavery." The only response seemed to many to be to extend the German empire eastward. After all, Russia loved German thinking. But Russia also loved sensations, a vague blend of thoughts and feelings. It did not know the true meaning of thinking. More important, the future was no longer a matter of "empires." The time for empires was past. Humanity was on the brink of a new global, cosmopolitan age. With Russia, the future called not for economic or political ties, but rather for the development of spiritual relationships between one human being and another. These, in time, would lead to what Steiner calls "an independent economic community."

With the West, in contrast, relations should be limited to strictly economic relations—to demonstrating how economics, technology, and production might be infused with truly human, associative, artistic values. Rather than commodifying all things, including art, all things should be produced in an associative, artistic way. In this way, foregoing the innate tendency to imitate the West, a creative spiritual life—arising from the free spiritual life of Central Europe—could begin to permeate the economic sphere. In the West, where everything becomes economics, including spiritual life, capitalism becomes wholly materialistic: capital is not understood as a spiritual reality, as the inspiriting force. As Steiner explains, it is up to Central Europe to show how this is the case, to inspirit social life through threefolding.

Social thinking—as a world-historical task—must therefore take into account "international relations." But the key is, on the one hand, a free, productive, creative spiritual-cultural life and, on the other, an independent, associative economic life. In a word:

> It is important that we see into the real necessities of life. This already shows us why we must have a threefold social organism—so that we can send to the West economists uninfluenced by the machinations of the state and the spiritual-cultural life. And we need a free spiritual life in order to arrive at a viable relationship with the East. So our international relations themselves depend upon it.

One of the necessities of life at the present, then, is to begin to move toward the integration of East, West, and Center through the recognition and implementation (from the Center) of the threefold nature of human society, consisting of a free, creative spiritual-cultural sphere; an economic, associative sphere meditating between nature and culture (work-production); and a rights sphere that recognizes the absolute and equal value of all human beings. For this, democracy itself, which evolved in response to Cromwell's puritan-theocratic revolution as "a sensibility for religious independence," must be reimagined. From a threefolding point of view, however, "a true concept of democracy will only exist once there is an organization put in between the spiritual and economic organizations, one that is based on the relationship between people and on the equality of all mature individuals."

*

Thus, the lectures unfold, filled with details and examples, both from contemporary life and from history. The breadth and depth of Rudolf Steiner's knowledge of history—at least, European history—is staggering and continuously filled with remarkable and thought-provoking insights. (The course is well worth reading for these alone!) He shows, for instance, how economics gradually developed within the guild system during the Middle Ages from a quasi-natural, self-evident process into one requiring regulations, aimed both at production and at protecting the consumer. Over time, however, the need for regulations grew more intensive, especially in those areas without great natural resources. However, concealed within the whole field of such regulations, which gradually succumbed to the power of vested financial interests, a crisis was looming. It was postponed temporarily by the opening of the New World and the development of modern technology, which ensured the continuing and exponentially increasing dominance of economics in its previously given form. With the catastrophe of the First World War, the bankruptcy of the entire system became evident for those with eyes to see it.

Sadly, however, those eyes were few. Thus historical events led to the present still-unexamined situation in which the three aspects of social life—spiritual-cultural, economic, and political-legal-statist—remain completely entangled in one another and under the hegemonic dominance of economics, still understood as the field of universal commodification. Given this situation, it is clear that the way forward has to lie in rethinking economics so as to transform it from its present, abstract, disembodied idolatrous status into a healthy expression of human connectivity. How precisely this is to be accomplished Steiner leaves unclear, almost certainly because if it were to happen it would do so through the free, creative, individual efforts of free, creative human beings. This is to say that, rather than prescribing a course of action, Rudolf Steiner concentrates in these lectures and others devoted to threefolding on "thinking differently" about the whole network of human-earthly-spiritual relations summoned up by what we call "economics": capital, labor, price, commodity. Frequently placing these in relation to spiritual-cultural life or to the rights-political state, and often in relation to historical and evolutionary development, he returns to these topics repeatedly from lecture to lecture, always treating them in a new light. As he does so, we too begin to see them differently; and the possibility dawns that we could actually "think otherwise" about things that, for the most part, we take for granted and think of automatically.

At the same time, interesting sub-themes continually emerge, deepening our awareness. One of these is the hidden presence of religious and theological notions implicit in contemporary society:

how religious, theological ideas have transformed into secular social norms. We have already seen, for instance, how the idea of democracy gradually metamorphosed in the modern era from the idea of "religious independence" and how economic "regulations," developed within the medieval, religiously inspired guild system into its modern form. To these, Steiner then adds, spiritual-cultural life, pointing out how the university "developed entirely out of the church" and how the nation state and its wars were simply a consequence of "the movement of religious institutions into political life." The same is true of philosophy and law. Natural science and technology, for their part, while they developed out of their own ground, nevertheless did so "in parallel," and thus took on "some resemblance" to what previously developed out of the church. Higher education likewise; that is why, as Steiner puts it, its structure is so "unnatural." What it amounts to is that spiritual life is inadequate: "only the exterior form is taken in." What is required is the emancipation of these things—and emancipation that can only occur through the separation and autonomy of the three members of the social body—spiritual-cultural, rights-political, and economic—so that each may develop its own natural, indeed spiritual, form out of their own essence or nature and our own human essence or nature.

For all this, what is required is clear thinking based on the actual realities of life, not on what has become the norm: "ideological" thinking, based on the spinning out of preconceived notions divorced from experienced realities on the ground. Such thinking—if one can call it that—results only in miring and entangling us deeper in a web of "empty phrases," slogans and catchphrases. In other words: propaganda of a kind that only lead to collapse. As Steiner says" "A reality that is guided and directed by empty phrases must quite clearly collapse upon itself. This is connected to the basic phenomena of our present evolutionary movement." To these phenomena, deriving from a near-universal dehumanizing materialism, anthroposophy is both the response and the answer.

Thus, as the lectures progress, Steiner tries to teach by example what it means to think and speak clearly and authentically out of anthroposophy about the human social-cultural situation, and how doing so leads inevitably to threefolding, as well as to other anthroposophical initiatives such as Waldorf education. Such clear thinking—re-thinking from the ground up— is not an easy proposition, especially in the economic realm (as those who have worked with Steiner's economics course well know). The fact is we are not used to thinking new thoughts. We are all-too-comfortable with what we know. Nevertheless, the effort is worthwhile; and Rudolf Steiner is an excellent teacher. Moreover, a great deal of what Steiner proposes is actually common sense—that is what makes it so radical. When, for instance, he explains with examples drawn from several converging points of view why the distinction between so-called "productive work"—that is, actual labor—and the technically "unproductive" work that teachers, doctors, accountants, and so on perform is spurious and basically nonsensical, we both understand right away and recognize the importance of what he is saying: that economically there is no difference between their forms of income, that each constitutes an essential transformation point in the economic process. He does so because his examples are drawn from reality. As he says, "The absurdity of these theories is never demonstrated in their logic, but only in reality." What he is asking of his speakers, then, is that they have penetrated and made their own the essence of anthroposophy and threefolding and that they have a sense for what is real: "Only a worldview and an understanding of life that takes hold of eminently practical questions will have any significance for the world as a whole."

On the other hand, Steiner is a realist in his advice to prospective speakers in other ways, too:

> It is also necessary for us to respect the habitual thinking of our contemporaries. You have to be clear about the fact that if you were to go out right now and talk with people for an hour, or an hour and a quarter, about the kinds of things that I am presenting to you, they would start to yawn and finally would leave the lecture hall, happy that your talk was over, longing for a healthy nap. They would find it difficult, much too difficult! People have grown totally unaccustomed to following along with thoughts that are taken from reality. Because people have heard

> only abstractions—as schoolchildren they got used to following along with abstractions—because of this, humanity has become mentally lazy. Humanity is terribly lazy in its thinking right now. And we have to be sensitive to this, but in a way that is useful.

Given this situation, Steiner advises them to tell stories about what they know—anecdotes, for instance, relating to the Waldorf School, eurythmy, the College courses or the anthroposophical businesses. To do so, of course, requires that in their lectures they "grasp our [anthroposophical] movement as whole"—again, not an easy task. By this he means, as he explains in lecture six, that one grasps the essence of anthroposophy, that is, the essence of the human being, both in the sense of what this means in the largest sense and, grasping this, what the human mission or task is, for this is the meaning of the "Movement as a whole." That is, this task is at once given as the human evolutionary role, and in that sense as a kind of absolute, and is at the same time historically contingent: it changes with the evolution of consciousness and its historical conditions. Hence the importance of understanding both the larger contours of evolution and the symptomatic nitty-gritty of recent history. Throughout these lectures Rudolf Steiner seeks to convey precisely this dual vision to his auditors.

It is important then to hold in mind the apparent paradox of the high role of humanity and the humble work called for in the present. Connected with this paradox, Steiner alludes to another: that of the free, creative individual and the community or association that human beings can form. While spiritual life, in the end, is an individual matter, that individual cannot realize the fruits of that individuality alone. In other words, "the individual human being is not in a position to do anything in economic life that might actually bring something productive into it." Individuals must realize their free, creative "I," but that I can only truly manifest in relation with others, to the needs of others. The ivory-towered individual is an anti-social being. "We err as individuals when we try to conduct ourselves in economic life on the basis of individual judgments. From this we can see with apodictic certainty the necessity of associations." Steiner is here speaking of economic life—and he explains the economic nature of associations in great detail—but, bearing in mind Christ's sayings "When two or more are gathered together in my name, I am there" and "For I was hungry and you gave me food; I was thirsty and you gave me drink; I was a stranger and you took me in," one can see that what he says of economic life is but a particular case of what, from a Christian perspective, is a universal spiritual rule—hence the importance of economics from this point of view. The end is the same as Christ's teaching—the community of all-humanity. None of this is theory. "Wherever we go, we must describe things that come out of real life."

All this takes faith in human beings: that human beings can come to healthy self-consciousness and become the stage upon which the true "directive forces of life are revealed." In other words, as Steiner tells the prospective speakers:

> We must find the ability to say to ourselves, "Everything external is superstition. The one and only thing that exists within us is the directive forces that must take hold in life!"
>
> For this, it is necessary to have the courage to overcome merely passive prayer and to actively pray for taking hold of the godly in our will. This transition to active prayer, to any sort of inner activity; this transition from skepticism toward human beings to faith in human beings, this is the zeal that must lie within your hearts and souls. We must feel that we are the ones who stand at the historical turning point when people will be lead from skepticism toward human beings to faith in human beings.
>
> You do not need to say this to people, but you must step up to the podium with full consciousness of this, with the awareness that, "I have to communicate to humankind that the directive forces of life must be actively grasped in our interiority; that life in the future must be administered so that people say to themselves, 'I must be the one who does things.'"

Here we have the necessary "conviction" with which the first lecture began. That we do not have faith in ourselves and in humanity is "the final superstition." At last, then, Rudolf Steiner calls us to trust in ourselves, and to trust life. There is no room for skepticism. We must have "faith in humanity, faith in the inner activity of the human being." This is what it means to be oriented toward the future, to midwife the future that is calling us. Thus Steiner concludes these rich, subtle lectures with these stirring words:

> My dear friends, I would like you to go out into the world as people of tomorrow and to imprint your words with the consciousness of people of tomorrow.

COMMUNICATING ANTHROPOSOPHY

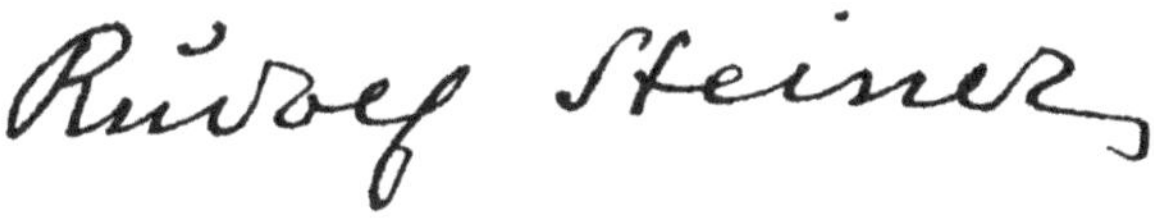

I

Working on Behalf of the Threefold Social Organism

A Training Course for Speakers

Lecture 1

Stuttgart, February 12, 1921

Today, we will first discuss the possible intentions of those individuals who are taking part in this course and how we might best gain a foothold in our tasks.

If you seek to fulfill the intentions connected with this course, then in the near future you all will go out into the world to do work on behalf of the threefold social organism. In our current historical moment, this work is of the most eminent necessity. And this conviction—that it *is* so necessary—must be our starting point. We must be clear that it is high time that we go to work for this threefolding impulse, which we must regard as an absolute requirement for the life of present-day civilization.

Since in the next few days we are going to discuss the requirements for doing this work, you must be able, from the very start, to shut out all skepticism in your hearts toward the importance of the threefolding impulse. You will not be able to do this work if you are skeptical about this at all. During this training course, you will come to see that it is not only what you do or say that has an effect in the world, but also certain imponderable, inexpressible things must accompany your speech and actions if you truly want to be effective.

Furthermore, we must be clear that all of the old forces of civilization to which this decadent age clings are rebelling against this threefolding impulse, forming oppositional groups; we have much to fight against if we want to use our power to bring the threefold social organism into reality. And the more success we have on one side, the more we will have to fight on the other. Such successes (as evidenced by the experiences with our opponents this week) do not lessen the intensity of the fight, but rather cause it to continue escalating. And we will have to arm ourselves for the fight that is coming, which is not to say, of course, that we should all go rushing into battle; doing so will not bring about any progress. But we must all be aware of how intensely this fight will unfold in the near future, precisely in the moment we achieve something in our work.

What I would like to offer today will come primarily in the form of several psychological starting points. Obviously, it can only be a matter here of describing the functional foundations for your work. I would like to emphasize from the start that it is not possible to offer some sort of handbook for speaking about political-social matters, or about anything else; what is important is that we create a positive foundation for working on behalf of the threefolding impulse. And for this reason, you may feel at first as though I am being far too general when I begin by introducing several very general rules; nevertheless, if we truly think through these rules concretely, they will prove to be of exceptional importance to us.

In the work that you intend to do, you will get somewhere only when you work out of two foundational forces in your soul. Since we are dealing currently with a more-than-ordinary degree of seriousness that must infuse these matters—must ensoul our work—we should first make ourselves aware—totally aware—that we will not progress at all if we do not develop these two fundamental soul forces. First of all, we must speak out of a genuine love for the subject; second, we must speak out of a love for humanity that is filled with insight. Be clear with yourselves about this: if these two preconditions are not met, or if they are replaced by some other force, such as ambition or vanity, you will still be able to deliver very logical speeches to people; you will be able to speak very cleverly, however, you will not be able to achieve anything. At the core, the requirements for working through speech do not lie only in the formation and use of words. You need only to start looking at the way things are most often achieved through words now, and you will see for yourself everything that I have been saying to you.

Imagine for a moment: two speakers are presenting in front of an audience. One of them is an unknown individual with unusually powerful insights, penetrating powers of speech, and full authority on the matter at hand. Then another speaker steps before that same audience—the way things are these days. This man has held some sort of public position for a long time, whether it be as Deputy of Such-and-Such or Statesman from Somewhere-or-Other, the Great Industrialist well-known in one place or another, or the Great Scholar of X. This second man would speak with far less penetrating motifs and themes, would articulate a position with far less authority and justification. The efficacy of a work in the world is necessarily dependent upon the content of spoken words. But we certainly cannot establish our work on the sort of rhetorical flourishes or authoritative positions that I have just described.

There are also two soul conditions that must characterize our speech. Those are the soul conditions that I just mentioned: the genuine love of the cause, which is the only thing that can support the necessary inner conviction, and the love of humanity. It is self-evident that these two soul forces cannot replace the content of the spoken word. That this content must also be indisputable goes without saying. But the content of our words will have no effect when it is not supported by the two soul forces of which I have spoken. For that reason, it is absolutely necessary in our time to say (since we are more inclined to, shall we say, dismiss such technicalities) that we must all examine the extent to which we have both of these forces within our souls. If we discover that we do not have them, it would perhaps be better that we not take part in the important actions that are to be undertaken, because all that we bring to them, all of our work, will be wasted. And we must also be of the conviction that any work coming out of other impulses can never be of great impact; whereas any work that has conviction and comes out of a love for the cause and also for humanity will perhaps only have a small effect at first, but it will nevertheless be a true effect.

My dear friends, the truth chooses all manner of invisible paths by which to enter humanity. It is the case that any time both of these imponderables (love for the cause and love for humanity) are present, an effect in the world will result, even if it does not come to light immediately. In one way or another, it will come into the world; of that we can be sure.

But other things must also be part of that work. A full insight into the inner nature of the subject must be present when we speak in public about something like the threefolding impulse. We also cannot allow ourselves to give in to any illusions about the soul constitution of the people to whom we are speaking; or about the conditions that exist in the world that require us to speak to people now. Among our contemporaries there is no shortage of people who are capable of taking up the things we have to say to them. But because the majority of leading figures at present are the way they are, it is also true that the powers of those individuals who would be capable of taking up the threefolding impulse are suppressed, and in a rather brutal manner.

If we avoid generalities as much as possible, we necessarily come almost immediately to a discussion of details. When you come to people with something like this, the most typical thing they say is, "Yes, but in Central Europe we are experiencing a crisis and a tremendous amount of poverty. We have to fight just to get stale bread. Our primary concern right now is economics. What good are high ideals? What is the use of things spoken on the basis of spirit?" You will hear this objection expressed in a wide variety of ways. And we cannot deny that it is spoken by souls in a truly desperate situation. From a purely material perspective, this objection has a certain justification. But if we allow the most important questions of the present to pass before our souls (the questions that could become the foundations for our work), we will see that the view that the only important concern right now is solving the economic situation, is based completely on illusion. It comes out of a different question (or perhaps the answer to that question), which people take to be self-evident; but it is not self-evident. It is based on the premise that humanity—not this person or that person, but humanity as a whole—is not to blame for the present conditions of the civilized world. We will talk about this in more detail shortly.

If we take a moment to consider the economic system that has overtaken the world (and it is necessary to do just this now), then we have to say to ourselves, "Nature will provide us with the same amount that it did at any other time in history, if we are able to properly harness it, and if we are able to bring the fruits of our labor properly into human life"; into all of human life, of course. That humanity is in a more desperate situation today than it ever has been before is not a result of physical changes; rather, it is a result of the human spirit. If humanity finds itself in a crisis today, that crisis is a result of a false spirit, a false way of thinking. For that reason, the only thing that can be done to bring us out of this crisis is to replace the false thinking with proper thinking. Neither nature nor any sort of unknown forces have brought humanity to its current position; humanity itself has brought about these things. If there is a crisis, then humanity has caused this crisis; if people do not have anything to eat, then it is people who have not provided this food. It is important that we not start with the false premise that some sort of unknown force has brought about this crisis, and we must first overcome this crisis before we can start talking about proper thinking. We must be clear that since this crisis was caused by the improper thinking of human beings, only proper thinking can bring about the end of this crisis.

We must consider from all possible sides this mistaken belief that if you can give people enough bread to eat, then once they have enough bread, they will arrive at proper thinking. This is a terrible misconception. And nothing that will actually bring about salvation can penetrate into today's civilized world if we do not all decide to turn away from this misconception; to replace it with the correct conviction that a reversal, a reformation, of thinking about the nature of the world itself must enter humanity now. This is precisely the conviction that must gradually find its way into a sufficiently large number of minds.

We, however, will find ourselves able to speak to these people only if we do not have any illusions about two things. The first of these is the fact that generally at present there is no awareness of the productivity of spiritual life. The nonsense that resulted in the saying, "Competence is all you need" (the saying is not nonsense, but the way in which it was used)—this nonsense must, in light of the things that are happening out there in the civilized world now, be altogether banished from the human mind. For the events of the civilized world show that a certain, select number of altogether incompetent people are always carried to the heights of leadership by some aspect of their nature.

We are living now in an era that particularly values incompetence. We will also speak in some detail about this and will have to seek the forces that led to this selection of so many incompetent people at this moment in history. I would, however, ask you please to remember that for as long as we are speaking here among ourselves and creating the necessary preconditions for our work we must all stand firmly on this conscious foundation: that the threefolding impulse is altogether correct, that we are not at all skeptical toward it; that we see in it the only power that can lead us out of the confusions of the present. Only by standing on this foundation will we be able to avoid taking the things that I am about to say as presumptuous, or something of the sort; these things are said because they are intimately related to creating the preconditions for our work.

Take my book *Towards Social Renewal.*† If you consider the way in which it is taken up by many people these days and if you take a look what is put forward by its opponents, and if you then try to make some sort of judgment about the things that lie behind what the opponents say, you will be able to arrive at these underlying things only by psychological means, through psychological observations. The opponents mostly talk over and around the content of *Towards Social Renewal.* For the most part, what they say has almost no relationship to the actual content of the book. For example, I recently discussed the content of *Towards Social Renewal* in Bern.† After my talk, the economist from the university spoke for three quarters of an hour. In not one single sentence did he succeed in addressing the actual content of *Towards Social Renewal.* That is an absolute fact. And he also did not properly address the content of my lecture. He was completely unprepared, not knowing *Towards Social Renewal* at all.

Now, what do people feel when they approach the ideas of the threefold social organism? Why is it that they build up these things from the deep foundations of their souls that are so out of keeping with it? They do this because they sense that it is something altogether unusual. Without being fully conscious of it, they sense what is active within themselves. They feel that if the threefolding impulse, as it is described in *Towards Social Renewal,* were to take root in the world, then it would elevate those who are capable and knock from their pedestal those who are incompetent. The impulse that lies within the threefold social organism is one that will have a big effect as soon as it is brought into humanity. But its effectiveness is such that it takes away the effectiveness of all those who are incapable. This is what people feel in the depths of their unconscious. Naturally, they are not able to say this, which is why they end up saying the things they do. If you take the time to examine psychologically the things that people say; that is, to analyze the ways in which they have an effect in the world, then you will arrive at a corroboration of what I have just said. And in the end, all of this is related to the fact that at present, there is no awareness of spiritual productivity. People have grown too accustomed to allowing the spiritual life to be borne by impersonal things, or by people who are not in the least bit spiritual; that is, by the state or by state figures who do not have their own living spirituality at all.

You need only take these things one by one; need only ask yourself: what do the people in theology departments want? In theology departments at present, people are far less interested in delving into the secrets of the primal spiritual forces of the world than they are in producing religious bureaucrats who are useful for the state, or for hearing confessions. In jurisprudence, it is not about seeking the foundations and the essence of law; rather, it is about teaching people what is customary in one state or another, about things that were established by people who also had no interest in the essence of law but who wrote laws on the basis of one set of interests or another. And it is possible to go through everything that plays a leading role in spiritual life and see that in every case an awareness of the productive element of spirit that must be borne up in civilization, an awareness of the living effect of the spirit on the human soul, is barely present.

Over time, people have been gradually nurtured toward a crippled intellectuality; toward merely thinking without filling their thinking through and through with initiative from the will. People are being taken in by crudely considered thinking. You will see this firsthand when you give your lectures. You will be able to experience again and again the way in which the people who listen to you are contented simply to have heard one thing or another. People have a certain "lustfulness" for thoughts; they feel content with them; they would like best simply to hear what satisfies a certain inner desire. But they actually become inwardly furious if you suggest to them that words should not remain merely as words; but rather, if the words are to truly have any results, that the entire being of every individual should be filled by them, and that those people should then take part in life from the perspective that the words open up to them.

In the last few centuries, people have simply grown too accustomed to taking up words in a particular way. When they sat themselves down in the church pews and listened to the priests in the pulpit, the sermon was supposed to be "beautiful"; it was thereby meant to warm (with a decidedly philistine warmth) everyone's inner lives. People came to feel a certain inner "lustfulness," to desire to fulfill a certain inner soul longing, in such a way that the fulfillment of these desires had to come from outside themselves. Then, after people had left the church for the day, they did not want to have something like what had been offered there fully penetrate their lives. This has been said often enough, of course, but for a long time nothing has been done about it.

The situation is similar in regard to other things that are spoken of these days—you can probably guess that as well. It would be wrong to say that most young people go through the doors of their universities with a certain inner glow; that they await what their teachers have to say, following up on the things said the day before, with a powerful inner warmth. In a far greater number of cases, it would seem, people sit through their lessons simply because they are obligated to do so (or maybe many of them do not go to their lessons anyway), and they are happy if they are able to cram enough to pass their exams. These exams really do not tell us whether a young man, for example, is going to be a capable, competent person; instead, they tell us whether he has within himself the things that will make him a good theological or juridical bureaucrat, meaning that he will be able to integrate in a prescribed way into the state structure.

We will see that under these conditions, which were active during the last few centuries and particularly during the nineteenth century, the understanding of the effect that the spirit has in human existence has been gradually lost. Think for a moment about how truly effective religion would have become if it had not moved away from this understanding for living spirituality. All the religions that have now become official religions did not originate in the place that official religious life now sees as its foundation; that is, in the idea that everything we carry within our spirit is just an ideology, a collection of abstractions. Religions originated in the understanding that an objective spirit present in the world revealed itself through certain individuals; and that in this way it had its effect upon the world; that spirit is something actual, a genuine power. Most people who are a part of contemporary religious life understand nothing about this.

Recently, it was very interesting for me to experience the following. I spoke out of the thoughts that are at the basis of the first chapter of *Towards Social Renewal.* That is, from a spiritual perspective, an essential part of the proletariat question is that the modern proletariat sees all spiritual life (customs, rights, art, religion, science, and so on) as ideology; and that in this understanding of the spiritual life as ideology lies the basis for an obliteration of the soul, which instinctively brings us, more or less, to the contemporary social movement. I outlined this in my book *Towards Social Renewal.* Recently, I spoke about it in a lecture, and a professorial discussion participant understood the matter so well that he said something like, "Now, you have said that in regard to spiritual matters the proletariat live in a kind of ideology; but one cannot say that because people in all classes, all life situations—the whole of humanity—are constantly living in ideology; it goes without saying that everybody lives in ideology!" The gentleman had absolutely no concept of what I meant, because any concept of the reality of spiritual life had already been lost to him. For him, it was entirely self-evident that our spirits and our souls are filled with nothing more than ideologies. As a good citizen, he thereby could not see any alternative except to say that we all live quite justifiably in ideologies; if the proletariat are living in an ideology, it cannot be the reason for the social impulses of the present!

You see, these things are so fundamental in our time, even in those who are "educated," that we have no choice but to say that people have absolutely no understanding of productivity in spiritual life. Above all else, we must give people some concept of this productivity in spiritual life; of the creative spirit, of the spirit's power. This is of the utmost importance. This is the one thing about which we may have no illusions; if we do, then we will not understand how we can speak to people now.

Another obstacle that is important to know is that, because of the particular form of social life that has appeared in the last few decades, any awareness of the needs of others has been fundamentally lost. Without this awareness of the needs of others, there can be no true form to economic life. Economic life can be truly formed only by people who, in their thinking about economic life, are capable of looking beyond their own needs, and who have a feeling for the needs of others, through which they learn to feel a part of the whole of humanity. An understanding that is full of insight for what we can call humanity's collective consumption—this is what is needed in economic life.

Economic life consists of production, trade, and consumption. But controlling production, assigning to production its proper power—this is not primarily an aspect of economic life. You will see it in *Towards Social Renewal*: capital is brought into circulation primarily by the spiritual branch of the social organism. The manner in which things are produced is thus a spiritual question. The question of consumption is, in essence, an economic question. Naturally, those who are a part of economic associations need to have the possibility, which comes from spiritual life, of controlling and organizing production; but the intensity of production, the means of production, can be truly recognized only when you have an awareness of the needs of other human beings, not only for your own small group.

But what has appeared in recent life? All over, in those *Schwätzanstalten*[†] that we call Parliaments (this is a literal translation, and so entirely justified; today, we will, without falling into chauvinism, use this German translation for Parliament), everywhere in these *Schwätzanstalten*, there has been a move toward the formation of interest groups: the association of industrialists, the confederation of countrymen, and so on. In the now-collapsed Austria, there were four economic interest groups at the root of the chinwagging [*schwätzismus*]. Thus, precisely the opposite of what leads to true economic understanding has actually been active in recent history. Interest groups, meaning people who were there and saying from the outset, "I am going to decide what I think is right based on my interests in the matter." In economic life, decisions can be made only when we are able to distance ourselves from our own individual interests and be aware of others' interests.

Several years ago, I wrote about this in the series of articles† that appeared under the title "Theosophy and Social Questions" ["Theosophie und soziale Frage"]. There, with a certain assertiveness, I formulated the things that I am saying now. But you see, when it comes to such things, I was not just speaking off the cuff (otherwise I might as well have said it in Parliament, in the *Schwätzanstalt*); I always meant to communicate something that found greater resonance, something that spoke to *all* of humanity. Back then, I stopped writing about it, because nobody took any notice. Of course, there were some interested in it theoretically. But for a long time now, it has not been enough to have merely a theoretical interest. The active social forces that appeared naturally in humanity in earlier centuries are gone now. At present, we need words that can also transition naturally into new active social forces. What I mean by this will perhaps be clear to you after I say the following. Take the most radical socialists, the Communists, the Lenins, the Trotskys† and the others—take them all. Do these people start with some sort of primary principle of social life? No, they take as their frame something that already exists. Even Lenin and Trotsky do not use anything even remotely objective as their foundation, but rather the pre-existing state. Even the Communists do not make use of anything objective—some field within a self-contained economic life or something similar. Instead, they take existing frames and go from there, because they do not trust themselves, no matter how radical they might be, to create altogether new frames. They do not trust themselves actually to begin at the beginning.

Just take a look at another area of society: great numbers of people now, even educated people, are converting to Roman Catholicism. There is a Young Catholic Party forming, and it will probably take on very strong dimensions. Why? Because people today do not trust themselves to seek the beginnings of spiritual life in their own souls; because they do not trust themselves to begin with something that is truly original.† They want to lean on something that already exists. They want to take shelter within something that is already there. Strong inner activity created out of something truly original is not something that people want. They do not trust themselves enough to pursue that. This inner activity, however, is precisely what we need. We must awaken an awareness of it in others. This is what we need now. It is high time that a sufficiently large number of people in European civilization come to an understanding of this. This is what we need: to begin with truly original principles, and not to lose ourselves in abstractions thereby.

At the time, I wrote in my article titled "Theosophy and Social Questions" that social life will be able to become healthy only through people who act on the basis of the interests of others. Those who are interested only in abstractions normally protest against this: "That is nothing new; that has been said for a long time now." If we then ask where and by whom it has been said, we then learn: by Schopenhauer.[†] He said, quite correctly, "Preaching morality is easy; founding morality is hard." Morality must be founded upon empathy for others. Yes, you see—here you have the abstraction! In Schopenhauer, you find an empty abstraction, which, such as it is, is entirely correct. If you wanted to be abstract, you could say, "Having an awareness of the interests of others is what it means to have empathy for them." But in saying this, you have taken the concrete fact that leads you to take it up in life, and turned it into a shadowy abstraction. And with this shadowy abstraction, you give people something that makes them very content.

When you present people with concrete ideas, as is attempted in the literature about the threefold social organism, then opponents come and say, "All of that is already out there!" If we then look up what they are referring to, we find that they are all shadowy abstractions. One person finds that Schopenhauer's lesson on empathy already contains everything that I have said to you today; another person finds it in Kant's categorical imperative, and so on. This is a point that we must examine closely in order to discover the possibility of seeing the essence of the matter.

And so, it is necessary that we not speak about what is true on the basis of any sort of prior judgments; rather, we must always allow the truth to be dictated to us by the things that surround us; must allow ourselves to be taught by what others have, and above all, by what they do not have. But in order to do that, it is necessary for us to familiarize ourselves truly with what lives in the present.

You see, it is true that we must defend ourselves against the attacks that are now being launched from various sides against anthroposophy and also against the threefold social organism. But defending ourselves is not all that we must do. We must be fully conscious of this. We can still defend ourselves against certain streams of the present out of which these attacking individuals come—individuals whose particular attacks are pointless to defend oneself against. Take, for example, a certain religious Dadaist who recently wrote an article in *Die Tat* [*The Act*]; Michel is his name.† A true religious Dadaist; this is actually the only way to describe him. Now, you can defend yourself against such an attack as much as you like, but with a person like this, you will never get anywhere. Because what is based in anthroposophy, what is based in the threefold social organism—he does not understand one word of them.

For example, this person has the idea that he should only express himself using nouns when he writes. Although he is always speaking about "grace" and everything that Catholicism has given him, in his feelings and in his way of understanding things, he is (as befits a religious Dadaist) entirely materialistic. So when he hears that someone has to dissolve these hardened nouns in order to think truly about the spiritual, he calls this the "explosion of good style." From his perspective, this makes perfect sense. But in a discussion or a defense against such attacks, you will get nowhere. Of course, you can give people who say such things a good slap on the wrist; that is all well and good; but you will not get anywhere in these matters solely by putting up a good defense.

And we must be wholly conscious of this if we intend to be effective in the world: it cannot be that we simply defend ourselves against attacks launched against us. That may be necessary sometimes. But what is really important is that we familiarize ourselves completely with the streams running through these times, with the directives that are out there, and that we then unflinchingly describe them to the general public. The mindset of an individual like Michel or someone similar is really not important; what matters is this particular form of religious Dadaism. That stream must be accurately described to the general public. Herr Michel is of no interest; of interest is this particular form of religious impotence that becomes an active stream at present—a trend.

We must describe this in such a way that those people (who are still out there) with a healthy feeling for the truth see what is really going on in the mirror we use, so to speak, to reflect these streams back to them. Naturally, this is much more difficult than simple dialectical defense. But it is also extremely necessary. We must familiarize ourselves with the things that underlie our present civilization. Then we can take them by the roots and set them in the light of the present.

As far as that goes, a good bit is already contained in the material out there from the lectures I have given since April 1919.† In those lectures, I always tried to point out certain active so-called spiritual streams and economic streams in a particular way, and also to describe certain individuals in the way that they must be described. But the things that I said have mostly been allowed to die since then. They are out there. They have certainly been read. But they need further work. The suggestions must be taken up, must be carried forward.

This is what is important in our time. Then, gradually (we do not have much time left, and that "gradually" cannot last too long now) in our threefold social organism movement, something will come into existence that will be a positive, fruitful critique of all present civilization. And upon this foundation of a penetrating critique of present civilization must be built what will put positive ideas into our heads and into our hearts. People must come to see the way in which those things that are found in current trends, things that are mostly just reheated versions of older trends, splinter our society. For if they come to see how splintering those trends are, they will be persuaded to turn toward the positive and concrete things that we can say to them; the people in leadership roles right now are all drifting about in illusions. As long as catastrophe does not come from one corner or another, people will be inclined to deny that there is any danger. This is one of the most characteristic aspects about the present.

Therefore, we must each renew our efforts every day to show other people the way that what they prefer to keep clouded and out of sight will lead to splintering. It is particularly interesting, with this in mind, to study how leading individuals' fear began to affect things even as we started to form our threefold social organism movement in 1919.† Even back then, although it was not more than a few weeks long, there was a general fearful hubbub. In those first weeks, you could see very clearly just how certain industrial and commercially-minded people half begrudgingly posed the question, which of course arose in a way specific to them. "How can we come to terms with the Socialists? How should we do one thing or another?" And they deigned (even though they are mostly working with caricatures of questions about Socialism), nevertheless, they did deign to speak about such matters. Then a few weeks went by, the Socialists did one dumb thing after another, and then the leading individuals of old were in charge again.

This is an interesting movement that can be observed currently, for it showed just how strongly people resist transitioning into inner activity and instead give themselves over to what already exists, working out of what is already there and not making it clear to themselves that we are dancing on the edge of a volcano. Even now, it is the case that most people do not understand this at all. This is why it is so necessary for us to call up an understanding for the fragmentation of society in all circles of the world. How you go about achieving that understanding yourself is what we will discuss in these lectures. Today, I wanted to highlight some of the formal aspects of our work and show you where we should be directing our thoughts. You will not come to represent a cause effectively through anything external alone.

For a long time, human education was necessarily a theoretical one. And now, all students have theoreticians breathing down their necks (including those supposedly learning something hands-on, since their practical experiences are really nothing more than routines). They each have some set of theoretical phrases that are then to be "implemented in reality." This is why so-called hands-on teaching (practical experience) is so ineffective now. It is completely ineffective because people are being taught to be theoreticians. Our entire school system has been constructed in such a way as to intellectualize people, to make them into theoreticians. And this is what we must come to: that when we act on something we stop doing so in a purely theoretical way; every word must be an inner action.

It is extremely interesting to immerse yourself, for example, in the debates that are going on in national economics about the fact that only physical work produces anything good, and that spiritual work does not; that spiritual work is wholly unproductive. In the national economic literature you will find this said in many different ways. And indeed, two of the most influential leaders in national economics in the nineteenth century took this statement as an axiomatic basis for their work: Karl Marx and Rodbertus.† Both supported the view that spiritual life does not produce anything worthwhile, that only physical labor produces anything worthwhile. This perspective should be understood as historical. But the way in which it is presented is based on a thinking that goes something like this: the portion of the physical labor that has been engaged to produce something is used up, and the exhausted power of that labor must then be compensated and recouped. An idea, on the other hand, is not exhausted when you have discovered something, when thousands and thousands more things can be based upon that model. This argument it is often made. But it is nonsense. If you really were to calculate how much energy is required to discover an idea, you would quickly see that the exhausted powers that must be recouped are no less than those used up in physical labor, because in fact everything that is carried out in thinking is as dependent upon the will as those things carried out by the hand. It is not at all possible to separate these two things. It is absolute nonsense to differentiate between head and hand labor in reality. But these have, over time, become empty phrases, because there was a tendency in the last few decades to make what was once factually real into empty phrases.

If you have experience in these matters, you can follow this process every step of the way. I remember, for example, hearing a lecture given by the socialist leader Paul Singer† to members of the proletariat. There were a few people there who had just begun to speak a little bit about those with a "writerly soul." You should have seen the way in which old Singer, in his corpulent state, rebuffed them, and responded that he would not stand for having the practice of spiritual work put on the same level as other labor. That was back at the beginning of the 1890s. Since then, it is possible to observe how reality has moved toward empty phrases in the general character of socialism as well.

Such observations depend upon your finding your way into life, and then speaking out of life itself. Naturally, not everyone can do this between now and tomorrow. But it is possible for us all to have an understanding of this idea. And if you have this understanding, then certain imponderables will find their way into your speaking. And then, your speaking will already turn into something that bears fruit.

This is what I wanted to say to you as a kind of formal introduction today.

Lecture 2

Stuttgart, February 13, 1921 (afternoon)

As of right now, we will move forward only if we are able to provide a satisfactory basis (meaning one that is illuminating for people) for what will heal present-day civilization. And in regard to the various questions before us, much depends on whether we begin with a valid starting point. First, a healthy understanding must be communicated of the actual reasoning behind the kinds of statements found in *Towards Social Renewal*† and everything connected with them.

This is simultaneously a matter of social relationships and the formation of socially-oriented judgments. When exploring these sorts of judgments, we are always dealing with the following: if you make judgments about actual relationships only on the basis of logical reasoning—relationships that involve people's feelings and will forces (since this is, of course, always the case when it comes to social relationships)—then you will only come up with never-ending debates; this must also be kept in mind during discussions. When it comes to the unstable reality in which human beings participate you must take experience as your starting place (a particular experience of one sort or another), rather than logical reasoning, because it is always possible to say a lot both for and against anything that you might consider. Only from the perspective of experience is it possible to make a judgment about something. The reason that so many different and contradictory socio-political perspectives have emerged recently is that the people who proposed them did not take experience, the observation of relationships, as their starting place, and did not form their judgments of the basis of it.

This is, in fact, exactly what was attempted in a comprehensive way in *Towards Social Renewal.* And we must make it intelligible to others that everything found at present in science and education has no foundation for these sorts of judgments, apart from the one found in anthroposophical spiritual science, which does not take logical reasoning alone as its basis, but rather begins in comprehensive experience. And in our spiritual science, you nurture in yourself the capacity to judge on the basis of experience, whereas the way that contemporary scientists beat the drum of experience is only posturing. Contemporary science speaks a lot about experience, but makes its judgments solely on the basis of purely abstract intellectualism. Our spiritual science does not do that. In that way, it fundamentally nurtures the capacity to judge on the basis of experience.

You see, the man I recently mentioned in a public lecture, the national economist Terhalle,[†] quoted a statement by someone not particularly authoritative in these matters, Georg Brandes,[†] who said that it is so hard to do the right thing in social relationships because the vast majority of people do not make logical judgments, but act out of instinct. It is easy to have the impression, if you believe that you stand on a certain infallible basis in all of your decisions, that everything occurring in the soul of a social group comes out of instinct and not out of reason. In a certain sense, it is even correct to say this. But it really does not get you anywhere. If, when considering the formation of judgments, you consider groups of people (whether nationalities or classes) rather than individuals, it is never possible for a judgment to arise from reason. The things that form a judgment do not come solely from convergences in what people think, but also out of what they feel and want. Thus, a one-dimensional judgment can never exist, absolutely never.

From the standpoint of reason, there are no unambiguous social judgments. Social judgments can only be made with a perspective on their representational quality. This is not something you can say to people without further explanation because otherwise it will be misunderstood. But in our times, you must know that when a person intends to develop and deliver a social judgment this act is possible only if there is some recognition of its representational quality; which is to say that a judgment allows itself to be bent and formed, that it very much has a kind of artistic structure (though the word is frowned upon), and not merely a logical structure. Only those judgments that have this kind of malleable form can be applied to social life. This is something that I had to say in order to give our intended subject its proper direction.

In addition, it is necessary these days to accustom people to having a certain breadth of horizon. We are worlds away from those who make judgments by looking at the smallest possible horizon and then hold to those judgments with the belief that they are absolute, are infallibly correct. They see only what is directly in front of them, but they make judgments about everything. This is the character of our age. From this, you will see that in the case of everything that I have attempted to present (this was true even earlier, since April 1919),[†] I did not strive to offer finished judgments, but rather to demonstrate certain things that would allow individuals to make judgments of their own. Ever since April 1919, my striving has been toward the creation of a basis for independent judgments made by each individual. This, too, is something that you should make clear to all circles of the world—that we do not dispense finished, dogmatic judgments, but rather offer guidance that sets the individual on a path that enables independent judgment. And you will improve your effectiveness, your speaking, by not setting much store in finished, dogmatic judgments; rather, your primary task above all else must be to see to the creation of a basis upon which one person will arrive at a judgment by one means, another person by another. Only when there is a convergence of these sorts of judgments will we have something that we can actually use in reality. It is unfortunately all too true that the world is full of judgments; and it is equally true that the world is far from having the foundations for the formation of proper judgments.

And now I come to a point that I would like to use as a preface to our considerations here; a point that absolutely must be clear to you, and that you must use as a starting point for the development of your talks, rather than simply repeating to others word for word what I am saying to you now. When developing your talks, you must begin with an awareness of what I will now attempt to present to you.

You see, within European civilization in the course of the last 100, 150, 170 years, a vast diversity of judgments, the broadest variety of unrest, has appeared in all areas of social life. Try for a moment to take an overview of everything that the nineteenth century brought to us in the way of perspectives on social life, and you see, if you really go through all of them, that actually every single one of these attempts always has several weak points. You will see in every case that a true overview of what is necessary cannot be found. The people who assessed and discussed social life during that period of time brought forward many shrewd observations, many exceptionally shrewd ones. But it was always the case that they finally had to admit all of that really does not have much effect on reality; you really cannot do anything with the things that national economists and practitioners have presented about one social institution or another. It was possible to do something with them in some small area, but never on a comprehensive scale. And the reason lies in the fact that for almost two hundred years, people have tried to "resolve" questions within Europe on the basis of rudimentary foundations (at least they believed they were solving them on this basis); problems that cannot be resolved in this way.

I would like to use the following comparison in order to make what I am trying to say understandable. If a man is building a house, and the foundation and the basement are finished, it is not possible for him to decide that he now wants an entirely new building plan for the second and third stories of the house. He must continue to build according to the plans that he was using when he built the foundation and the ground floor. Once something is already underway, you cannot make something entirely new and unrelated out of the foundation you have laid.

This, however, is exactly what happened in Europe. National economists, socialist activists, bourgeois agitators, practitioners, and others wanted to resolve economic and legal questions, but in actuality all of their so-called solutions were built in the air. But it was not possible simply to go back and start from the fundamentals either. If we really take into consideration the whole life of civilization (a life that is increasingly a whole, from which it is impossible to extract individual parts), one can only say, "Yes, in truth, we live in the midst of an ongoing evolution." We cannot ask ourselves at this point: what are the primary fundamentals of legal relationships in the civilized world; what are the primary fundamentals of economic relationships in the civilized world? This is something that people of our time always forget to bear in mind.

Things are rather curious in Switzerland, for example. The belief is that it is possible to consider distinctly "Swiss affairs" separate from those of the rest of the world, and then to think about legal and economic affairs in that bubble. This is what people there have done for more than two hundred years. And this is the fundamental reason why such chaos has now arrived. You see, people tried to "resolve" —I always have to say "resolve" with quotation marks—questions that, to make use of my earlier comparison, had already been built up to the ground floor by the eighteenth century. You can only build the next story of that building on top of what has already been built. This all goes back to the fact that within European civilization people have lost the ability to have a proper feeling for historical experiences, particularly for those historical experiences that have laid the foundations for the life that springs forth from them. And the most important historical experiences must be properly judged if one intends to make judgments later. You cannot always make judgments by going back to the fundamentals.

And by that I am pointing toward two important experiences that, although they lie in the distant past, must now be carefully considered. Our spiritual life, as well as our rights-political life, as well as our economic life in Europe are based on such experiences, and you cannot think about modern civilization unless you are clear about what was brought into Europe by these occurrences. The first of these is from 1721. It is the Treaty of Nystad[†] that ended the Great Northern War. The second is from 1763, the Treaty of Paris,[†] which brought an end to the conflict between France and the North American colonies and England. These two occurrences are actually, in the world of factual reality, very much part of the life of European civilization; you can see their effects everywhere. But Europeans have completely forgotten to think about these events in the correct way. As a result, they all make incorrect assessments constantly. The facts that I have presented to you are hidden within all of them. I would put it this way: the way we eat breakfast every morning has come about as a result of these events. But people do not want to know about it, just as they do not want to know anything about reality, but want only to make judgments with their heads and logically set their heads spinning (I mean that literally). Most of the judgments that are made now really do put a spin on things, in the colloquial sense of the word.

You see, if you appraise these two events properly, you will have to see a connection between both of them and the European catastrophe in which we now find ourselves. In human evolution, it is not the case that you can make a judgment about something over the course of a few years, because facts and occurrences stretch themselves over vast periods of time.

The matter stands as follows. In 1721, in the Treaty of Nystad, it was first decided that Russia was a power in spiritual life, as well as rights-political life, as well as economic life; one that had a hold in European affairs. Now this is of no small significance. Because Russia, in regard to its spiritual constitution (I say this not to insult, but to present the reality of the matter), Russia, as far as its spiritual interests are concerned, is to this day an Asian power, a power with an Eastern morality. Its soul life is in a form that is familiar to us only through its similarity to the Eastern soul life. Inserted into this Eastern soul life is an exception, that which was brought about by Peter the Great, which in turn led Russia to expand into the Baltic Sea region.

With that, all later things were already decided. And this, too, is something characteristic: Europe had discussed whether Russia should come to Constantinople, or not.[†] And this question was decided in 1721 at the Treaty of Nystad. And this is one of the essential characteristics of European discussions: that people are always trying to answer questions that have already been more or less resolved. The question was already answered to a certain extent back then, and yet people continue to start over without paying attention to the fact that these things happened.

What did this bring about? If you consider the whole history of Europe and the division of Russia in the nineteenth century in relation to it, then you will have to say to yourself, "This division of Russia" (just think about the pan-Slavic and Slavic movements), "this division of Russia led necessarily to the spiritual questions of European life taking an Eastern turn." Rome, for example, had to capitulate to the East, to a certain extent. The East wanted to retain the constitution of its soul; thus, Eastern Catholicism divided from Roman Catholicism. This is a wholly different world in regard to soul constitution. It is, above all, a world in which there has always been a tendency to blend the things that come forward in spiritual life with those that are part of the worldly, secular, governmental regime. There was, to some extent, a desire to seek religious leadership in the state leadership.

So it was through this that European civilization's relationship to the East arrived at its current configuration. Questions were raised that did truly exist, meaning not the ones that have been dreamed up, and about which so many people have given in to illusions. Simply consider the constant stance the Czech Slavs and the southern Slavs had toward Russia, to which Russia responded with something that of course was, in the external realm of political power, nothing more than an empty phrase, but that still had an incredibly misleading effect on the hearts of the Russian people: freedom for the people of the Balkans. Everywhere there are spiritual forces! Into the mix come other things that are again part of spiritual-national relationships: the antagonism between the Polish-Slavic element and the Russian element. Thus, the entire situation of Eastern Europe is defined.

And everything that was reflected there in the spiritual realm is dependent upon the life of the collective civilization. It is not possible to speak about the things that play out in human evolution if one looks only at a part of the story. You cannot simply say that there is, generally speaking, a perspective on how the spiritual life, the economic life, and the rights-political life should stand in relation to one another; one can speak about these questions only by considering certain actual conditions. And the way in which Eastern spiritual life affected things, transplanted as it was into Europe, is wholly dependent on the fact that Russia is largely an agrarian empire that has not fully come to an end; that conditions there still lead people to say, "Nature provides people with everything that they need." Such a soul constitution, as it came over from the East into European life, is necessarily dependent on the things that were made possible by the agrarian lifestyle in Russia. The individual Russian man, regardless of which class he belonged to, would not have the soul constitution that he has if his external daily life were not so intimately connected with the natural world. For the whole of Eastern life, a true question of economics (and thereby the third branch of the threefold social organism) is simply not present.

Everywhere, all over the world, there are these three branches of human social life: the spiritual life, the rights-political life, and the economic life. But the soul constitution of the people under the influence of these three branches always expresses itself differently according to whether those in question are inclined to look toward all that the land offers, or whether they are not inclined to look to all that the land offers. The farther we go toward the east, the more self-evident it becomes that people make use of the natural world and cull from it the things that it offers up, and in this way they have economic activity without doing much to organize an economic life as such. And the situation in Russia did not necessitate (or it was not found to be necessary) the organization of an economic life as such. This comes out of an Eastern way of thinking.

When it comes to these matters, the Eastern way of thinking expends as little effort as possible (if I may put it this way) to go beyond the perspective of another "population" on the Earth. That population is, namely, the animal world. Anyone who believes that this animal world does not also have a spiritual life, and even, to some extent, a rights-political life—that person is altogether on the wrong track. Animal life absolutely has a spiritual life and some form of rights life. But it does not have an economic life. It simply takes what is given to it by the natural world. And the Eastern population raises itself as little as possible above this earthly population, the animal world; the Eastern population has this distinct spiritual life, which follows the imagistic and the intuitive, because in its economic life it takes what the natural world offers and does not spend much time discussing that economic life. Everything that is part of the social structure there is established on the basis of things other than economic relationships; on the basis of class and of lineage, but not on economic thinking. This particular soul constitution—this is the precondition that allows one to give so much over to the nation-state element, as happens in the East.

Europe has been discussing national and social questions for two centuries. But in regard to both matters, the discussion has been conducted on the basis of these two elements without taking into account the things that were really already there. One could simply no longer think about things as they were thought of in the nineteenth century, and especially in the second half of the nineteenth century and the beginning of the twentieth century, after the national element had been given the nuance with which it had been imbued through the influence of an Asian element, of the Slavic-national element (as it had come to fruition). And so, people were actually talking about national questions anachronistically. The things they continued to discuss were long since over.

People should have already been conscious of the fact that one day the big question might arise whether the East and its way of thinking about spiritual life might be able to overpower the West. Even today, the first signs of this are showing. In the East, in Asia, discussions are taking place about how to make it happen that all of the technical-scientific thought in Europe, with its abstractions and its exploitations, and so on, disappears, allowing for a takeover by the Asian element of human feelings and sensations—what is associated with the soul.

In the abstract, you might even be in agreement with this idea. But the fact of the matter is that the soul life and the spiritual life of the East are in a state of decadence. This does not contradict the idea that the forces of the future are in the Russian soul. But everything that was there is in a full-fledged state of decadence. You cannot count on anything resembling a solution coming over from the East. You see, through the Treaty of Nystad in 1721, all of Europe came under the particular nuance of national thinking that had been thrust upon the Slavic nations. And all the results contaminated Europe to a certain extent; Europe was contaminated by Russia's ability to take part in its affairs.

And the experimental nation (if you truly concern yourself with world affairs and do not simply stop at the borders of your own country, then you will see such things), the experimental nation in this case was Austria. And Austria failed because people there continued to have discussions about questions that, to a certain extent, had already been taken in a particular direction. Austria has not been able to come to terms with its Slavic problem because Austria could do so only if it had developed an understanding for its original productive spirit, for a spiritual life that came out of its own elements.

It is true that you cannot talk about such a spiritual life to the liberals, for example (them least of all). They would always respond (and in countries that are republics, this was always the response), these liberals would always say, "Well, if we turn our schools over to a free spiritual life, then Catholicism will take over these schools, and we will have resigned ourselves to clericalism." This is their argument! But this argument is based on the idea that people will think that their only possibility is to appeal to a spiritual life that was productive centuries ago, but that is now anachronistic, decadent. In the moment that one becomes conscious of the need for a freely created spiritual life, then one finds it to be self-evident that this must, of course, be given to the life of our schools. Because people do not take part in the creation of civilization with their own will forces but rather desire merely to give themselves over to something that feeds them—be it the state or a premade economic life—because they do not infuse their will with creative powers, because of all this, damaged organizations like this will result. It is a matter of being able to free oneself without giving the schools over to an old way.

The people who talk in the way that I have mentioned also say, "But we will not ever bring about a new spiritual life, and so the old one will simply overrun everything." In that case, you can easily becomc a follower of Spengler and his book *The Decline of the West.*[†] There, it makes no difference whether we do anything at all, or whether the Catholic Church takes over everything. But a new spiritual life must be there! It was not wrong that at one time the church ran the schools; for everything that we now have in scientific life came about in one way or another from the old church. That the church ran the schools is not what is wrong; what is wrong is if the traditional church were again to run schools when in fact we are standing before the historical imperative to achieve a new spiritual life.

So, it was only Europe's inability to imagine a new spiritual life that brought about the discussion of national questions. It would have been necessary from the perspective of productive spiritual life for Central Europe to have an effect on the East. This would certainly have frozen in their tracks all the things that came about in the pan-Slavic and Slavic movements. This spiritual life was there in its beginning stages. Around the turn of the eighteenth century, people had begun to create a new spiritual life, and it was called "Goetheanism."

But people did not have the courage to hold to it; this is one side of the story.

On the other side are the issues that people discuss and understand as social-economic. Since 1763, ever since certain territories had to be given to England by France, thus deciding that North America would be Anglo-Saxon, and not French and Spanish, the economic-social question has been directed down a very specific channel. There were many decisive moments in the eighteenth century: in the East, there was the 1721 Treaty of Nystad and, in the West, there was the 1763 Treaty of Paris. These two important decisions, hidden within the whole spiritual and economic life of Europe, must be kept in mind, because you will never arrive at any judgments unless you do.

And you see, you cannot make value judgments about the things that come up in world history, as so many people do, from entirely subjective perspectives. Sometimes you can do nothing other than make use of certain radical words and descriptions. The East had, at one time, a great and powerful primal wisdom. Today, it is the case that, to some extent, the East, with its decadent and old primal wisdom, has fallen into barbarism. For "barbarism" (in Schiller's sense of the word)[†] is nothing more than the rationalization of primal human instincts, the directing of those instincts through understanding and mere thought life. If, however, we call the East barbaric and speak of the barbarism in the East, and particularly in Russia, then the further west we move, as we pass England and cross over into America, then by the same token, this Western civilization must be called not "civilization" at all, but rather "savagery." This is the opposite of barbarism. The barbarian tyrannizes the heart and the feelings with the head; the savage tyrannizes the head with all that comes from the rest of the human organism, with the life of instincts. And this, in essence, is the Western life, and this Western life is the site of savagery! If you look past the gilded layer of European culture that you find in America, you have to ask yourself, "What is the American culture, at its core?" It is, to put it radically, savagery.

But there is no chauvinistic agitation hiding in these words! If you truly want to recognize this American life for what it is, then you have to say, "The Europeans have not actually conquered the Native Americans there inwardly (externally, certainly!), but inwardly the Europeans have immersed themselves in the Native American life. Instincts have become the ruler." And this is what lies at the core: the altering of Europeans by Native American instincts. It is not only the case that the Europeans, after they have lived over there for a while, have longer arms, and so on (this has been anthropologically confirmed); the constitution of the soul is also changed. It is not a matter of what people have as concepts and mental pictures, but rather what, as a whole human being, they possess as their constitution. And in that regard, one has to say that the farther west one moves, the more the essence of the Anglo-Saxon being crosses over into savagery.

This savagery definitely exists. And it is once again based on the fact that the economic question is actually not a part of the discussion. In the East, the collective social structure, due to the particular situation that I described to you, becomes absolutist. In the West, it becomes anarchistic.

Just take a look at what happened in the West. People were banking on the inexhaustibility of economic life; they were simply feeding off the colonies; they were working on the basis of this inexhaustibility without thinking through this economic life. The Western economic life was absolutely built on the principle of taking as much as possible from the colonies, regardless of whether the colonies lie within or without. It is quite telling if you follow the way that during the 1880s and the 1890s more and more territories were gained in America for the purpose of growing wheat and other crops. People took from the natural world. It was not particularly necessary for them to think about economic life. Consequently, it made no difference to them what it meant to have associations in economic life, because the economic life there operated on the basis of inexhaustibility. But, all the same, something happened: an economic structure was formed. England's structure is based on the fact that it controls India. In America, a certain kind of economic life was formed. This in turn impressed its structure onto all of the West's social life. Something came into being that has led to a way of conducting economic affairs arising only from the principle of inexhaustibility.

In the East, the decadent social life that pays no regard to economic life tends toward absolute dominance in all areas of social life; in the

West, what I have just described to you developed out of the Anglo-Saxon's ability to assimilate. In this opposition between East and West, modern civilization was erected.

It is interesting, for example, to compare two completely opposite people with one another: Rodbertus, the German national economist—who, despite being a fairly open-minded man, could one day end up in the ministry (which many people are claiming)—and, let us say, Karl Marx. A person like Karl Marx was possible only because he first learned to think in Central Europe and afterward witnessed economic affairs in the West. Karl Marx could never have achieved what he has achieved for the proletariat if he had never spent time in Germany. All of that came about only because he learned to think in Germany; then became familiar with the way people conduct themselves on a daily basis in France, in Paris; and then became familiar with the economic life in England based on the principle of inexhaustibility, and all that comes with it. And it was upon this final piece that he could begin to build his work.

In the same way, it is characteristic of Rodbertus (this is why we are comparing here two people, Rodbertus and Karl Marx) that he assessed things like (and this is, of course, an exceptional case) like a Pomeranian manor house lord who had suddenly became socialist. This was how he looked at things, and it is interesting; for when you take a look at two extremes like Rodbertus and Karl Marx, much of interest comes out of it! But Rodbertus must be understood thus: as a suddenly-socialist Pomeranian manor house lord! Such a person knows well that one can never fully dispense with agriculture; he knows what significance it has for the national economy. Others say all sorts of nonsense that is pleasing to those who in their youth did not learn to tell the difference between barley and wheat, because they grew up in the city. But a man like Rodbertus knows better. A man like that knows the significance of agriculture being overstressed by mortgages. If he still has any socialistic pretensions, as he once did, then he does not allow the one to contaminate the other very much. Something questionable does indeed come to the fore. But one side corrects the other. And the result is something halfway brilliant, revealed in the person of Rodbertus. And so, compare this with what Karl Marx said, and you will say to yourself, "The members of the proletariat today, in the broadest sense of word, find that what Karl Marx said is immediately clear to them." Why do they find it so? Because it was thought of in the context of a purely economic life, and the proletariat find themselves solely within economic life; and also because it is particularly astute thinking, since Karl Marx learned to think in Germany. But a German could not form any concept of the way that economic life would be if everything was thought of only economically. Germans today cannot do it either. A contemporary German could do this only by saying, "I must create a reality in which it is possible to think purely in terms of economics." This is found within the threefold social organism.

Everything else that appears in the West (take Darwinism, or men like Spencer, Huxley, or one of the American scientists, or even Emerson, Whitman,† and the others)—all of it, *all* of it in the spiritual life has a fundamental quality that leads us to say, "The thinking head begins in the stomach." Everything is a transformed, transplanted instinct. Everything is actually just thought of as economics. They think only through what they eat and drink. This is the case all over, and to a very high degree. Certainly, a lot of people do not notice it these days. And if you say this, then they take it as an insult. But it is not meant as an insult. It is, in fact, something of great significance; it is the only thing of great significance in recent, in contemporary civilization—this way of thinking. But it is the case. And European civilization has, in fact, been squeezed between these two extremes since the eighteenth century. Only the people that have been excluded from European civilization, that have simply been put in front of machines; only these people have brought to the world a way thinking on the surface level of things that would seem to have nothing to do with these same concerns, but that in fact has everything to do with them: this is the world of the proletariat. And it is most interesting when you consider these things as they really are.

Austria, as I have already said, was the experimental country.† In the 1870s and 1880s very strange things happened in the life of the Austrian nation. On one side, there was much discussion about the Slavic question. Some called it, more accurately, "Austrian federalism." The entire spiritual life in Austria (spiritual life being one branch of the threefold social organism) was given its structure entirely on the basis of these discussions about the Slavic question. On the other side, terrible fruits were born (you will find this in the subordinate clauses of the Parliamentarians' speeches much more than would seem to be correct or necessary), terrible fruits were born out of the collapse of Austrian economic life under Americanism, under Anglo-Saxon economics. You can see everywhere in Austria the way in which their exports (for example, their exports of grains to Hungary) were infringed upon by what came from the West. Back then, very insightful people in Austria said, "The flow from West to East will flood our country with debts; agriculture will gradually die out." This was, in turn, a hint at symptoms that bespoke deep historical causes, so that at the time in Austria there was a lot of talk about what, in regard to spirit, was shining through as the Slavic question; and what, in regard to economics, was shining through in the question of agriculture.

And then, for example, a strange plan turned up in the heads of a few people (I think it was around 1880) that will actually make quite an impression on you; it was even discussed in the Austrian Parliament. A plan for a League of Nations was put forward; or in any case, a plan that called for a League of Nations that would actually have to be referred to as a League of Western European Nations. But leagues that actually incorporate the whole world cannot actually be formed in this way; that is nonsense. It could only come about in the head of an abstract man such as Woodrow Wilson,[†] that one would form a league that incorporated the whole world. If that were possible, then you would, of course, no longer need such a league. So anyway, the idea for a League of Nations had already turned up in the 1880s. Again, you can see here something about which you can then say, "In the course of the nineteenth century, impulses periodically appeared that were actually needed, but they were always overrun by the impractical solutions that are always brought forward without any regard for their historical reality." Wherever reality has shone through into human realities, it has always been immediately obliterated. For the contemporary human being is a theoretician.

And this is the idea that I would most like to entrust to you: if you all do not succeed in casting off your theoretical selves before you set out on your work, then you will achieve nothing. You must set aside the theoretical self; you must attempt to speak out of reality. Your work will sometimes succeed, sometimes not—that part does not matter. What matters is that you speak on a foundation of reality. To that end, it was not my intent to present you with judgments today, but rather to point out to you the facts. I said to you: consider what has come about as a result of the Treaty of Nystad in 1721 and the Treaty of Paris in 1763. Everything that is historically described about these events is yours to consider: you have a perspective to look at. Everywhere, you will find things from these events that continue to play a role in the spiritual life, the rights-political life, and the economic life. I wanted only to illuminate one aspect of this. For if you let your words come out of your own judgments of the matter, then you will achieve something; if you only repeat what you have heard, you will not.

Lecture 3

Stuttgart, February 13, 1921 (evening)

From the proceedings currently out there in the world, you will naturally see that all conversation about social conditions lacks the proper foundation if it does not take into account international relations. For exactly this reason, I have chosen the course for these remarks to follow the lectures I gave yesterday and earlier today. I want to start with a short description of certain matters in international relations and then, with this as our foundation, be able to move on to our actual task.

My earlier hints will have left you with the following question: "How are we to think about all of this if we want to arrive at a possible solution to the enormous, world-historical questions of today and of the near future; how are we to think about the West on one hand and the East on the other?"

You can, of course, easily see that all human thinking at present is, for the most part, one-sided. Is it not true that a person making a judgment about a particular question of world relations at this time thinks according to the following schema?—saying, "When you look toward the West, you are looking at efforts that in the coming decades will enslave Central Europe. They will force Central Europe into slavery." And the only response to the threats over there is to take the same orientation (meaning more or the less the same orientation that the West takes toward us in Central Europe) to take the same orientation toward the East, meaning that we should form economic ties with the East and seek replacement sources in the East for all of the things now produced in Germany. Because everyone has gotten used to considering things only from an economic perspective, they simply extend this schema onto the East.

Actually, considerations of true reality speak against doing this. And for that reason, I wanted to begin by expressing exactly how the East and the West are involved in the life of modern civilization, so that a way might be created by which this judgment could be made. The question is: Is it prudent for the leading economic figures who have integrated into a configuration that under the influence of the only genuine economic life is supposed to embrace something still being called the "German Empire"—is it prudent that in this situation economic relationships (meaning economic relations as such) be directly established with the East?

Anyone who thinks about these matters in the way people currently think will say, "Yes!" But anyone who pays attention to what the spiritual life, the rights life, and the economic life of the nineteenth century (and the previous era generally) taught us will probably arrive at a different judgment. For, just think about the real facts that lie before us here. We have many opportunities to see how devotedly and gladly Eastern Europe takes up the spiritual life of Central Europe, if we look at the relationships that played out in the last decades of the nineteenth century. For if you turn toward the spiritual life of Russia and ask yourself, "How did this actually come about?" you will see that something with a dual nature is living in this Russian spiritual life.

First of all, the reflexes of good Central European thinking that live in us oppose everything that is found in true Russian spiritual life, in everything that has come from that spiritual life, and in everything that Central Europe has taken up out of a certain "lust for sensations" (a lust that appeared in the last decades of the nineteenth century). With great willingness (more than is to be found within Germany itself), German intellectuals and everything connected with German thought were taken up in Russia. Already in the first half of the nineteenth century, Germans were being appointed to permanent posts directing Russian education. Everywhere you can see how what is to be found in the form of concrete thoughts and institutional goals in Russia have come about through the influence of Central Europe, and of German individuals in particular. This was an influence that came into being long ago with the legendary Rurik brothers, which you always hear repeated: the Russians have this and that, and everything is possible for them, but they lack order; for that reason, the Russians turned to the three brothers and asked them to help create order.

This was more or less how it was throughout all of the nineteenth century in regard to all the spiritual sources for life in Central Europe. Anytime someone needed to take up something concretely, they always turned to Central Europe or Western Europe. But the reaction to these calls from both regions was completely different. Central European life entered into Russian life with a certain self-awareness, although nothing substantial resulted from it, and it continued to live its own life. But when Western European spiritual life entered into Russian life something substantial *did* result from it—something that took on a certain concrete, sensational quality, something that lived there with a certain pomp, with a certain decorative flair. This must absolutely be taken into consideration.

Consider for a moment the significant Russian philosopher Solovyov. Such a philosopher has an entirely different significance within the context of Russian life than he does within the context of Central European life. Everything that you will find in his thinking is Central European—Hegelian, Kantian, Goethean, and so on. We find only the reflexes of our own lives in all of these philosophers when we turn and look at their concrete thinking. You could even say, "All of the concrete thinking that one finds in Tolstoy is Central European or West European," but with all of the differences that I have just mentioned. Even for Dostoevsky, the same is true, despite his stubborn, nationalistic Russian chauvinism. This is one side of the story.

But at this point, at the end of the nineteenth century and the start of the twentieth, we are seeing protests in Russia (and I would like to suggest that they are nearly unanimous) against the influence of the economic machinations of Central Europe. Just think about the way in which certain aspects of business contracts and other similar things have been taken up. And think about how much the Russians (apart from all the yelling) how much the Russians have acted like a shrinking violet in their protests against what has turned into an out-and-out economic invasion or takeover.

All of this must be taken up as guidance. All of this must prove to us that if you try to base a relationship with the East solely on trade or other economic relationships, it is like trying to shake someone's hand with broken fingers. Despite the great difficulties connected to these matters because of the Bolshevik opposition, what must be achieved is, above all, to bring the spiritual element (one resulting from a productive spiritual life) into Russia. Everything that comes out of a productive spiritual life stretches across all worldviews and sentiments related to the spiritual life itself, as well as the rights life and the economic life. All of that will be taken up well by the Russians.

Because the second of the two elements, aside from the first which involves only the adoption of concrete (namely German) thoughts—the second element of Russian spiritual life is one that (how shall we say this) one that is undifferentiated, vague (this is not meant to stir up bad feelings; again, it is just terminology), a vague blend of thoughts and feelings. This is precisely what can, for example, be characteristically observed in certain typically Russian philosophers like Soloviev. His thoughts have German origins. But in Soloviev, they turn up in altogether different forms than in the German thinkers. Even the Goethean element turns up in an entirely different form in Soloviev. It has been mixed around, re-imagined, turned into a blend of feelings and thoughts that lend a certain nuance to the whole. But this nuance is also the only thing that distinguishes this spiritual life. And this nuance is still passive; it is accepting and open. And it relies on taking up Central European spiritual life.

In this exchange between Central European spiritual life and the Russian people, it is possible that something awful could develop for the future. You also have to keep in mind how generative this interacting is for civilization. But it is important that the back-and-forth occurs only in the purely spiritual element. It must play out in a certain element built on the relationship between one human being and another. This is the kind of relationship that we must achieve with the East. And when this fact is recognized, then something else will arise all on its own from what happens in spiritual life; something that we might call an independent economic community. We cannot start with this, because if we do then it will absolutely backfire. Everything that economists might do with the East will surely bring us absolutely nothing if it is not built on the foundation that I have just described. It is a social issue of eminent importance; we must keep this circumstance in mind.

The other side of this is our relationship to the West. You see, educating the West from out of our Central European spiritual life is impossible. And we should reckon with this impossibility, irrespective of the fact that it is already incredibly difficult to simply translate the things we think in Central Europe, the things we perceive in Central Europe, as well as the things they perceive in the East. The whole way of looking at things when it comes to purely spiritual matters is completely and totally different in Central European regions than it is in the West and in America.

People were amazed that Wilson understood so little about Europe when he came to Paris. They would have been less amazed if they had taken a look at a thick book that Wilson had written back in the 1890s; it is called *The State*.[†] This book was actually written entirely under the influence of European scholarship. But you should just see what has come of it, this European scholarship! You would not have been amazed had you seen the precedents; you would not have been amazed that Wilson understood nothing about Europe when he came there. He simply could not. For whenever thinking as such comes into consideration it is futile to try to arouse any sort of direct impression. On the other hand, it would be very significant if you were to imagine the matter such that you said to yourself, "Well, when you try to do business from culture to culture with the West, you will never get anywhere." If, on the other hand, you shut out the scholars and, even more so, the statesmen from the exchange; if you do not send any statesmen to the West and instead send only economists, then the people there will understand these economists and something fruitful will result. Only when it comes to economic life will we get anywhere in direct exchange with the West.

This is not to say that when having an exchange with the West we should simply limit ourselves to everything that belongs to economic life. No, no; this is not necessary. It is, for example, highly interesting to take a look at many of the concert halls, big concert halls, in Western Europe, and to look at the famous composers being played there: Mozart, Beethoven, Wagner, and so forth. Generally, you will find only German names. However, you can be sure that if you want to make some sort of impression on Western Europe using only what comes out of the substance of Central European thought, you will not get very far in either the Romance cultures or the Anglo-Saxon culture. This does not preclude talking with people in those areas about what is thought in Central Europe. It goes without saying that you can do this. But you must speak in a different way than you might in Central Europe, where the life of the imagination, the thought life, is the primary consideration. Take a look at a larger example: Western Europeans (and perhaps also the Americans) will understand our building in Dornach much more than they will understand what we are talking about within it; that is to say, they will understand everything factual about the building.

Of course, when one is speaking it is also possible to put things in a way that allows the factual aspects to emerge from the subject at hand. This was certainly true prior to the war (once again, I bring this up not out of immodesty), so much so that in Paris, in May 1914, I gave a lecture in German.[†] It had to be translated word for word, but all the same, I was able to give it in German. And this lecture (this is simply a fact) was more successful than any lecture that I had ever given in Germany. We have come that far. But it is necessary to couch what is said in such a way that it deals, shall we say, more with the surface layer, with the appearances, with the results, with the potential effects; it is necessary to present everything that way. In this instance, we are dealing primarily with the question "How?"

And, therefore, it is not at all unrealistic but rather a very concrete thought when we say to ourselves, "We will have a big impact on the West if we understand our task in the proper manner; if we, for example, really manage to get away from the things that are not working and will never work because we will always be behind compared to the West; if we get away from the simple imitation of the West." You see, it will make absolutely no difference if we imitate the machines of the West; we will not make them as precisely as they do in the West. If we make false teeth the way they do, we will not make them as elegantly; it is pointless! If we simply imitate, we will never really establish the right relationship with the West. They will have no need for the things that we create by imitating. But if we take hold of what we can do, and what the West cannot do; if, for example, we were to fill technology with artistry and artistic understanding; if we were to arrive truly at what has long been forming within our Anthroposophical Society, which we have not been able to bring to completion due to failures of the individuals that have given themselves to the task; if we were, for example, to imbue the locomotive with an artistic form; if we were to give an artistic form to the train stations where they arrived and departed; if we were to impress upon ourselves the things that we alone are able to apprehend—then the people in the West would take it up and would understand it too. And then they would have open exchange with us. But we must have a picture of what this exchange might look like. This is something that each individual must do on his or her own, but it must be done. And we must begin this task presently, so that we can recognize how the impulse for threefolding emerges out of genuine, actual relationships.

We must have a spiritual life whose nature makes it able to affect the East in the way I have just described to you; this is the only way to have a productive spiritual life. By doing this, we will already trump the Lunacharskys[†] of the world, and all of those like him. People like that will not be able to enslave the Russian soul forever. If we had this productive spiritual life, we would already have begun to have an effect on the East. We must only muster up the strength to bring this spiritual life into being ourselves. We must defeat all of the base people who have stepped forward wanting to trample over this spiritual life.

The animosity toward the spiritual life has reached such a point that recently in Dornach I read a statement saying that in the conflict with spiritual science, the spiritual sparks have been enflamed enough that actual sparks and flames might take hold of this building in Dornach.[†] So the enmity toward spiritual work is taking on the most brutal forms. What is crucial to understand is that this is altogether necessary. We must bring into reality this productive spiritual life, this wholly concrete, productive spiritual life, paying no mind to how life might sneer or push it around. You must know that this productive spiritual life that is able to come into being in Central Europe could call forth the great brotherhood that could then expand into the East and unite it with Central Europe; whereas all of these brutal economic machinations will only open up further chasms between Central Europe and the East. It is exceptionally important for us to see clearly into such matters, and it is important that such ideas become popular. It is particularly important because if you win over the public, then (simply because they will grow accustomed to thinking in this way), people will arrive at a whole new way of thinking about the other social questions as well.

But this must be established on a broader basis than it has been thus far. For this reason, it is necessary that we work with all the flame and passion available to us, so that the things we strive for are not forever wasted efforts. I must stress, my dear friends, that right now we have a wealth of material in our journal *The Threefold Social Organism*,† but it is fundamentally entombed, because it is only in written form. This is why we have had to work continuously. But this is impossible to maintain. We must develop a broader foundation of many different people who can handle all of the things that are faltering in one way or another. We must be clear about these matters.

We must be entirely clear about our need for a productive spiritual life, and clear that we must cultivate it so that we can establish a viable relationship with the East.

And we must also have an economic life in which the state does not interfere, in which only the economists are active, in order to have any exchange with the West. The economists alone must tend to this exchange. Only in this way will anything good come of it. It can be done, indeed, it should be done for as long as no other means is possible. Otherwise, though there can be an exchange from state to state with the West, nothing fruitful will come of this. Something good will come from the exchange only when our statesmen disappear from the economic dealings, no matter how much they kick and scream about having to do so. Let the statesmen over there in the West do business! Over there, the statesmen are right in the midst of economic life. But here in Central Europe, if the economists become statesmen, they lose all of their economic bearing; they become men who think only politically.

It is important that we see into the real necessities of life. This already shows us why we must have a threefold social organism—so that we can send to the West economists uninfluenced by the machinations of the state and the spiritual life. And we need a free spiritual life in order to arrive at a viable relationship with the East. Our international relations themselves depend upon it.

What form this takes in each individual case is something that each of us must determine ourselves. What I offer here should be taken only as a guide. It is, however, a guide that comes out of real affairs. And you must take up these things that are so often said in a deeply serious way. It is not true that today's practitioners truly understand anything about practical life. In fact, they basically understand next to nothing about true practical life—and it is precisely because they are practitioners! The practitioners nowadays are actually the biggest theoreticians, because they live entirely within the schema of their own thoughts and theorize about praxis within that space. This is precisely what must be examined in the deepest sense of the word. And this is what we must wholeheartedly place at the foundation of our so-called agitations: that we work out of an understanding of actual affairs.

You see, we must above all be clear that modern economic life necessitates threefolding. And this is because this economic life is chaotically intermingled with the impulses of the East, the impulses of the West, and the impulses of the Center. And the following is true. Economic life consists fundamentally of three elements: everything that nature provides (as I discussed in the previous lecture); everything created by human labor; and all business conducted through capital. Capital, human labor, and natural resources, with everything that can then be furthered through production—these are the things that figure into economic life.

But you see, it is the same within the social organism as it is within the threefold human organism, which consists of three parts but which also has a threefold structure within each part. In our head, we have a human organ that is primarily an organ of the nerves and the senses, but the head also carries out processes of nourishment; it is, in a certain sense, filled with organs associated with nourishment. In everything that makes up our purely metabolic organism, in the midst of metabolism, of everything that serves the metabolism, we likewise have something from the nerve- and sense-organism, the sympathetic nervous system. The same is true in regard to the threefold nature of the social organism. In each of the three parts, the whole is once again repeated. But currently, this repetition within each part is wholly inorganic. It is inserted into each part in a way that destroys life, rather than building life up.

First of all, nature is tucked in there, and production is, of course, only a furthering of nature. And insofar as nature is inserted, a whole way of feeling is introduced that is wholly Eastern, that comes entirely from the East. The people of the East will not understand that it is possible to incorporate human labor into economic life. And even if we go back to our earlier economic relationships, infused as they are with Eastern affairs, you will nowhere find that human labor figures into the economic life.

It is also impossible for this human labor to figure into economic life. You see, it is possible to compare apples and apples. You can get something from those calculations. You could also compare apples and pears by counting them both as fruit. You can get something from those calculations. However, I do not know how you would ever compare, for example, apples and eyeglasses. Now, what is within a useful object, what is found in a commodity, is fundamentally different from human labor, which, to use a Marxist phrase, "is congealed within that commodity."[†] That is total nonsense, but it has become popular these days to say it: that which "is congealed within the commodity." To take human labor and then equate it with everything contained within a useful object, within a commodity, is as nonsensical as trying to compare apples and eyeglasses. But modern economics has done just that. It has accomplished a great artistic feat in economic life: it has, so to speak, made eyeglasses edible and turned apples into ocular ornaments.

This is not something that you will notice in human life. You notice it in the secondary natural realms. It sounds paradoxical to say something like this, but in reality it happens constantly. Insofar as you have any money at all in economic life and insofar as that money carries a certain value, which is found again in the price of the commodity as though this somehow occurred naturally, in this transaction, you have effectively compared apples and eyeglasses. It is impossible. It is unthinkable.

Although the three areas of the social organism (spiritual life, rights-political life, and economic life) were indeed ordered around old relationships, the economic life, in an Eastern way, and although people produced only on the principle of inexhaustibility without giving it much thought (I suggested in the previous lecture that they thought little more about it than animals, who also take only what nature offers to them), in previous times, people did not necessarily try to compare commodities and labor, even in our regions of the world. Work was organized in a different way: a man was a landowner, a noble landowner; he inherited this social position from his forefathers. If he did not have such blood in his veins, then he was a bondsman, a serf, a slave. In other words, people had a legal relationship to one another. Whether you had to work or could just tend to your belly and watch from the balcony as others worked was not determined by issues of price or money; instead, these matters were based on legal relationships. Work was ordered around entirely different fundamental principles than the trading of goods. The two things were necessarily separated from one by rules of older relationships that we can no longer use. In the East it was twofold: commodities and human labor. For that reason, it has always been thought that legal work relationships are shaped by different fundamental principles than the ones that shape the movement of goods. This resulted from these old legal relationships, to be sure. But back then work was not somehow quantified; rather, a person was established in a post and then did the work, and the work that was done is what circulated. But some aspect of that human labor did not "flow into the product."

So you can see that the rights-political life is already hidden in what has come about in economic life, specifically through labor, which has such a share in it. If, in economic life, we speak of what is purely economical, we must speak of goods, of commodities. Insofar as we speak about the evolved economic life (meaning the economic life that touches on the participation of work), we must add to this a legal element such that the regulation of labor is something rights-political. It thus crosses over into another branch of the social organism. And capital is, in fact, fundamentally a part of the economic life, insofar as it carries this economic life spiritually. Capital is what generates the economic centers, what generates the activity. It is the spiritual element of economic life. Now, it is the case that in modern materialism, this spiritual life within economic life has taken on a materialistic character. But it is nevertheless the spiritual element of economic life. Capital is the spirit of economic life.

This leads us to again seek a threefold structure within economic life itself. In other words, everything from the economic life (in which the production, circulation, and consumption of goods takes place) that flows into it as labor can be brought into relationship with the rights-political life; and capital, which is the actual spiritual element, can be brought into relationship with the spiritual life. You will find this described concretely in my book *Towards Spiritual Renewal*,† where it says that the transfer of capital, the circulation of capital must stand in a certain relationship to spiritual life. This is the key: that we learn within economic life itself to treat these three areas separately and distinctly.

We will form for ourselves a proper picture of what is actually true only if we know, on the one hand, that we must create regulations in a certain area that the East easily bypassed: the relationship between human economic life and nature. In the East, this relationship was self-evident. We have to regulate it. For people in the West, the whole of spiritual life, as I explained to you earlier, has become wrapped up in economic life. Even Spencer† thinks economically when he is supposedly thinking scientifically. Everything there is put into the economic life. Spiritual life is economics. Consequently, capitalism as such becomes materialistic. The idea of capital has to be there, as it says in *Towards Social Renewal*; but the connection between the spirit and capital will experience the starkest resistance in the West. There, capitalism, as it currently exists, corresponds so completely to the Western mode of thought, where everything spiritual is brought into the material. And so, everything that is currently being demanded of Central Europe by the West, about which people say such unjustified things, on a fundamental level, this is nothing other than the effects of Western capitalism, which has now spread a very wide net for itself. Though the

Western states have all fallen under the capitalist purview, people believe that they are just dealing with the West's political structures. This is not true. The statesmen, too, have basically become economists there, just as the academics are economists. And so we have to tell these two things apart. First, there is, I would like to suggest, everything that we have to think about in economic life, things that the East is not accustomed to thinking about; and then there is all of capitalism, which must be inspirited; everything that the West would never think to inspirit. This is precisely the task of the Central European regions. Thus, something has come into being in these Central European regions that must be very carefully considered.

It always happens here in Stuttgart and in Switzerland (and other friends have also experienced something similar), it always happens that you encounter people who say something like, "Yes, well, if one were to agree with the need for a free spiritual life and a free economic life, then there would be nothing left over for the rights-political limb!" In fact, the way that political life is these days, having taken in spiritual life, which has no place there, and taking over the economic life more and more, in this form, true political life is stunted. In that situation, actual political life, namely the life that should exist between people, between all mature individuals, is simply not there. And so naturally, people like Stammler[†] can only manage to stammer out something like, "The essence of political life is that it gives form to economic life." But in actuality, the essential fact is that political life will develop properly, since it encompasses everything that exists between mature individuals, simply because they are human beings; meaning that, for example, the whole realm of labor regulations belongs to it; the essential point is that political life will develop properly only when the two other limbs have been separated from it. Only then will a truly democratic political life be able to form. It is no wonder that no one has any true concept of this political life, for these days no one has any true concept of an independent democracy because they only think abstractly, and then they use their abstract thinking to define a democracy. One can always define things, right? Definitions bring to mind that old Greek example that I have often mentioned in which someone defined the human being very concretely as: "a living being that walks on two legs and has no feathers." The next day someone brought a plucked goose to the man who made this proclamation and said, "This must be a human being then, for it walks on two legs and has no feathers." With definitions, anything is possible. But the key is not to have definitions, but to find reality.

Take the concept of democracy as it currently exists, in the form that originated primarily in the West; how did this concept come about? You can follow the development of England. Trace it through the older English lordships, and you will find there a striving to escape from bondage. But all of this has a religious character. And then this striving took on an entirely religious character under Cromwell.[†] Something developed there out of the puritan theocracy—out of the concept of freedom of belief—that was then taken out of the context of theocracy, of faith, and became the concept of democratic political freedom. This is what people in the West call the democratic sensibility. It was derived from a sensibility for religious independence. This is how one arrives at a true concept of democracy. And a true concept of democracy will exist only once there is an organization put in between the spiritual and economic organizations, one that is based on the relationship between people and on the equality of all mature individuals. Only then will a true political relationship result.

But you see, it is telling that primarily in Central Europe, without already having arrived a concept of the threefold social organism, people have already started to think: "How should a state really be established?" It is extremely interesting that, working with certain concepts from Schiller and certain concepts from Goethe, Wilhelm von Humboldt[†] (who might even have become a Prussian minister—that is a strange thing to think about) wrote this beautiful essay in the first half of the nineteenth century: "The Limits of State Action." In that work, he wrestles with the possibilities for establishing a state structure, a true state structure. He attempts to sort out everything from social affairs that can actually be solely political and legal. Wilhelm von Humboldt certainly did not succeed at this in an unbiased way, but this is not the question. Such things would have to be improved upon. And we will get no further until we come to create something real and actual for the things that are political (and meanwhile Stammler keeps stammering about political life existing only for the formation of economic life).

These things must absolutely be brought before the public at large in a far-reaching way, and as quickly as possible. Only by bringing healthy thinking to our contemporaries and spreading these thoughts as quickly as possible will we be able to move forward.

For the opposing forces are strong. They scoff and assert their will to destruction from all corners of the world. And we should not give in to any illusions about the powerful will forces amassed on that side. If the venture on which we are currently embarking is to have any meaning then we must say to ourselves, "We have tried to gain a social impulse out of anthroposophical spiritual science." Is it not true that everything that makes up anthroposophical spiritual science has the advantage of time; that it can go slowly, that it can pay attention to what people can tolerate in a given moment? This could lead to the formation of cliques. These cliques exist only in the physical world; the spiritual movement supersedes them. Everything that lies at the root of the pure anthroposophical movement in the form of life force—that has significance, holds content in the spiritual world. And so it does not really matter whether cliques form, whether there are different sects and the like within that movement.

These are the details that naturally come under dispute in our current, serious age. But this is not as terrible as it will be if the proper things do not happen in practical areas, where calls for immediate action have been made to the anthroposophical movement, as is the case, I would suggest, in the groups that do work pertaining to society. In this case, there is no time for waiting. In this case, we cannot establish leagues for the threefold social organism organized to be merely copies of the old branches of anthroposophy. In this case, we must be aware that if we only begin work on it tomorrow, then no matter how good that work is, it might be worse than whatever we manage to do today. In this matter, it is crucial that we begin to be effective in a strong way immediately, in the present moment, because the next day it might be too late. And in fact, the things happening around us demonstrate just how, from week to week, it might suddenly be too late. Thus, this initiative has been introduced, and it is for these reasons that so much significance has been placed upon this initiative—because it is essential that these things happen quickly. Europe has no time to lose.

The necessary thing is to bring into people's heads the possibility of thinking such that reality plays a role in their thoughts. Humanity has developed in such a way that, generally speaking, an unreal way of thinking has become the predominant way, even in regard to practical life. It is unreal thinking when, for example, people come forward and say, "We should cultivate the law; we shall somehow make progress in social life by way of an ethical standpoint." This is a very beautiful thing to say, of course, but it is very abstract. The spirit has value only when it takes hold of material life directly, when it is able to bear and to subdue material life. Otherwise it has no value. We must not let ourselves be somehow captivated by the kinds of tirades that people like Förster[†] and others are speaking to the world. They are certainly beautiful words, but those words do not penetrate through to material life because the people who speak them do not actually understand material life themselves, but rather believe that the current material world can somehow progress simply through preaching.

And this is the mistake that the bourgeoisie has made: in their soul lives, they have retreated further and further into a realm of luxury. For six days in the week, they sit in offices. In the front of the account books they write, "In the name of God!" But then on the following pages, everything is done with little interest in God one way or the other; that "In the name of God!" is entirely abstract. But then, after they have worked in that all-too-familiar manner throughout the whole week, they go on Sunday to hear a sermon (spoken so as to fill a soul with soulful longing) about eternal salvation and the like. In other words, they make spiritual life into a luxury and then try to spiritualize material life! The bourgeoisie has progressed far in this direction. They have driven themselves toward this more and more, so that in the end, the whole of spiritual life has truly become an ideology.

On the other hand, it is no wonder that the proletariat should come forward and theoretically declare, "Spiritual life is an ideology." And no wonder that it is now trying to rearrange all of economic life by paying attention only to the modes of production. These two things go together. Truly, the way things are now, the fight between the bourgeoisie and the proletariat consists in nothing more than how the one is worse and the other better, and vice versa. It is merely a fight.

Going deeper into the matter will not lead you to find a way to give a fruitful form to life. You will find a way to do that only if you have a comprehensive impulse, one that encompasses the human being as such.

For this, you must either engage with the threefold social organism, if you recognize that; or you must understand things well enough to put something better than the threefold social organism in place. Everything else out there right now does not reckon with the human being as such. For that reason, it is essential that we rescue our movement in the very near future from everything that our opponents have in store. Their plan is make our movement impossible through machinations of their own. And these machinations will be very carefully laid out. Just think about all of the carefully crafted things currently lying on the battlefield of the *Berliner Tageblatt*† [Berlin daily paper]. Is it not the case that the *Berliner Tageblatt* printed a fabricated article in which all manner of idiotic "occultists" are mentioned? Included among them is anthroposophy, which has absolutely nothing to do with all of that. But people spare themselves the trouble of dealing with anthroposophy by simply putting it under the same heading. Of course, everybody can understand all of that nonsense printed in the paper; when you have something like that, then you do not have to bother with anthroposophy at all.

In fact, that sort of thing is happening all over the world; you encounter it everywhere—in English newspapers†—everywhere. This is just one example. In the near future, we will see the beginnings (it has already begun, actually, but it will develop even more) of a war of annihilation against our entire movement. So we must familiarize ourselves right now with all that is to be done. And if some sort of drastic action does not occur in a far-reaching way, then, my dear friends, then we must say to ourselves, "We might have a concept of something that could happen in society from the perspective of anthroposophical spiritual science, but we are not bringing the proper force to bear on seeing it through." Indeed, if we see the consequence of what the opposing side is working toward, sometimes resulting in wickedness, then we must say, "We must all see to it that the will forces for our movement come forward!" Those in the wrong have the will for it; why should those in the right be unable to bring forward the same powers? Why should we allow it to be justly said, "An intention existed to bring about something healing for humanity; but the enemies were of a different stripe—they had decisive wills that drove them forward until those intentions were extinguished!"

My dear friends, if we do not stand our ground until our will forces, too, are extinguished, then it goes without saying that we will be able to accomplish nothing for the present. We have arrived at a point of "either-or" in our movement. For that reason, this initiative has been undertaken. I urge you to think of this. I urge you to take this up in your will forces before we go into further description of what we will be using these will forces for.

Lecture 4

Stuttgart, February 14, 1921 (afternoon)

THIS is the first theme recommended for your speeches: the great questions of the present moment and the threefolding of the social organism. It is necessary for us to select these particular themes so that you have an opportunity to familiarize yourselves as precisely as possible with what is presently necessary and also with what the impulse for threefolding the social organism has to offer in response to the great questions of the present; furthermore, to allow for an opportunity to point out that anthroposophical spiritual science must provide the foundation for the kind of social thinking brought into the world by threefolding; and finally, so that organizations like Der Kommende Tag (The Coming Day)† and others always have the opportunity to participate. Their work must extend into our movement as a whole, into spiritual as well as practical activities. On the one hand, they have the task of making the spiritual world into something plausible because it is necessary now to cultivate a truly productive spiritual life; on the other hand, they have the task of reckoning with practical matters because as a movement we must move into social life, into economic life, and to that end we simply have to become stronger financially (as much as possible), not for our own sake, but for the sake of the progress of economic life.

Today, I would like to present a few things relating to the themes prerequisite to our broader considerations. It would also perhaps be best if I name a second theme along these lines: the freedom of education and its development, and its relationship to the state and to economics. And then we will take up something like this as our third theme: the economic system of associations and its relationship to the state and to free spiritual life. By taking up these three themes, we will then have the opportunity in the next few weeks of laying out before the world, in an effective way, everything that collectively belongs to our movement.

Now, I shall begin by saying something fundamental about the first of these themes. It is important here that you show people that actually the demand for the three limbs of the threefold social organism already exists, that we are actually not suggesting anything other than putting what is already there into its proper form. Although in a different form, everything is there that should be there, and will be there, once it has been re-arranged. A demand for three different things exists; but they are chaotically intermingled, and inwardly at odds as a result, like some kind of disastrous birthing in which the head ended up in the stomach and the digestive organs ended up in the heart; a birth in which the three systems of the organism have gotten all mixed up with one another. And so, the proper form should simply be given to everything already present, everything that already wants to have an existence.

In order to make this more apparent, let us begin with the third limb of the social organism, the economic life. This economic life, as it currently exists, can be accurately characterized simply by tracing its development through the last few centuries. It is only in the last few centuries that true economic life has taken on its current form, a form that has given rise to all the social questions. Of course, it has been a somewhat long and gradual process. Economic life, as it lies before us, even if we are to look back as far as we possibly can, that economic life still cannot be traced back any farther than sometime in the thirteenth or fourteenth century. During this period, we find that European economic life underwent a kind of crisis; a kind of subtle and creeping crisis, shall we say. It was during this period of time that the foundation of European economic life readied for a transformation.

If we go back farther, into an even earlier period, we find that this European economic life was necessarily beholden to the continental exchange of business and goods between Asia and Western Europe via Central Europe. And we also find that in this prior period, economic life all over the world was carried out as a self-evident process, even trade was practiced as something entirely self-evident. By and large, economic relationships were not yet so intensively developed as to necessitate that the freedom of exchange, the freedom of trade, be regulated or organized. But as the Central European population grew ever denser, as economic life grew ever more intensive, the need arose to organize everything. And from the more independent economic life of that prior period emerged an economic life that was more much bound up. The more independent economic life of an earlier time is characterized by the fact that individual economic activity was governed by independent sensibilities, with the farm hands, with the indentured populace—which was mostly limited to domestic economics according to the instincts of the landowners—and that more expansive trade, which was conducted with Asia, also did not require any particular regulation. It could be carried out freely because back then economic life was not yet so intensive.

But as I said, with the increase in population as well as the development of other relations (which we can discuss in a moment), the intensity of economic life continually increased, and certain protective regulations had to be established that were not necessary before—regulations that were all intended, more or less, to somehow protect the consumer. This is somewhat peculiar, that in the period of time when economic life underwent a kind of gradual crisis (around the thirteenth and fourteenth centuries) there actually developed a tendency all over the world, though not by any general conscious effort, to establish measures that protected the consumer. What else is it except a protection of the consumer when the cities through which merchants traveled, through which the trade routes passed, instated the so-called storage laws, forcing the merchants passing through to stop for a certain number of days before being allowed to continue on and freely sell all of the goods that they were unable to sell in the city? This is about protecting the consumer; all over the world, the concern was for protecting the consumer.

Though this may not be immediately apparent, there is something else from this period of time that must be reckoned against these efforts to protect the consumer. I have just been spending a good amount of time applying myself to this question and recently found that the establishment and development of the guilds, though superficially concerned with organizing production, was also undertaken to support the consumption of the products made in those guilds. If you go to work on this problem without any preconceived notions, it is impossible not to find this. This happened by taking a detour through the process of organizing the means of production. Despite the fact that the guilds were formed through an incorporation of businesses that produced the same goods, this was not done initially with the intent of organizing the production of those goods; rather, the merger was undertaken so that all of those businesses who were incorporated within the guild could sell their products at a price that protected the consumption of their goods, as I have suggested. The guilds were, in fact, a means by which the consumption of goods was protected. If you simply take a few books out of the library and compare the dates that you find there, then you will say to yourself—if you keep in mind the guidelines that I have given you here—this is what characterizes the economic life of that period of time.

And now this economic life has developed through several centuries under the influence of these various regulations. But it had always a kind of subtle and gradual crisis within its being. It has grown ever more intensive. And this is the peculiar thing: an economic life that grows ever more intensive in one particular territory creates a need for ever more limitations, regulations, and organization. An economic life that is somehow open, that has access on one side or another to inexhaustible sources—namely agriculture, the economics of the earth—does not have the same compulsion to organize itself. An economic life that is closed on all sides, one that becomes ever more intensive, feels the drive to organize in this way.

Now, this European economic life would, as the centuries passed, have been driven toward a decadence of unimagined intensity if a certain event, known to all of you, had not occurred. What staved off this decadence was, on the one hand, the opening of the world seas, and on the other hand, the discovery of America. This opened up economic life again to the West. We cannot accurately say, can we, that this was akin to the opening of a release valve, because the opening that was created was simply too large. That would be a very big valve!

But it is this event that steered economic life down an entirely different course. Now, the opening of this path to the West also happened to coincide with the arrival of modern technology. But the expansion of this modern technology was made possible through an entirely different set of relationships than the ones that enabled the opening of economic life to the West. With simply these two things, the opening of the seas and the discovery of America, you have everything that gave to modern economic life its basic configuration. To that can then be added what I presented to you yesterday as the most significant political events of recent history.

Within this European economic life, we then find two separate tendencies. The first tendency developed under the influence of the intensive economic life of the second half of the Middle Ages and beyond, and since then it has taken on a particular manner of economic thinking. People learned how to think economically under the influence of the relationships that developed, let us say, from the thirteenth century through the sixteenth or seventeenth centuries. During that time, people began to take up the task of thinking about how one should practice economics. It was during that time that the now current economic ideas developed; first in trade, then more slowly in industry, and finally even in agriculture. These thoughts were all more or less established during that era. You could also say that all of the classes of the population that were and are called to practice economic thinking—primarily, at least at first, within the European territories—these people developed their economic thought life under the influence of the experiences from that time. This lies deep within each human being. It was because of this that the constitution of the human soul became conservative. All of the conservative thoughts that lie within the human being can, at their core, be traced back to this period of time.

Economic life then opened toward the other side, as I have described to you. And because of this, something came into this whole imagination of economic life that was not immediately or unconditionally incorporated into that way of thinking; instead, it gave that way of thinking a particular economic impulse. I mean by this the connection with the West, with America, with everything that came about through access to the seas. This made economic life powerful.

And so, I would like to propose that the thought content of economic life and the driving impulse of economic life were thus formed. These circumstances were so potent that they gave current social life its entire configuration, including its materialistic form. And this modern civilization took on more and more the character that necessarily resulted from these same two factors.

So now we have an economic life that preponderates and dominates, simply due to the force of historical events; one that has a profound impact on human beings and on human evolution. Economic life takes on the character that only it can, for it is naturally the case that each of the three limbs of the social organism takes on its own lawfulness according to its nature and being; in the economic life, commodities and prices are the guiding forces.

This can, however, lead to a disruption of social relationships, if the economic life is intermingled with the two others limbs of the social organism. In that case, each limb simply follows its own laws in conflict with the others. And this is what has occurred: because economic life predominates, it has drawn the other areas of life, other social limbs of life, into its system of lawfulness. And this leads to the appearance of other relationships that have subsequently led us to the great questions of modern society.

If we look back into the history of our evolution, we see that the whole proletarian movement, in the form of a movement specifically demanding better pay, a movement against the enslavement of labor, simply did not exist historically. Yesterday, I said to you that the division of labor (whether one was a lord or a serf) was established out of a rights-political perspective in olden times. Now economic life has arranged it so that everything takes on the character of a commodity. Everything became a commodity. And for the first time, human labor became a commodity. Prior to that, it was service—voluntary or compulsory service. But only in this modern period did it become an actual commodity. And economic life can do nothing other than turn everything that falls under its purview into a commodity. And in this sense, I think, we have actually always had a threefolded society. We must only actualize it; we must only take what exists in a false form and establish it in the world in its true form. In the false form, it does us harm; it will lead to our downfall. If we are in the position to give it a true form, then it will lead us forward.

But it is not only the labor force that was turned into a commodity, the materialistic spiritual life was also turned into a commodity in the form of capital. At some time, please take a look at the capital market, at the accumulation and use of capital in modern times, and compare it with the treatment of capital in, say, Ancient Greece! In Ancient Greece, the man who had the power to make something happen was the one who held political power; he had the power to build this or that. On a political basis, he was able to find those who would carry out the task, and his capital was based on the fact that through his earthly relationships he was the ruler and could give orders to a large number of people. That was what capital looked like in Ancient Greece. In modern times, which we are now considering, everything that results in any sort of undertaking has also been fundamentally transformed into a commodity. What else are you doing when you buy or sell products on the market? What exactly are you dealing in? At the core, you are dealing in the spirit of an enterprise. Everything that we can call the spirit of enterprise has been essentially transformed into a commodity. You do not have the specifics, the particulars of an undertaking before you; you have no idea what you are buying or selling, but in reality you are buying or selling the spirit of an enterprise. You can observe this yourself in the redistributions of the capital market. To put it briefly: wherever the economic life predominates, everything is invested with the character of a commodity. Everything becomes commodity: the labor force becomes a commodity, spirit itself becomes a commodity. This has been the course of recent evolution.

Now, something entirely different is happening at the same time. The modern state has been formed on a political basis. We see at first, do we not, that these modern states form out of certain pre-existing, free relationships between the surrounding rural populations and the existing cities, which formed around church epicenters in Italy and with a somewhat different mindset in France and England. And so, the things we call states are formed from these conditions.

Whereas in the West, this concept of the state is already taking form, in Central and Eastern Europe we continue to see something else, namely, relationships that are still somewhat freer. As a result of the older relationships, we see that the existing cities, which formed around churches or something similar, become market epicenters. And as these old cities gradually turn into markets, new cities are simultaneously forming. It is interesting to see how these cities came to be in the eleventh, twelfth, and thirteenth centuries under the influence of economic life. First, in present-day southern Germany and in Western Europe, they started to form about five or six hours' journey from one another. In Northern and Eastern Europe, they form about seven or eight hours apart. In older times, this made perfect sense. Why? Because the farmers who did their business in the area needed to get to and from the city with their products in one day. This came about as a result of an inner necessity.

But when something like this happens in history, then something else not motivated by the same inner necessity comes about simply because of the principle of imitation. First, there comes the need to have cities that lie about five or six hours from one another, or perhaps even seven or eight hours. And then afterward, people look at that and says, "Now there's a good idea!" And they imitate it. This brings about things not motivated by necessity. It compromises some people's ability to think about these things healthily. The historians treat one city as though it were just like any other, meaning they treat those that arose out of economic necessity in the same manner as those that did not arise out of economic necessity. Everything then starts to get confusing and messy. You must have a feeling for the difference in order to look at this properly. People might be able to argue very convincingly that this city or that city did in fact come about due to economic necessity. But, to be sure, this is not always true. Some cities did not come about due to economic necessity, but rather because of the principle of imitation. The general truth is correct regardless. This circumstance, that cities formed as marketplaces, was the case for much longer in Eastern Europe than in the West, where centralized states developed and then sought to incorporate everything into their established frames.

Historically considered, it may seem fundamentally uncomfortable to claim that the territorial regions as well as a certain federal system developed out of the spirit of the patriarchal togetherness felt by rural and city populations in Italy, whereas a different system developed in France, Spain, and England. And whether or not it is uncomfortable, as I have suggested, for you to think in this way, it is nevertheless true that as you move toward Central and Eastern Europe, the formation of the countries, as was true of the cities earlier, occurred more through imitation than anything else. And here we arrive at something that you cannot say to people yet, because it would result in fourfolding, rather than helping toward threefolding. But it is the truth, regardless. The fact that the Western countries developed into unified states was of course an economic necessity, but it was also something that emerged from the dispositions of the various peoples living there. But the Central and Eastern European countries actually developed only because of imitation. For them, there was no historical necessity. The German and Austrian Empires finally fell because their inner organization was based on imitation; there was no historical necessity for them. And North America, which is entirely dependent upon incorporating into economic associations, is yet another outward imitation that has not even arrived inwardly at what the Central European countries have achieved. Anyone who takes a proper look at the economic relationships of North America will be able to definitively predict the course of events there.

Now, you see, beside everything that developed primarily from the original system of economics, the modern configuration of trade arose under the influence of the kinds of relationships that I have described to you. And this was where the fusion of political life and economic life occurred—not in industry, but in trade. Industry was only just getting underway. It is cheap and easy to argue against what I am saying now. One need only protest, "But industry had to be there first, because only then could people start trading things." This is not the point. Even if you consider some of the most developed industries now, most of these have not yet grown beyond the commercial sector. People simply create their own products for the trade that they engage in. We have not yet gone so far as to find the bridge that will carry us from original production (based in nature) through trade (which prefigures business) to what currently predominates. For in the moment that business becomes predominant, associations become a necessity. The structure of present-day commercial trade is still determined by the principles of trade; even industry comes from the principle of trade. In essence, industrialists are tradesmen, different only in that they produce the goods they trade. Even in their industrial establishments, their perspective is always directed toward simple commerce; these are the predominant principles. In the moment that business takes hold in simple commerce, associations become a necessity. The fusion of the state and economic life has actually occurred via a detour through commerce.

And on the other hand, each of the three limbs of the threefold social organism has its own laws, and fights against the others if they are not properly detached from one another. As you can see, the rights-political life has been fighting with the economic life for some time now over matters like economic regulations, pension funds, and so on. What can else can this mean except that people are trying foolishly to separate labor from economic life? It would be a clever thing, if anyone were actually able to detach it fully! But in an attempt to do just that, the states are "on the march" (if I can be permitted to use a phrase that, as you know, was misused by Wissel†), on the march for an independent rights life. By creating things like workers' protection laws or laws regulating pension funds, they take the organization and regulation of labor and the working day away from economic life. Now, we see here that the second limb of the threefold social organism is on the road to emancipation from economic life.

The matter of spiritual life is a bit more confusing. All true spiritual life is, at its core, an outgrowth of the ancient theocracies. You need only to study university life in the twelfth and thirteenth centuries to see this. This university life developed entirely out of the church. And it was an emancipated spiritual life. Only gradually did it grow together with political life. A large part of the European wars consisted of nothing more than the movement of religious institutions into the political realm. And regarding these ancient times, you must say to yourself, "The freedom of educational institutions was much greater under the old church system than it was and is under later political systems." For these institutions are developed, and with full consciousness, out of the spiritual life. For example, it was with full consciousness that, at the ecumenical council in Constantinople in 869,† the church disestablished the spirit—that is, they elevated to the level of dogma the assertion that the human being does not consist of body, soul, and spirit, but rather only of body and soul, and that the soul has certain spiritual qualities. At the time, this was done with full awareness. Now philosophy professors preach that the human being comprises body and soul without knowing that they are only proselytizing a bit of church dogma. What we call philosophy has developed out of older church life, and so consequently Herr Wundt[†] in Leipzig is merely a scion of old church dogma, even though this might no longer be apparent in his manner of presentation.

But the same is true of other things that developed out of the older theocratic mode of spiritual life. The theology departments—well, just take a look. They have really grown apart from earlier spiritual life, so that they really present only a caricature of that former state of being; the same with the law departments. Anyone who looks around will find the shell of older theocratic existence in modern civilization. I do not even want to talk about medicine. It is blatantly obvious that it has grown out of other connections with the older spiritual life that developed in churchly, religious ways. We have there a stream, a branch of spiritual life that grew entirely in relationship to a church life free from state influence, which was precisely the one true spiritual life in a previous era.

This brings us to something, I would like to suggest, that develops not out of spiritual life, but parallel to it—modern natural science and technology. There, spiritual life has grown in its own ground and merely taken on some resemblance to what previously developed out of the church. This is why everything that developed fitfully, if I may put it so, in imitation of older constructs, appears so strange. Through imitation, people built more and more vocational high schools, commercial schools, economic schools, and so on. All of that haltingly took on similar forms to everything that had developed out of earlier church life. And this is why the structure of higher education is so unnatural: something that in many ways has a kind of braid-like, pleated quality—the actual essence of the university—instead displays its antique, churchly inheritance. And then we have those schools that are actually somewhat humorous when you place them beside their precedents; that is, the modern economic schools, the vocational schools, the mining colleges, and so on, all of which have sought some similarity with the universities (even in superficial things like their names).

So on the one hand, we have the spiritual life and how it turned from an older, free church life into one that was slowly absorbed by the state; and on the other hand, we have the intrusion, shall we say, once again originating in a certain state of freedom—for spirit must indeed be free; genius cannot be manufactured by the state—the intrusion of spiritual life finding a new place for itself in political life. It would have been consistent with the ideals of many people to cultivate true artists at art schools. But you know already that the educational program that cultivates the genius or the true artist does not yet exist, despite the fact that people want it. And thus we see how the spiritual life is absorbed altogether inadequately. Basically, only the exterior form of it is taken in. The content is constantly forced to be, shall we say, restrained, or to be completely curtailed. For is it not true that if you find yourself in the position of having a bit of spirit—which is a wholly unpleasant position to be in now—then you have to protect it (at the very least keep it secret throughout all of the terrible torment of exams and other things), so that it does not freeze and harden inside of you; so that you can let it unfurl afterwards. Indeed, you have to keep everything belonging to true spiritual life hidden under your hat. This is how it is. And this, at its core, is nothing other than a kind of emancipation of that spiritual life, a latent form of self-emancipation.

We stand here before a brewing crisis. The final consequence of socialism is no less than Marxism—Bolshevism in its radical form. Everything becomes "socialized"; the whole state becomes one big industrial establishment, a giant business venture—at least that is their ideal. Now, if people undertake to see this through, then it becomes necessary to organize all of the technical knowledge that is part of this whole menagerie—excuse me, "machinery" is of course what I meant to say. Without this technical knowledge, you cannot move forward. Modern technology is absolutely necessary. But Bolshevists and all of the other groups that want to bring Marxism to bear upon reality can bring about nothing other than its ruthless exploitation. By this I mean that you can enslave technically gifted people for a period of time, but they will slowly fade disappear if not first allowed to cross over into an independent, emancipated, free, productive spiritual life. The whole world is standing before precisely this crisis in every region where the "socialization" of spiritual life is taking radical strides forward. Just as the other two limbs of the social organism (rights-political life and economic life) have their own governing laws—the way in which economic life makes everything a commodity, the way in which rights-political life encloses everything economic, even what does not fit within its purview—so too must spiritual life, according to its own laws, emancipate itself from the two others.

So there is a demand for these three limbs of the social organism: the spiritual limb, the rights-political limb, and the economic limb. For this reason, these comprise the three great questions of the present. The three great questions of the present are: the question of the proper form for spiritual life; of the proper form for rights-political life; and of the proper form for economic life.

And we encounter this everywhere that other attempts at answers are being made. Simply take a look at, for example, what is coming out of the various denominations in Central Europe and Germany, where people in the evangelical unity movements and in the young Catholic movements, among others, are trying to galvanize the older generation, to squeeze something that still has life out of that older generation in the hope of having some sort of spiritual life, because they do not have the courage for a truly productive spiritual life. You see everywhere these clumsy attempts at bringing to birth a new spiritual life. Naturally, the attempt to squeeze something more out of an old lemon cannot really lead to any true spiritual formation. The only thing that can lead to that is a turn toward a productive spiritual life. But we are seeing these sorts of clumsy attempts being made everywhere. We are seeing how the Americans are turning out for a re-renewal of Christianity, because they believe that humanity cannot recover on the basis of old state principles. But nowhere will you find those with the insight to see that producing a new spiritual life must come out of its own original sources. Everywhere, people are cobbling together the things that are already there. This proves that people are already instinctively on the right path, but that they have not yet found the courage to establish a truly independent spiritual life in a pure form.

On the other hand, we are seeing how the old state principles that have developed in Europe since the fifteenth and sixteenth centuries are dying in their sleep. What else would you call the monstrosities that people call peace treaties[†] and the like, that have occurred since Brest-Litovsk and Versailles? What else would you call that but a snoring, suffocating state principle, one that cannot give form to anything except terrible things; one that creates structures that have no chance at existence? Czechoslovakia, for example, will have no chance at existence, because it does not have the things it needs. The Polish state is to be restructured once again. It is simply not possible for the political life to recover when it is built upon the democratic principle of "all men are equal"—in other words, when it encompasses all of the concerns of each and every adult.

For as long as contemporary life is so chaotically intermingled, we will not get anywhere. Here we see that, in fact, the political life is dying in its sleep, on one side, while trying to prove, on the other, that it absolutely must take worker regulations under its purview. And so we can say that we have the spiritual question, demonstrated by the fact that clumsy attempts at moving forward are being made (for example in the evangelical unity movements and the young Catholic movements); we have the rights-political question, demonstrated for example in the peace treaties; and we have economic life standing before us as the third great question of the present, out of which (at its core) the great war against the West really arose, and which readily invites itself into groups discussing revolutionary impulses and other similar things.

This matter must therefore be addressed from all sides of the problem. You will find among the lectures that I have given here[†] one that addresses these things directly. Now, from the perspective of these three great present-day questions, we must address our first theme. We must embrace the idea that these great questions are out there (the spiritual question, the rights-political question, and the economic question) and therefore the threefold social organism is not something that has been invented, but rather something that has been read and derived from these three great questions of the era; and on the other hand, we must also embrace the fact that everything that has been prepared through anthroposophical spiritual science is a foundation for a truly productive spiritual life.

All spiritual life from earlier periods, found in the religious denominations, of which the branches of the present-day university are simply descendants—this old spiritual life—has outlived its time. The other, new spiritual life—meaning the one that has grown out of natural science and technology—has not yet been able to begin its life. It has not been able to spiritualize itself. It must be driven toward spiritualization by the same kind of thinking that led to the development of the older spiritual life. Spiritual science will eventually become as productive as earlier spiritual life, which is now in a state of decadence in the religious denominations.

This is what gives spiritual life its content, its purpose. And when you can see into the matter thus, you will properly recognize that the question "Where is free spiritual life supposed to come from?" can be answered in full confidence by saying, "We have to speak not only of the demands of free spiritual life, but also of something that can be placed within the framework of this free spiritual life; something that produces spirit, something that is in fact living spirit." You will then be able to point to the anthroposophical sources related to this. In that moment, you can develop something that if you want to bring it to the public at large must be brought forward with a certain enthusiasm, so that our interior lives turn outward, so that really everything that you are as a person, everything that has brought you together, enters into the public. This must be the only tone that you strike in your lectures. You must be clear about this: that anthroposophy gives to free spiritual life its content and its sustenance.

On the other hand, you will find a different tone when you deeply feel that economic life turns everything into a commodity, and that everything that should not be made into a commodity must be removed from economic life. Then you will find the dry tone of sober consideration that must run through your lectures when you speak about economic life. In those moments, you can speak soberly and dryly; you must speak in that manner, as though you were doing computations.

And this is how you will find the two different nuances that you need for your lectures, and you will find them to be entirely different from one another: the dry, sober tone of the dry economic analyst, and the enthusiastic tone of someone who is speaking of free spiritual life not merely as a political ideal, but rather speaks as though knowing what wants to enter in.

And then you will find, between these two rhythmically alternating tones (no need to have any convulsive rants or anything like that), the third tone; the tone that you will need for handling the rights-political realm.

But it is necessary that in your voice itself you become intensively threefolded, so that you recognize this properly: that in your soul you have a different bearing toward spiritual life; a different bearing toward rights-political life; a different bearing toward economic life. When speaking about spiritual life, you speak with inner strength and conviction; you speak as with the true knowledge that every human being is an authorized participant in the harmonious spiritual life of humanity, in the harmony of human spiritual life. When speaking about the rights-political life, you speak in a way that allows the soul to swing like a pendulum from one side to the other: duties—rights; rights—duties! You speak with a certain cool deliberation, which need not have any resemblance to the pretentious mendacity of old statesmen; but it does come with a certain deliberation, in so far as in the rights-political life justice befalls one person just as it does another. And when speaking about economic life, you speak as though you did not have merely your own purse to look after; it may seem to be nonsensical, but you should speak with the feeling that you have other people's purses in your bag and are responsible for tending to all of them. You should speak with this feeling because you must go about your work as carefully as possible; because unexpected things that you had not thought of can sometimes happen. The secure feeling that you have in relation to spiritual life (in spiritual life, so long as you have grasped it properly, nothing can go wrong); you cannot have this same secure feeling regarding economic life. It is very possible for things to go wrong there. This must be present in the tone that you use to speak about these matters. This is why you will find that in *Towards Social Renewal* spiritual life is spoken about with absolute certainty and definiteness; when it comes to economic affairs, only certain examples are used, so that the reader has the feeling that it could always be different.

This is what will give your speech a certain inner strength: being intensively threefolded in your inner life. And what I am recommending to you is meant to lead you a little bit toward this inner state of being. Since most of you are young, if you become aware of this threefolding of the human orator, this will be a source of strength for your work.

Lecture 5

Stuttgart, February 14, 1921 (evening)

IT would be good to bring in a few more formal matters now, so that we can then go back to other considerations relating to content.

I indicated earlier that by placing yourself completely within the sense and being of one or another limb of the threefold social organism you can find the proper tone for speaking. If you live into this correctly, it comes naturally.

Now, on this point, I would like to present a few more things to you. But I would like to remark at the start here that, when it comes to pieces of practical advice, situations can always be somewhat different than they were in this presentation; so that one can really speak about such things only as examples. It goes without saying that you might handle things one way in a certain situation, and in another way in another situation. But when I imagine what might be fitting for the situations that you will face in your public speaking in the next few weeks, I find that I would first like to make you aware that having a very particular inner approach in each individual situation is of great importance for the speaker.

You see, if you were to select a theme, such as, let us say, "The great questions of the present time in relation to the threefold social organism"; and if, because you had a number of speaking arrangements at various places that week, you were to present this theme by repeating at your lectures a number of specific statements that you had mastered through memorization, this would be the worst thing that you could do. For inner reasons relating to the content of the material, this is probably the worst method that one could choose for such matters. You can actually develop a responsible form of speaking that supports the content only when every speech you give is also new for you personally. Even if you give a speech thirty times in a row (or, in a more extreme and seldom case, one hundred times in a row), it is necessary for you to experience it as something new—even if only in the way that I will shortly describe. It is necessary to have great respect and attention for the content of that speech; to allow it to present to your soul all of its fundamental nuances (not so much its particular structure, its particular formulations, but rather its fundamental aspects) before you deliver it; to allow it to live once again in your thoughts. How you are able to approach your speech depends on the relationship that you have to the material. I have known top-notch actors and actresses who have told me with great conviction that they begin to feel as though they have played a role well only after they have played it for something like the hundredth time. Now, a certain kind of illusion is naturally hidden in such a statement, for they probably had that feeling after the ninety-fourth time, and after the fiftieth time as well, but only in relation to the performances that came before that one. And at the most basic level, this feeling is simply what maintains the necessary feeling of freshness toward the act of speaking: that you can simply never get enough of the material you are speaking about, even if you are repeating it almost exactly.

Someone who must give a speech and who feels that it already bores him; or that the act of giving a speech bores him because he has talked about the same material so often, seems to me like someone who has eaten for a whole month, and on the first day of the next month, says, "I am bored with eating, because it is just a repetition of all the eating that I did for the last thirty days; I do not want to do that again." In its most basic functions, the human organism does essentially the same monotonous thing every day; at most, you vary the food that you eat a little bit. You can give the same nuance to the way you think about a lecture, so that a change is brought into it much in the same way that you vary the meals you eat day after day. But basically, that monotonous pairing of hungry/eating, thirst/drinking, and so on, remains, and at the root it never seriously becomes boring.

In encounters with the lively growth of the natural, even spiritual, forces present in the deteriorating world, our intellect—our whole soul life, in fact—turns away from this fact; it turns away out of a belief that to receive something once is then to "have it" completely. If you progress in soul development, then you return to things found in nature and in the original, spiritual, elemental forces: the rhythm, the repetition of the self. And we must participate in this particular return to everything that stands near to these original creative forces, nearer than our deteriorating intellect and our soul life, if we are to work in the spiritual world, in the sphere of the spirit.

The religious denominations have already taken this up at a basic level. They do not have different prayers for every morning and every evening, but rather the same prayers. They take it as given that this is not boring, that it has the same relationship to the entire soul development of the human being as eating and drinking has to physical development. We can relate to everything that we do in the realm of the spirit, particularly in the case of something like public speaking, in such a way that we go through the content of our work with the same inner interest again and again before presenting it, even if we have already done so countless times. Only then, when we have run through the content in this way—even if only for a few minutes—only then will we achieve the proper relationship to what we want to say. We will also achieve the proper feeling of responsibility only through this method.

This feeling of responsibility is something that you will need when you find yourselves in a position like the one before us in the coming weeks. You must make yourselves conscious of the fact that in your talks you are not speaking merely to the people who are present; rather, you stand in the midst of a world-historical moment, and your talks hold something of meaning for this world-historical moment. You must hold up before your soul the weight and significance of what you are doing. You have to say to yourself something like, "I have something to bring to people that if it strikes a chord with them will truly serve as the only means of elevating the world, while all around us are the forces of its downfall."

If you stand in this relationship to the matter, then you will also be able to properly assess all of the opposition coming toward us from every corner of the world, shouting loudly on all sides of the path that you are now planning to tread. Within our movement, most people, including many members of our society, will pay no attention to this opposition. They do not like to worry themselves with it, and this reflects a lack of interest in history. But we must speak and do our work *out of* an interest in history. Only then will our words take on enough weight for us to work with them. We may not take this opposition lightly. It is actually quite horrifying sometimes to see how people within our movement remain so impassive when faced with the terrible attacks that are made on anthroposophy, on the threefold social organism, and even on the Kommende Tag. In this regard, the opponents are, if I might be allowed to say such a thing, a beast of a different stripe. Some of them are truly ruthless rogues. But their roguery is filled with an incredible zeal. And they find words that are motivated by a certain enthusiasm, often by the enthusiasm of wickedness (even most of the time), or even by the enthusiasm of inability; an inability that protests because it cannot come into being opposite what is being brought into reality. But there is vigor in it, to some extent; even in their complaints, there is vigor. You do not find the right words when you just set them down with artistry. But you find the right words if you can arrive at them through your whole bearing and feelings toward the subject. This is what we must move toward both in written and in oral practice. We should not turn away in fear from the very harsh criticisms that are shamelessly being levied against anthroposophy and the threefold social organism. And we must become conscious of the fact that the shadowy outline of something positive emerges from this experience.

Also of relevance here is what we bring into our positive speeches against our opponents; the fact that we talk about these things is done with no consideration for defending ourselves. You must certainly defend yourselves sometimes (I have done it in the past); but what does a defense really mean against an individual like Max Dessoir[†] and others like him? In an instance like this, it is very significant to point out what damage it does to German educational and university life to have such people as instructors. Putting this general cultural phenomenon in the proper light is something for which we must find the proper, nuanced words. And in that case, it is definitely a good thing to, shall we say, paint a particular picture of these things. You then have to seek in your life experiences the right shades, the right colors, with which to paint this picture. There is karma to it, if you simply attend to it in the proper way. This karma will hold for you the necessary nuance.

In my book *The Riddles of the Soul,* I refer to the unusual fact that Max Dessoir mentions, in that thick book he has written, that he is one of those people who, due to some particular bearing in his soul, has to pause sometimes in the middle of a thought, unable to go any further; this can even happen to him when he is giving a lecture. He is suddenly so filled up with the power of what he is trying to express that his mind just stops dead in its tracks (he does not say it quite this way, but it is as though this happens). I brought this up in my *Riddles of the Soul.*[†] A few weeks ago, I received a letter from a friend[†] who was in one of Dessoir's courses in Berlin during which precisely this happened—that Dessoir's mind suddenly stopped dead in its tracks. The students called this peculiar piece of university furnishing "pretty Max," because it was a tradition of his (according to the friend that I mentioned) to put on a different colored vest each week for his lecture in class.

This is nothing more than imitation, you see. Greater men than Max Dessoir have had the same sort of weaknesses. For example, it happened once to the famous philosopher Kuno Fischer[†] that a young student went over to the barbershop that was right next door to the university buildings there in Heidelberg. And this barber was quite understandably interested in the university and the young men who attended it. And so he started to have a conversation with this crass young chap who was planning to enter the college so that he could study with Kuno Fischer. The young man confided in the barber that he wanted to study with Kuno Fischer. "He is writing on the board today," said the barber. "How do you know that?" asked the young student, astonished. "He was here just before and had me tidy his hair in the back. He always does that before he plans to write on the board; he has to turn around to do that, you see."

Now, "pretty Max" found himself in the situation one day where the thoughts just suddenly flew out of his head. When this happened, he started to get a little wild (and it goes without saying, he was wearing his vest of the week). There was a student sitting in the front row who had a newspaper in his hand, and he went at this student, started screaming at him that it was all his fault because he was reading the newspaper that Dessoir had lost his train of thought. Five minutes later, he picked up the thread of his thoughts again. This all really happened; it has been documented!

You can easily make careful use of such things. And you will find often that you can bring in some very particular colors if you want to describe the strange state of education as it is carried out at universities these days. Aside from its terrible parts, the ones that are aggravating and destructive, it also has plenty of bizarre aspects. I myself, if I may be allowed to mention it, knew a chemist† who was a professor of organic chemistry and technology. Every year that he was at university, he said, "Yes, there are in fact only three great chemists: the first is Liebig,† the second is the more recent Gorup-Besanez,† and modesty forbids me to mention the third."

Now, as I said, for us it is important that we not place emphasis on the desire to defend ourselves, which can naturally spring up in these situations. What is important for us is that we present cultural phenomena for what they are, in all of their negative aspects; that we make ourselves thereby strong enough to arrive at a judgment of these so-called spiritual streams of the present. We can then allow this to flow into our positive presentations, and we will more effectively bring this into others' souls in this way. If we want to get through to our contemporaries, then we must be able to cultivate in their souls a feeling of repulsion toward certain present-day phenomena. We must be able to cultivate a proper judgment about the terrible things that are spreading in the world from incompetence and, more especially, from dishonesty.

In order to be able to do this properly, we need only demand of ourselves that we keep a sharp eye on the world and not let people get away with certain things. We have to criticize the symptomatic things going on in the world. Particularly in the realm of so-called science, a certain dishonesty predominates at present—and we will continue to see this. And this dishonesty, which actually only continues to grow stronger the more we move from natural-scientific and philosophical faculties through medicine and into other provinces; this dishonesty is something that we must not fail to describe again and again in our presentations to our contemporaries. This is of the utmost, of an absolutely highest importance. People these days do not really have a strong feeling against what this dishonesty actually does, how corruptively it works in the feeling-thinking core when someone who is otherwise a scientist is consumed by a certain dishonesty while working. And in the long run, if not immediately, we will have already achieved a great deal if we make our contemporaries aware of the presence of this dishonesty in the educational life. We will find the proper rhetorical approach to this if we take up the kind of attitude toward the matter that I have described to you here.

Particularly when you find yourself in a position like the one in which you will be during the next few weeks, one thing seems important: that you live actively within the material that you intend to present; that you actually always struggle with it to a certain extent while speaking; that you allow your preparation to be such that the intentions, thoughts, and subject come before your soul, but not the specific wording, because you must always struggle to arrive at the right words only once you are standing before the audience. Therefore, it is good not to prepare the specific wording you will use, except certain key sentences, at most, depending on how you are individually—you might be the sort of person who writes down key sentences. But not mere slogans! As a rule, slogans will only lead you astray. Rather, key sentences, mostly things that will be the themes of particular of sections. So you might write for example: "Economic life has its own rules; it turns everything into a commodity." And then, since you will not take this just as a starting point, but as the theme of a section, you will talk about it in such a way that everything you say crystallizes around it. You speak to build things up around a key sentence like this. Then you transition to the next key sentence.

It is really good to have only the first five or six sentences as well as the last five or six sentences of the lecture written out word-for-word, and not just in your memory but in your whole intellect and mind. Having the others written out is not good under any circumstances, because it significantly hampers your active, inner relationship to the matter. But it is necessary to have the first and last five or six sentences formulated rather exactly. Anyone who stands before an audience as a human being, and not an oratory machine, will usually have stage fright during the first five or six sentences. This happens precisely because one is a human being and not a machine. So it is a good thing to get stage fright. It can take many forms. It might be that stage fright gives us inner liveliness during the first five or six sentences, which if they are well-formed then provides us with the right inner relationship. On the other hand, if we have not formed the sentences well—it can too easily happen that something just does not occur to you, can it not? For example, I knew a man, an otherwise excellent lecturer, who always read his lectures off a sheet of paper. But one time (it is as though he is standing in front of me now, I remember this so clearly); one time, he wanted to present at least the first few sentences, the first sentence, from memory, but it did not come to him. He had grown so accustomed to having a manuscript that he had to read from the very first word on. So when it comes to the first five or six sentences, it is good to really live into them fully, down to the level of the exact words themselves.

So, for such "opportunity lectures" as the ones that you will be giving (in the best sense of the word; I mean to say that they come from the opportunity of this present moment), it is doubtless best for such talks if you bring the first five or six sentences along, already written down; then the key sentences; and then again the last five or six sentences at the end. But if I might be permitted to give you all a piece of advice. I ask you not to take this up in such a way as to think that you always have to follow it under any circumstances and always have to do exactly what I am telling you with the piece of paper that you bring along. My advice would be: make up a sheet for yourself upon which you write down the first five or sentences, then the key sentences, then the last sentences. Hold yourself to that. And then—burn it! Do the same thing the next day, or for the next lecture. And then burn it again. It is better to do that fifty times than be content to bring the same sheet of paper to fifty different lectures.

This action belongs to the inner enlivening of the relationship between the person and the material. You must, as it were, be finished digesting the living material of the lectures that you give; it must be as digested as the food that you ate on February 13 is on February 14. This should be considered a rule.

You see, in certain areas of work, it is important that we rediscover the way back to elementary relationships to life. This is the only way we can tear spiritual work out of its moldy state, which it is in because in the life of abstract reasoning there are ideas like this: a person wants to experience something only once; and once a person has experienced something, then it no longer produces a sensation. If you get used to doing things like what I have just described, you will gradually come to a place where you can receive everything produced spiritually from far deeper places than the questionable places that are prized most highly by people thinking of external expansion. And it is enormously important that what is most exalted spiritually does not come out of this heady, intellectual place. This region is colorless, it is prosaic; it is such that (even if this sounds paradoxical) it actually concerns no one other than ourselves. Everything reason is able to achieve in clarity concerns only the person who bears that reason.

What we have to say to the world is not based on what we understand, but rather on what we have felt our way through and experienced; on things that have caused us pain and sorrow, and joy and feelings of triumph. And, my dear friends, the content of what you have to say to the world in the coming weeks, you will be able to re-experience anew every day. If you go through this content in your soul you will feel triumph and sorrow and, in a certain sense (if you feel what shall be), also happiness, redemption. Above all else, you will be able to feel a strong sense of responsibility. All of this can be done every day. And this is a much better preparation than any other, and much better than anything you will find in most books on rhetoric. This living inner relationship to the matter is what actually truly prepares us to develop those imponderables that exist between us and our audience, no matter how large it might be.

In general, it can be noted in regard to this just how much we have become abstract and theoretical. I once heard a lecture given by Hermann Helmholtz[†] at a large gathering. He took out his manuscript and read the whole lecture from the first word to the last word. Afterward, a theater director with whom I was friendly came up to me and said, "What was that? The lecture has already been printed; he could have just handed a copy personally to everyone who was listening.

And if Helmholtz, who is certainly very prized and honored, just went around and shook everyone's hand, that would have been a much greater pleasure than listening to something that you could just read yourself, since it is printed."

We actually need to hold this fact up before our souls: the printed word, including everything you read out in a speech that you wrote down earlier, is something entirely different from the spoken word. And even if it has already happened often (for reasons other than purely artistic reasons, or something similar) that the spoken word was then written down—that this ahrimanic art was practiced—and then the written word was read again, we should not conceal the fact that this whole procedure is, in essence, a whole lot of monkey business. For certain reasons, this has to be done; but it is monkey business all the same. For those who take up these matters artistically, what is spoken is not the same as what can be printed or written down in the same moment. So I was deeply sympathetic when that theater director said to me that it would have been better if Helmholtz had just shaken everyone's hand and had his printed lecture passed out.

These are things that must be held up before the soul, because this is what constitutes rhetoric at its most basic level; whereas what you find in books on rhetoric are mostly the sorts of things that cannot really be filled with content. They are thickets of brush, they are dried-out straw; things that you cannot actually do anything with when you intend to live actively into the matter at hand.

These are the sorts of formalities, shall we say, that present you only with recommendations. You nevertheless can—I do not want to say "think through"—you can sense and feel through and through these recommendations. And if you do this, you will be able to prepare yourself in the best possible manner for your task in the coming weeks. Out of the feelings that you will develop toward such recommendations will grow a vision of how you should actually approach the material that you will be working through in the coming weeks. And in regard to this, I want to add the following.

In the kinds of talks that you will be giving, even if you grasp the themes in the way that I have just described, it is good to start with something that belongs to the current moment, with some sort of current event that is also symptomatic of this whole historical moment. We are living in a time in which such events happen every day. If we keep up with current news even a little bit, we will notice these sorts of symptomatic events everywhere. We can use these as a starting point. By doing so, we immediately create an atmosphere of commonality between ourselves and our audience. For the audience knows about the event, we know about it, and we create a kind of communication that is of particular significance for contemporary historical talks; or to say it a little better, for talks that are meant to have an effect on history's unfolding. Or you can describe a symptomatic event that lies a little farther afield. It is often a particularly suitable way of properly concentrating the audience's attention when you describe something that seems to have no connection whatsoever with the topic, but that has a deep inner connection with it. This makes the audience perceive a kind of paradox, not knowing why you are talking about it; and then you try to find the transition from this to the topic that you actually intend to discuss.

Another recommendation is this: in certain cases, it is exceptionally good if, at the end, you come back to the beginning. You can do this best by formulating something at the beginning that you present as a question—not asking the question pedantically, but posing something question-like—then the lecture becomes the exploration of the posed question, and at the end you finally come to the answer, so that the whole thing is closed in a certain way. Doing this often has a very, very positive influence on the souls of the audience. They will retain everything more easily than they otherwise would.

With certain things, it can even be good to have a kind of motif that you return to after certain sections, albeit in a different form. If you formulate something in the same way every time you say it, you will not be very effective; but if you return to something in a different form, you could thereby achieve something quite good.

Then we will also have to effect a kind of reforming influence on the audience through the structure of our talks; I could also say a kind of "pedagogical" influence, if it did not offend people to hear the word "pedagogical." You can have a reforming influence through the structure of your talk. You see, people will demand of you nowadays that you define things as much as possible. But we want to limit ourselves when it comes to defining things. We do not want to make the concession; there are other concessions as well that we do not want to make, but least of all do we want to give people pedantic definitions. Instead, we want always to characterize things. Indeed, we want to characterize some things from two or more sides, in order to bring forth a sense of how any particular thing can be characterized from multiple sides. We have to put forward the impression that everything that comes from a spiritual foundation, everything that stems from spiritual science, must come forward also in a different form before our contemporaries than what comes out of materialism. Everything that comes out of materialism will be materialistic, even if it is saturated with apparent religiosity; even if it is colored by the religious, it will speak in hardened, fixed nouns. What comes out of the spirit cannot speak very well in these hardened nouns. For the spirit does not work in that way. It is in constant motion. Spirit is necessarily comprised of action words, of verbs. It dissolves the noun form. It prefers to form clauses, rather than making use of fixed nouns. In this way, it avoids treating beings like pieces of wood; it avoids placing them next to each other like pieces of wood or stakes. Placing things next to each other like stakes—that is materialistic. What is grasped in the spirit dissolves the hardened noun. And it is important that we not make any concessions in this regard to our materialistic time. In any case, this will probably not be the case for you. It is much more likely to happen to contemporary poets, not so much to people who say the kinds of things that you have to say—in any case, when something emerges from the visionary realms, it can also come in the form of these hardened nouns. For there the imaginations are figures. Every style has its own particular character for its own particular area. But what is needed in a certain sense is to bring something new to your fellow human beings as teachings, as insights—this, if it comes out of the spirit, will never feel compelled to merely line up hardened nouns side by side.

Then it will be good for you, I would like to suggest, to really go through something moralistic. When we were beginning our anthroposophical movement, people were proudly saying, "When I was somewhere or another, I presented theosophical or anthroposophical insights without saying where they came from and without using the word theosophy or anthroposophy." This denial of the ground upon which you stand has become a true nuisance in anthroposophical circles; this desire to disavow oneself of the matter at hand. Now, I would like to say to you that the people who have been won over because someone avoided speaking about the matter clearly and openly have either not truly been won over; or if they have, then the victory is worthless. The only things that have any value for our movement are ones that have been achieved with complete truthfulness and absolute honesty. And if we make that a clear guideline, then perhaps we will suffer a loss here or there. And wherever we do achieve something, it will be a good victory. Under no circumstances should we avoid holding up the spiritual-scientific and anthroposophical foundations of our work to people. Even if for a large number of people this is like waving a red flag in front of a bull! The trouble is not the red flag; it is the bull.

These are the things that must belong to the moral nuances of our zeal on behalf of the movement in the coming weeks. And we need true zeal. We do not need to have the feeling that we are to be martyrs for something. But we should have a feeling of great responsibility. We should have the feeling that we are speaking out of an evolutionary and historic moment. The more we feel this, the better.

I could remind you again today of something that I have said often in the past. I wanted some time ago to make clear to two Catholic clergymen how unjustified they were in the particular demand that they made of me after a lecture. I had given a lecture in a southern German city (which is today no longer a southern German city)[†] about the wisdom of Christianity. Two Catholic priests were present at the lecture. It was during the period of time, a long time ago now, in which the demand to fight intensively against anthroposophy had not yet gotten as far within Catholic circles as it has today. After the lecture they came up to me. Now, it is true, is it not, that when it comes to anthroposophical matters, one can speak objectively about a theme for a long time, even if Catholic priests are in the audience. If they have not been told beforehand that they should dispute everything that has not been constitutionally sounded out by the church, they would not notice that there was anything to complain about. The opposition coming from the church must come from places other than truthful ones. So the priests came up to me and said, "Well, we have nothing to say against the content or your lecture"—at that time, the cry from Rome had not yet gone out—"but the way in which you speak is no good. For we speak in such a way that everyone understands us, but you speak only for a particular circle of people who are already prepared." I always have the feeling that one is not dishonest in external life if one speaks to people in way that is customary in external life. I address every *Hofrat* as *"Hofrat"* (court councilor), and address every Catholic priest as "your reverence." So I said, "Your reverence, it is not a matter of whether you or I think that something is for everyone. It goes without saying that you and I think that subjectively. This is not the point; rather, it is a matter of whether or not something is carried out from the impulses of the moment; whether, regardless of our subjective understanding, it should be brought forward or not. And so I ask you now, since I am presupposing this good, subjective knowledge, whether all people who want to know something about Christ come to your church these days? If all of the people come to your church, then you do indeed speak for all people. So totally objectively, I ask you: do all people come to your church?" They could not say yes; it was not true. Then I said, "Now, you see, those who do not come to you in church anymore, but still want to hear something about the Christ—I am speaking to them. That is objective. We can believe subjectively that you and I speak for everyone. That is not important. What matters is that we resolve to learn from the facts about how we are to do so." Of course, the two priests did not really take this in, but it is true all the same.

So, those are the things, largely formalities, that I still wanted to say you. They are not rules, nor are they recommendations meant dogmatically. I said at the beginning of my remarks that they are meant more as examples. They can be altered in many ways. It might be that you will find yourself in a position where it is necessary to follow other guidelines. But I was just thinking about what those of you who are sitting before me might have to consider, finding yourselves in the position that you might be in during the coming weeks—one of you in one way, another with a different nuance, depending on how you carry it out—

in order to step before the public in the proper way. Above all, in order to place yourself in the right relationship to what is to be accomplished, either completely or not, how you should relate to the things that you must present. And this is how I arrived at needing to tell you about the sorts of formal things that I have just discussed.

Lecture 6

Stuttgart, February 15, 1921 (afternoon)

It will all come down to the fact that the whole approach to the lectures that you are to offer the public is different than what lies behind almost all of the usual discussions out there currently. The approach that you will need take up will be determined above all by the fact that you always must point out the significance of the human being itself in the whole of social life.

You will find social analyses everywhere now that are based on something other than the human being. You will find social analyses based on the concept of capital, the function of capital (and so on), within the social order. You will then find that capitalism is spoken of as though it were a force moving through the world, and you will find also that at the core of all this talk of "capitalism" there is little attention paid to the essence of the human being.

Furthermore, you will hear people talk about labor, about the social significance of labor; and you will be able to sense that when people speak about labor the human being does lie somehow at the core, since the human being is the laborer, but that, as before, the concept of labor as such is detached from the human being—that is to say, from humanity—and that people are speaking about "labor itself."

Thirdly, you will find that people talk about commodity. This is certainly a meaningful concept within economic life, but it only leads to confusion and mistaken social concepts if we do not always pay attention to the essence of the human being.

To be sure, if you start off with threefolding the social organism, you have to differentiate starkly between those spheres of human activity that must be carried out in the spiritual realm, those that must be carried out in the rights-political realm, and finally those that must be carried out in the economic realm. But we will not correctly form these concepts (which must be grasped in such a one-sided manner regarding human action and activity), if we cannot turn our gaze toward what is essential about the human as a whole being. It is precisely this turning of the gaze toward the essence of the human as a whole being that instills in us the necessity to divide the external social order into the three spheres described in the writings that I have mentioned.

Now, the human being has, in fact, been slowly removed from consideration in our modern worldview. You will find everywhere that the human being has actually been cut out. You find this first of all in the most narrowly spiritual realm—that of science. Science regards the kingdoms of nature: mineral kingdom, plant kingdom, animal kingdom; it observes the evolution of the animal kingdom up to the appearance of the human being and then presents the human being as a complicated, transformed, metamorphosed animal. But it never starts by looking at the human being as such. It only presents the human being as the conclusion of animal evolution. For some time now, this has been the goal of science. But this is merely a symptom of the casting out of the essence of the human being from our feeling and thinking. If, in modern times, we had a strong feeling for what is purely human in all the various realms of life, then we would not be in a position to cast the human being out of so-called science; we would not be able to treat the human being merely as the conclusion of animal evolution.

You can also see how the human being is disabled in the institutions that lie at the core of modern spiritual life. We are held fast by regulations that do not come from us, or we are tossed into the effects of forces coming from economic life, but very, very little worth is place on the real existence of the human being as a human being in social life. And this is how people arrive at definitions of all manner of things—capital, labor, commodity; but the human being falls completely out of these considerations.

In Central European countries, it is quite strange how the feeling was very recently lost for how everything comprising the state or other community exists because of human will, rather than the human being existing due to the will of the state; how all institutions arising in this community must ultimately have as their goal the development of the human being into a full human being, into a full individual, insofar as that is possible.

How often have we heard repeated recently that the human being must sacrifice everything to the interests of the collective! My dear friends, if this were actually to happen, though at first it sounds quite beautiful—"the human being must sacrifice everything to the interests of the collective"—this would only lead to a stark atrophy of communal life. Nothing would lay a better foundation for a community than having the individuals within it develop, in every way and in the fullest sense of the word, into unique, human individuals. All those who say the opposite usually do not take the main issue into account.

Those who develop into full human beings, who are able to bring their human individuality fully into being, are directed by this development of theirs to give as much as possible to the community; they lay the foundation for community in the very best way through everything that lies within them. What can be developed in a human—provided it is led and directed properly—does not, therefore, result in egotism. Egotism is actually generated from without, not from within. Egotism is generated primarily by the community itself. This is too little considered when it comes to social questions.

And consequently, a true misunderstanding has developed recently between the natural lack of egotism and generosity in spiritual matters, and the egotism and greed in all matters material. When it comes to everything that human beings bring forth spiritually, they are, according to their natural disposition, not at all greedy; they only want to give as much of that as possible to everyone. Someone whose inner self is a poet would like most to give away everything he or she produces, generously and not egotistically, and not horde it. People do things differently when it comes to external, material goods; they want to keep those things for themselves. But this drive never comes from within; rather it is created by everything that surrounds us. A truly social art would consist in taking everything that surrounds us externally and gradually transforming it in such a way that we could treat other human beings in the way that we treat those things that belong to us inwardly—what flows from our individualities.

To this end, however, it is necessary that people make this way of thinking, which I have indicated now in a few abstract sentences, into their own sentiment. They will never be able to do this within the context of modern spiritual life, for present-day spiritual life tosses the human being into the external rights-political and economic orders and does not take as its basis the need to develop in each human being everything that flows from the individuality. In pedagogy, it is only an abstract guideline when people say that everything that is taught or used in training must be based on the human being. This abstract guideline helps nothing. And those who most often preach this guideline are—in the actual practice of teaching, for example—by and large, the ones who sin against it most.

What will fill a person with a sentiment that is oriented toward the human being as such can only be anthroposophical spiritual science. This spiritual science leads us in the direction of recognizing the essence of the human being. It places the human being in the absolute center of all its considerations. Take, for example my book *An Outline of Esoteric Science.*† You could just as well use something else as a foundation, too. There, the evolutionary development of the Earth is followed through its pre-earthly stages: through the Saturn stage, the Sun stage, the Moon stage, and so on—the particular names are not important. But not one of these stages has been traced in the hypotheses of modern natural science.

And what has modern natural science found? First of all, there was some kind of a nebulous stage back in the impossibly distant past; there was nothing resembling a human being there. And for a long time, throughout the various evolutionary stages, according to the thinking of natural science, there was no trace of the human being. Then one day the human being turned up, after the other beings had consolidated for a while. Someday in the future, the human being will vanish, and the Earth and everything will vanish with it. And finally, the whole of evolution progresses toward a dead and empty space. This is what science thinks about the world, about the cosmos—dehumanized. And if science were not otherwise obligated to slip the human being into this picture of the cosmos (which it is, since this two-legged animal is now walking around on Earth and since, after all, it does manage to do this rather inconsequential thing called thinking); if it were not therefore compelled to do so, science would simply lay the human being aside because there would really be no need to have the human being there at all.

But now consider my *Outline of Esoteric Science*; from the very beginning, the human being is there. Nothing in the cosmos is considered without simultaneously considering the position of the human being within it. Considering things in relation to the human being is the only way it makes sense, and simultaneously the only way in which we have a foundation for our knowledge. The human being is never excluded. This anthroposophical spiritual science leads our consideration of the world back to a consideration of the essence of the human being.

I am touching here upon a few thoughts that will be important to you as you get ready to go out and give your lectures; they should prompt you to pursue a line of thinking that will shift the human being into the center of the social process. And I hope that you will color your talks in such a way as to shift the human being into this central position and avoid excluding the human being from this central place.

You see, the theoretical considerations of recent years have from the start left out the human being; they consider the human being only as a kind of luxury object for knowledge. Even the national economic considerations of recent times have taken a similar path. Simply go back: Marxist thought, as well as others, go back to this; go back to Adam Smith.[†] You will see that two things have been placed at the center of his considerations: first is economic freedom, second private property. The human being is nowhere to be found among these central points. The human being is incidentally a part of the considerations, but first and foremost it is not there; the human being is not placed in the center.

But, of course, economic freedom is not something that the human being can have! Economic freedom is not something that you possess as a human being, but rather as the owner of some sort of property or goods. As the owner of property, you move within a set of social processes, and insofar as you own that property, you can, in a certain sense, possess the thing that Adam Smith calls freedom. But you do not market these processes as a human being; rather, you set the property in motion, you undergo processes with the property. And these processes—the plowing and harvesting, if you own property, and whatever one does in industry—these are free, independent; but the human being as such does not play a role in these considerations at all when you are speaking about economic freedom.

And private property? Here we must remember that this property has to be acquired in some manner, whether through theft or conquest or inheritance, or what have you; so this means that it has had something to do with human beings. But Smith does not consider the ways in which human beings develop a relationship to the things they possess; rather, he considers private property as a kind of absolute given. This is how the human being treats all private property; the human being, too, might as well be a herd of pigs. People consider the human being as though they were not really directing the main part of their attention toward the human being as such, but rather toward the property as such. This is how national economic thinking has tossed the human being out of its considerations.

But this does not come simply from what one might call a poorly developed knowledge or a lack of knowledge; rather, this comes fundamentally from the fact that economic life itself has taken on this form. Under the influence of current abstract ways of thinking, economic life has developed automatically. The human being has progressively removed itself, has gradually given itself over to something that takes on a non-human form. You could quite easily consider this yourself in the following manner.

Simply choose, shall we say, some lordly estate and then follow its history, disregarding everything that external forces of technology brought to it during that time. Follow its history purely in regard to the human realm (which has, of course, been excluded) through a series of generations; start with the owners at the end of the nineteenth century, then go back to the owners during the middle of the nineteenth century, then back to beginning of the nineteenth century, and so on. In so doing, you will be able to follow this history as this process is completed, as the estates get taken into the economic process. You will be able to follow it without having to pay much attention as to whether you are looking at the owners at the end of the nineteenth century or the beginning of the nineteenth century. They go for walks through their property, do the things that one would expect them to do to make their mark in the world. But it makes no difference; you cannot distinguish the owners at the end of the nineteenth century from the owners at the beginning of the nineteenth century. What you are seeing here is the non-human process at work. The objectiveness of the process has already developed to such a point that the human being is excluded from it.

The human being is excluded only on one side, but this is precisely where we arrive at the current disastrous state of affairs. The human being is not excluded, however, from a certain area of spiritual life: the technological, natural scientific realm. The human being has taken hold there, but the two things do not fit together. One has simply shoved its way into the other. The human being has also taken hold in a number of other ways due to the fact that as result of the disregard of the human being more and more people have become proletarian-ized. All that is proletarian-ized—which has no other aspect than the human being itself—all of this has come to the forefront. And thus, in recent evolution, the significance of the human being in the economic process, indeed in the whole social process, has not undergone a unified development; instead, the individual areas have worked inorganically upon each other. One realm shoves its way into another, mechanically. It would be accurate to say that nowhere and at no time has technology, for example, evolved in such a way that those who owned property were the ones who had the technology in hand; rather, I would say that technology pushed its way into the workings of property from the side. The result was, naturally, not something organic, but rather something that finally had to stand in stark conflict with itself. Everything that battles with itself in our time can be traced back, finally, to these facts.

In your lectures, you must now bring this around from precisely the opposite side, for the effect of this is that people progressively lost sight of the connections in the economic process and directed their attention more and more toward sub-processes, for example, the way in which capital comes about and functions, or how labor plays into the national economic process, or how goods are produced and circulated. But the ability to see the connections is simply not being developed. You see, if we want to consider the unified process, the process of social life as a whole, we can do this only by placing the human being at the center, by relating everything back to the human being.

The only thing that will give us the proper feeling for this is a proper spiritual science, because it always and everywhere places the human being at the center. This is why in my book *Towards Social Renewal* I did not have to ask, "From which means of production did modern social life emerge?" This is Marx's question, and others like him; this is the question asked by Rodbertus. Instead, I had to ask, "Where did the modern proletarian come from? Where did the impulses of the modern proletarian come from?" This makes up the content of the first chapter in *Towards Social Renewal*: how did this important fact—that the proletarian sees all spiritual, moral, scientific, religious, and artistic life as ideology—how did this idea find its way to the proletarian? The human being is placed at the center of this. And you will find the same thing in later chapters.

Only in this way do the concepts of commodity, capital, and work receive their proper meaning; just as natural-scientific concepts receive their proper meaning only when we bring the human being into all of cosmic evolution. And so your lectures must be colored by this; that you have the human being at the center of all of your thoughts and feelings, and also call forth in your audience the feeling that it is the human being, and not capital or the commodity, that matters.

I would like to speak a little about precisely this nuance in your lectures. You must be familiar in a certain way with the concepts that you will find in the usual handbooks and pamphlets on national economy. You are probably familiar with them already. It is not at all difficult to be familiar with them; if you have read one, you have read them all. Just take some of the little collections that appeared in recent years, like *The Natural and Spiritual World* or the Göschen collection, and you will have the sense that they might as well just have given you the table of contents. If you want to become familiar with the national economy, and if you are not too weak up in the top floor but have some grasp of concepts as they have evolved, then you really do not need to distinguish between one collection and another; you can just pick one. If you want to study national economy, then take the little booklet from the Göschen collection—but it is not necessary that it be precisely this booklet; you could just as well pick up another collection, it makes no difference. They do not differ fundamentally in their content. It is all uniform. It is not only soldiers that are in uniforms; even the scholarly books are all in uniforms now. The only ones where an inner life is present (or in any case, an inner life in the sense that I mean here) are those collections that come from publishing houses like the Herder Buchhandlung in Freiburg im Breisgau, for example. There, something of an older spiritual life—now noxious to the present day—is still hidden within; that is, some piece of ancient Catholicism. Concepts are hidden there that, at the very least, differ from the others and have a certain inner drive, even though it is a force that drives in a direction that we do not want to go.

It is ultimately the same phenomenon that you will see when you pick up a biography of Goethe that has come out in recent times. It really does not make such a difference whether you pick up one volume or another, whether it is the Heinemann or the Bielschowsky, or the Meyer. The authors of course tell the story a little differently: Heinemann writes like a schoolmaster, Bielschowsky like a bad journalist, and Meyer like a collector of scribblings. I think another of them is named Gundolf. He writes a bit like, shall we say, a coquettish, cultural dandy; but you will not find anything new that is not in the other biographies. Not once, I think, do you really learn anything consequentially new in Emil Ludwig's volume; but he nevertheless distinguishes himself substantially from the others insofar as the others write like philistines who grew up indoors, whereas he writes like a street urchin. But this also does not really affect the actual foundations in a substantial way. By contrast, pick up such an inwardly stalwart book as the one written by the Jesuit Father Baumgartner about Goethe (wherein he insults Goethe and complains about him, incidentally); in this book there is spirit, spirit indeed, leaving us with no need to wish for any inner drive!

And so we can say that we must absolutely become aware of what is being produced during this present age. We must know how people are thinking about labor and capital and so on. But we must become aware that we will always have to turn the matter around and place the human being in the middle of our considerations.

You might well be saying to yourself, "All of this could really make a person nervous. Now we are supposed to get out there and give talks, and do everything that has been said here!" But this is not how it is! It is a matter of having the right attitude, and not a matter of sitting here and thinking long and hard about how to bring the human being into the center. Now is the time for us to set about doing the things that have been indicated here. And consequently, the important thing is that you leave with the attitude described here, and try to do what you are able to do, according to where your development has brought you at this point. I must, all the same, present things as they would be ideally—at least according to me. And you can take from that all of the things that you are actually able to put to use.

Now, if you direct everything toward the human being, if you go forth anthroposophically in this manner, if you sometimes weave into your speech what comes out of anthroposophy, then do so without bringing in so much that you make your audience dumbstruck: when you are dealing with economic life you do not need to talk about the division of the human being into physical body, etheric body, astral body and "I"; people cannot follow all of this these days. We have to try to put things into the language of the modern individual. So if, for you, anthroposophical life does not merely stand in the background but rather is present in the way that you speak, and if what only anthroposophy can give is incorporated within your remarks—particularly if you take as examples from anthroposophy the things you use to make apparent certain aspects of the social life—then you will call forth a certain impression in your audience, and you will also be in a position to avoid any one-sided understanding of concepts.

I want to give you an example of how certain concepts in contemporary social thought are being worked on one-sidedly. I have already mentioned how, for example, the Marxists speak about labor and commodities. They say that labor has congealed in the products that appear on the market; when we purchase a product that has appeared on the market, we are purchasing "solidified labor." The time contained in this object is also mentioned, but this is not important here. The laborer labors. Through this process, the product comes into being, and therefore, the product is "solidified labor." The raw material offered up by nature has no effective worth in human trade. Labor flows into these materials and is thereby "solidified," and establishing how much a commodity is worth is essentially a matter of seeing what quantity of work has solidified within it. The quantity of labor that has solidified there is imagined to mean an exertion or expenditure of a certain amount of brute human strength that must then be replaced. This replacement is carried out via wages; a man must be paid for his labor so that whatever he loses through labor, whatever runs into and solidifies in the product, is replaced by the wage on the other side. This seems to be entirely plausible if you consider the workers and their relationship to the product one-sidedly, from the perspective of physical labor. You could therefore say, considering only this particular aspect of labor, "A product that appears on the market is worth as much as the work that has been put into it." Certainly, this is something that from a certain perspective is indisputable; something that is strictly logical when seen from a certain angle.

But now take another perspective. Take a man who, shall we say, has worked for years on generating certain products. Due to some change in economic relationships, someone on one side or another is now inclined to give him more for the work that he does than he received before, because some boom or prosperous economic cycle has made it possible to give him more. He announces that he will give his labor to the person who is able to give him more money. As a result, he starts to procure more goods for his labor than he had before. This causes him to value these goods differently, to value them in a fundamentally different manner. He stops looking at things from the perspective of the commodity's value being equal to the labor that goes into it. Now the opposite perspective becomes more compelling. He starts to value goods in such a way that he says, "A product is more valuable to me the more work I am spared; the less work has to be put into it, the less I actually need to work for it."

Consider the fact that it is possible to obtain goods through conditions other than labor: you can steal them, you can find them, you can obtain them through yet other means; if you consider that the words "steal" and "find" are only figurative, and the result, economically, is the same as labor, then this other way of looking at things becomes normal! If you have a commodity obtained in this manner, what does that mean for you? It means that you can give it to someone else in exchange for the execution of a task. You have done no work to acquire it, but you can give it in exchange. In our economic connections to one another, other people do work for someone else; you can have a certain number of people do a job for you. Here you have the most prominent expression of how the worth of a commodity is measured by the reduction of labor. And this reaches such a point that certain goods are created entirely under the auspices of this perspective of reducing labor, of not carrying out a job. If I paint a picture and then sell it, the economic worth of this is that I do not need to make my own brush, nor sweep my own room, nor do a variety of other things, but that I spare myself this labor. Here, the measurement of worth is based on what labor one avoids. Here, the value must be measured according to the reduction of labor.

And so, I can say that there are two perspectives with which you can define the relationship between labor and goods, between labor and commodities; or at least, with which you can define the value of that relationship. You can say that a commodity is worth as much as the labor that is put into it. You can also say, however, that a commodity is worth as much as the lack of labor in it; as much as it makes it unnecessary to put labor into it. And the first definition, which deals with solidified labor, is more applicable the more one deals with purely physical labor and its products. The other definition is more applicable the more one deals with goods in which thinking, speculation, or other valuable spiritual forces are a factor. Both of them can be applied to life as a whole, the one just as much as the other.

But it is important that you not be fooled by the fact that one definition is correct in certain instances, because then you might try to contest the other. In life, there are two opposing views for everything. We must therefore try not to look at life by starting with concepts. For if you have some really great and correct concept, and then you try to reach life from there, you will discover only one part of life. If, on the other hand, you take life as your starting point, then you will find that it is always possible to describe things from opposite poles, just as you can photograph a human body from the front and from the back, from the left and from the right. Proper contemplation of knowledge really does not differ at all from the process of artistic creation. And we must replace the theoretical perspectives brought into humanity in recent years with a view toward life.

But when people have a certain viewpoint, they take all of their cues from it. And people have for the last three, four, five hundred years relied on perspectives that originate in concepts, and according to these perspectives have established our social life. People create social life! As a result, we have not only one-sided imaginations of the world in our human concepts, but in life itself we also have one-sided institutions that do not fit together or agree.

For example, the proletariat has a way of working in which the relationship between labor and commodity truly is one in which the commodity represents a certain quantity of solidified labor; but if we then turn to the capitalists, we see that the essence of the commodity value is based in how much it reduces and spares one labor. As a result, we have within the real processes of social life two things that cannot be compared. The capitalists work in a different manner than the proletariat. The proletarian not only thinks, but also labors in such a way that the results of the labor are valued according to the work put into them; the capitalist works in such a way that the work is valued according to the principle of labor reduction. The one must expend labor in order to generate wages; the other spares labor. And these two links intermingle and skewer each other. And in this skewering lies the social grievances of the present moment. And there is no other salvation than to see into the real underlying process, to understand life as such; and to admit to oneself that it is necessary in the social process that there be human beings. You see, here we come to the human being; human beings who work in such a way that their labor runs into and solidifies in the product; and people who work in such a way that labor is reduced and saved—an act of labor cannot serve others unless this principle is followed. It is not possible to be a leader without following this basic principle: do less work.

It follows that it is entirely impossible to integrate the regulation of labor into the economic process; regulation of labor must happen in the social sphere, which is the rights-political life.

If you follow such lines of thinking, you will see where it leads. It is crucial that we clarify all concepts (since the world today is filled to the brim with unclear, nebulous concepts, even in practical areas), so that people can get things right again in their institutions as well as their thinking. If we do not have the courage to cry out to the world, "You may no longer think in the way that you have up until now because you are ruining the external world with your thoughts; you must put the human being at the center of your considerations, and not commodities or capital"; if we do not have the courage to cry this out against the delusions of the present, then we will not get anywhere. This has to happen in those areas where people are otherwise still talking about the old imaginations of the world, particularly in the area of national economy.

In the kind of presentations that I give, you see the way in which life, in all its particulars, must come under consideration. This is precisely what is not considered in the typical literature on the national economy, which is why reading any one of those little books is as good as reading any other. It makes no difference if you pick up Göschen's book on national economy or the one called *The Natural and Spiritual World.* In all of these books you will find what you need, along with the possibility of schooling yourself in how not to think. And in every case you will need to oppose what you find that is against a way of considering the world that deeply affects the human being; one that takes the human being as its starting point. The only way to develop this in yourself, and the only way to develop this in other people, is through something like anthroposophical spiritual science. Therefore, make no mistake, the salvation of external social life is possible only if a salvation comes about of one of the limbs of the threefold social organism—the spiritual realm, of education, development, and the like; only if such a salvation comes about and is able to make clear the way to a productive spiritual life, one that fills the human being completely.

It is difficult to make yourself understood when speaking about such things, but at the very least, those of you who are sitting here now must understand them well. You see the way in which, over and over again, the message is put out there that schools need to be formed according to the model of the Waldorf School.† Some people will say, "We could develop such schools as soon as we had the money to do so." Then, I always ask these people, "And what would you do once you had the money?" They answer, "We would ask you which people we should hire as teachers." I say to them, "I would only have a partial say in the selection of teachers because there are regulations that only people who have passed the state exams and been approved as teachers may be hired." This means that the results of an effort to develop Waldorf schools would not be what *should* result from such an effort. We first have to make it so that there is complete freedom when selecting teachers and no barrier saying that only state-approved teachers can be hired. This requirement that only such teachers can be hired cannot be present, because otherwise we do not have a threefold society.

It is not a matter of simply establishing within the present system schools in which you create surrogates of the lessons, in which you believe that you can just follow the course of study that I have laid out; rather, it is a matter of following this one principle: free spiritual life. Only then do you create a beginning for the threefold social organism through these schools. So do not call up false imaginations in people, leading them to believe that they can carry on in their old way of doing things and still found Waldorf schools; instead, call upon them to understand that in the school in Stuttgart, a truly free spiritual life exists. There is no program there and no course of study, but only the teacher and his or her ability; not an edict regulating how much the teacher should be able to do. We are dealing with genuine, real teachers. It is always better to have a bad but genuine teacher, than a teacher who is within the regulated establishment but is not genuine. And during the lesson, we are dealing with the students and with the work that is displayed on the walls of that classroom, not with things like teaching materials or teaching methods that come from the establishment. And this is precisely what we must point out: that we should always be dealing with reality.

When it comes to the "program" for such an institution, in my opinion you can just get together about twelve people, it could be a few more or a few less. I assure you, if these twelve people are even a little bit disciplined, then they will be able to come up with very clever things, will be able to develop reform plans; it could be incredibly clever, incredibly reasonable, what they come up with. They will be able to say, "This has to happen this way, this that way," and so on. When it comes to such things, it would be right to say that there are countless people who could tell you the best way to handle a particular branch of knowledge or how to put together a journal. But this is not what we should be thinking about. It is a matter of working from the basis of reality.

What is the use of having beautifully arranged school regulations and maybe even a set of teaching materials that is somewhat liberated from these things? With these sorts of regulations and prearranged materials, you just end up fooling yourself for a while; whereas you represent reality when you simply take up the material that lies before you. You have to reckon with reality, and avoid such statements and programs if you really intend to create something.

This is very hard for people to understand nowadays, and it is therefore necessary to make this point very strongly. By working so much with programs in every area of life during recent years, people have fundamentally contaminated life.

For example, if you look at the development of social democracy from the Eisenach platform[†] to the Gotha platform,[†] you will see a kind of flattening. The Erfurt platform[†] is worst of all. It prescribes the way in which everything should be organized; for example, the socialization of resources. But this is brought about through the exclusion of any consideration of life. And this was started by someone whose founding principle is something like, "What do I care about life? I care only about the Marxist program! Life can end as long as the Marxist program is fulfilled. As far as I am concerned, thousands and thousands of people could go to the gallows in a single day as long as the Marxist program is fulfilled!" This man is Lenin. He would be capable of sending thousands of people to the gallows daily as long as the Marxist program was fulfilled.

Of course, this is all said radically, but it is a proper characterization of the situation nonetheless. And where does this man come from? You see, the unrealistic way that this man looks at life comes from something that only individuals with genius say. Lenin is of course a genius; though his is a pig-headed genius, a genius that is stubborn as a bull, it is genius all the same. In his manuscript *State and Revolution*[†] you will find that he says something along these lines: "Of course, the fulfillment of what is to come will not follow from the Marxist program. But my Marxist program will ruin everything that is currently in place. Then a new humanity will be cultivated. It will not have a Marxist program, but will live according to this precept: each according to one's needs and abilities. But a new humanity must first be cultivated!"

Our programmatic life has become so incompatible with reality that we now have an individual who, with the help of his accomplices, is establishing a vast empire not on the basis of life, but on the basis of a program professing that the very establishment of this empire is fundamentally pointless; for healthy conditions will come about only when those human beings who are currently here are no longer here, but are replaced by other human beings. I would like to suggest that, in this, we encounter the current state of our mental imaginations and emotional life in a very palpable way. We must not underestimate such things, but rather look them full in the face.

Lecture 7

Stuttgart, February 15, 1921 (evening)

EARLIER, I described to you how the human being must be placed in the middle of the considerations to which you will be applying yourselves in the near future. If this occurs to the fullest possible extent, then it might be able to put right a number of things in the current worldview that will lead to catastrophe, as I also showed you in my last lecture. Now we must turn toward a few things that, at least by way of example, will illustrate what is connected with this claim: that the human being must be placed in the middle of our social considerations and the actions to be taken in the social realm.

We have among us now a huge number of slogans and catch-phrases, and the like. What people express to their fellow human beings is filled ever more with these phrases. We are living in an age of empty phrases. And a reality that is guided and directed by empty phrases must quite clearly collapse in upon itself. This is connected to the basic phenomena of our present evolutionary moment.

From the great number of things that are present in social life, let us take one particular example and consider it, as it is discussed quite often now. We are hearing from several people who want to participate in discussions of social questions that the proletarian movement is revolting against unemployment income, against unemployment benefits. Now, it is certainly the case that something real lies behind such a claim. But by and large, that "something" is entirely different from what the people who make such claims think. You must first be clear about the fact that you have to get behind the scenes through observation of social events, and not through concepts, until you see what "unemployment income" and "unemployment benefits" actually are.

People have talked about these things in a great variety of ways. There are people—even Bismarck is among them[†]—who spoke about this quite differently; they spoke of "productive classes" but meant working classes. They were, however, of the opinion that farmers, tradesmen who work with their hands, for example, and people in other similar lines of work are "productive people"; but that teachers, doctors, and the like, for example, are not "productive people." That what a teacher does, therefore, does not count as "productive work."

You know perhaps that Karl Marx made an economic discovery that has been much talked about precisely in the interest of setting this "productive work" in the proper light. Karl Marx's discovery is of course the famous "Indian bookkeeper." This is the man who, somewhere in a little Indian village where the other people worked with their hands, sowing and reaping and picking fruit from the trees, in this village his job was to keep the books for all these various activities. And Karl Marx decided that all the other people in this village were doing "productive work," and that this bookkeeper was deriving the means for his unproductive life from the "surplus value" taken off the top of the output from the others' labor. And from the case of this unlucky Indian bookkeeper, many conclusions have then been made that have now become fairly typical of a certain kind of economic thinking.

It goes without saying that the activities of a teacher can be categorized within the social process as "unproductive activity," just as Karl Marx categorized the activities of his unlucky Indian bookkeeper. But let us consider the case in this light: we have a teacher who is an able man, as able as any full or complete human being. He teaches and nurtures very young children, elementary school age. And to make things simple (our theory will not be hampered by this), let us say that all of the children that this teacher nurtures and teaches become cobblers. And he enables them to be even more clever through his expertise, through the fact that he is able to develop the capabilities in his students that allow them to think cleverly and move neatly into their life of employment as cobblers through his practical use of all manner of educational techniques; and now they become such terrific cobblers that, let us say, they are able to produce in ten days as many boots as others produce in fifteen.

Now, what do we have here? You see, all of these cobblers who were taught this way are doing "productive work" in a true Marxist sense. If this teacher and his expertise had not been present, if he had been an incompetent teacher, then the same amount of productive work would have been done in fifteen days rather than ten. If you count up all of the shoes made by these now-grown children during those five extra days that were spared because they had a skillful teacher, then you can rightfully say, "All of these boots were, in essence, made by that skillful teacher, and at the very least in the economic process, in everything that belongs to this economic process, which is to say everything from it that supports human beings, in all of this, the teacher was actually a productive element. His being lives forth in all of those boots produced during those extra five days!"

What is happening here is that people have taken such a shortsighted view of things that they identify Marxist "productive work" only with the work of the cobblers and see the work of the teacher as "unproductive work," meaning work that supports itself on the surplus value of others' labor. But reality is rendered false by this way of considering things.

We can take up another consideration that does not tend one-sidedly in one direction or another, but rather takes up the whole process of social life. If we think about it economically, purely economically, then we have to ask, what actually connects the teacher to his physical livelihood? In economics, is it really any different, economically speaking, any different from other sources of income? Does it really differ—this is my question—from something that (speaking as a Marxist now) is otherwise abstracted from physical labor and given to another person? Economically speaking, it is absolutely no different! We are dealing with the following here.

Let us assume that something that is called "surplus value" is spent on teachers; this value circulates productively, in the manner I have just described, into the whole economic process. Let us assume that it is given then to a financier, to a man who we call a pensioner in the truest sense, who actually does nothing more than what we typically expect of a "coupon clipper." Well—is the economic process depleted by the fact that he clips those coupons? Is it not the case that this person eats and drinks and clothes himself, and so on? He cannot live on what is given to him as "surplus value" alone. He lives on the things that other people do and make for him. He is simply a site where work, where the economic process, is transformed.

If we consider the matter objectively then we can really only say the following: such a person, living somewhere as a well-financed pensioner—this transformation point of the economic process—is a part of social life the way in which a still, fixed point is part of a scale, of the scale's arm. This point has to be there—this fixed, still point on the scale's arm. All of the other points move; the one fixed point on the arm of the scale does not move. It must be there, though. For things must be able to go through this process of transformation. In other words, from an economic perspective we cannot say anything definitive on the matter. At most, we can say that if the number of these fixed points, these "coupon-clipping" pensioners, grows too large, the others will necessarily have to work more, work longer hours. But in reality, this is not the case anywhere because the number of these pensioners in relation to any population as a whole does not approach that point, and because little more than nothing can result from an attempt to change anything on the basis of the current state of our social life and process.

So we cannot really even think about things in this way. And if you go through the Marxist literature, you will see that the demands laid out there to find something that is responsible for all of the so-called ills of social life, such as so-called unemployment benefits, that these demands lead to a slew of conclusions, to conclusions that are not justified. They do not prove anything. They would be able to prove something only if somehow the economic process were altered in some fundamental way: if the pensioners were to suddenly not receive their pensions. But this might never be the case. So we cannot get anywhere near the real issue with this way of thinking.

What we really need to be doing is making sure that we see clearly that such fixed points must necessarily exist in order to bring about the needed transformations, the turn-over of economic life. There is in fact a surplus value that is economically consonant with all of the definitions that Karl Marx gives of surplus value; one that is also consonant in all of its functions (insofar as one thinks purely economically) with the functions of surplus value in Marx: namely, taxes. In both its origins and its functions, a tax is exactly the same as Marx's surplus value. And the various socialist governments, wherever they have taken power, have not exactly proved to be particular strong opponents of surplus value in the form of taxes! It is precisely when it comes to such things that this theory reveals its patent absurdity.

The absurdity of these theories is never demonstrated in their logic, but only in reality. Anyone who strives to assess things from the perspective of reality must say the same. So long as we remain within economic life, it is impossible to give the concept of "surplus value" any sensible meaning. For as long as we remain within the realm of economic life, we are always dealing with the turnover of economic processes. And this turnover can occur only because there are fixed points of transformation. Whether these are found in the state or in individual pensioners is of secondary importance when we are thinking about things purely economically. Therefore it is necessary to point out that everything connected to a concept like "unemployment income" or "unemployment benefits" has nothing to do with economic thinking, but is simply a question of resentment; you look at someone who is receiving unemployment benefits and see them basically as nothing more than someone who is lounging about, not working. A legal or perhaps even moral concept has been smuggled into economic thinking. That is the originating phenomenon here.

In reality, we are dealing with something quite different; namely, that our human life process, the process of our civilization itself, cannot be maintained if people actually bring about the things that some are striving for when they make up empty phrases like "the right to the whole produce of labor." There is no real possibility of speaking about a "whole produce of labor" if you consider the following example. Suppose I became a cobbler and worked with more expertise than I would have worked had I not had a skilled teacher. Any possibility of claiming my right to the "whole produce of labor" is cancelled out. Because where does that whole produce of labor come from? Certainly not from just the collected product of the present! The teacher who taught me might be long dead. The past merges with the present and the present flows then into the future. Trying to get a picture of the kinds of things people create within the whole economic process, trying to see this with short-sighted concepts, is absurd.

Something different comes about as soon as we say to ourselves, "Well then, thinking about it purely economically, there can be no talk of someone receiving the 'whole produce of labor' because it is impossible to even understand this concept. You cannot draw its boundaries or contours. It does not exist. It is impossible." But something different comes about the moment that we consider reality. In reality, we find these points of transfer: people who receive part of the output of another who does physical labor. Now, assuming this recipient is a teacher; in that case, the teacher also does productive work, as I described to you earlier.

But then let us assume that the person is not a teacher, but rather a proper coupon clipper. Let us even assume that we have not just one coupon clipper, but two. One of them clips coupons in morning, then smokes a few cigarettes after breakfast, reads the morning paper, goes for a walk, has lunch, sits down in his rocking chair and rocks for a while, then goes to the club and plays whist or poker or something like that, and this is how he spends his day. Now let us consider the other who, let us say, busies himself with the establishment of a scientific institution; someone who, in other words, turns his thoughts toward the establishment of a scientific institution that would not have come into existence if this man had not been a coupon clipper. If it was to have been established by the people who are around and doing the work that allows him to clip his coupons, then it would certainly have never been established. He establishes it. And in this scientific institution, after ten years or perhaps even twenty years, an extremely important discovery is made. By the means of this discovery, productive work is still carried out in a similar way, but through an even more productive process than what the teacher was able to teach his children who became cobblers. In this case, there is a certain difference between coupon clipper A and coupon clipper B; a difference that is extremely significant for economics. And we have to say that the coupon-clipper's process was an extremely productive one in the whole of human life.

This question cannot be decided from a purely economic standpoint. It can be decided only if something else is there outside of economic life, detached from economic life, unaffiliated with economic life, that leads people who derive their livelihood from the output of the whole to give back what they have taken away; in other words, when a free spiritual life is present that moves people to become, not simply financiers, but to make some use of the spiritual powers that they possess, or even the physical powers that they possess.

At precisely this moment, when we see through to things as they are in actual life, we will be led to the necessity of the threefold social organism. And above all, with this complete vision of life, we will be made aware of the fact that all of the nonsense that is brought forward by national economics, and even by pragmatic people, is fundamentally useless; that ultimately something different must enter the minds of human beings; namely, a complete consideration of life. And this complete consideration of life—this is what finally leads to the threefold social organism.

Therefore, we must make an effort to make these ideas ever more widespread. We also must not disdain to point out just how shortsighted modern-day practical life is. We must make a connection between these two activities: presenting what is positive about threefolding, while being the harshest critics of the various spiritual streams that exist at present. We have to become familiar with these spiritual streams, and become harsh critics of them. This is the only way that we will be able to hold up a mirror to the absurdities that exist today; this is the only way that we will move forward, that we will be able to succeed. And what we are able to teach people through these means, we must simultaneously present to them in such a way that they are able to sense that we work with real concepts.

You see, a person who makes boots is absolutely a productive person. But according to Marxist concepts, someone who makes little beauty items is just as productive. If you are guided simply by the idea of physical labor, then making these is just as much a physical labor as making boots. It is thus a matter of looking at the whole process and taking from that a picture of how what someone does fits into the whole process of social life. People must develop a feeling for these things. There is no other way forward.

However, it is also necessary for us to respect the habitual thinking of our contemporaries. You have to be clear about the fact that if you were to go out right now to talk to people for an hour, or an hour and a quarter, about the kinds of things that I am presenting to you, they would start to yawn and finally would leave the lecture hall, happy that your talk was over, longing for a healthy nap. They would find it difficult, much too difficult! People have grown totally unaccustomed to following along with thoughts that are taken from reality. Because people have heard only abstractions—as schoolchildren they got used to following along with abstractions—because of this, humanity has become mentally lazy. Humanity is terribly lazy in its thinking right now. And we have to be sensitive to this, but in a way that is useful.

Therefore, we should allow stories to enter into our lectures about the things that have already developed from anthroposophical spiritual science. Maybe we should tell people fewer anecdotes! It can certainly be very helpful for the mentally lazy people of the present to occasionally interrupt a complicated lecture with anecdotes, but we have better ways to spend our time. In those in-between moments, being careful to introduce it properly into our train of thought, let us tell them about our Waldorf School,[†] about eurythmy,[†] about our college level courses,[†] about the Kommende Tag.[†] These are things that interrupt the course of thinking, which is first and foremost a pleasant diversion for people; they do not need to think as much. And then, is it not true that the essence of the matter can follow from this? We can spend some time describing how the Waldorf School came about, how it was established; we can describe how thirty instructors in Dornach in the collegiate level courses attempted to fructify science in the ground of spiritual science. In this case, when you say to them that science should be fructified, people do not have to think about how this would specifically happen in chemistry or in botany, but they can have faint imaginations about it while you speak. And so then they have a little time to put their thinking to bed in the midst of the thoughts that you are presenting. We have then reclaimed the possibility of talking about somewhat complicated things for the next five minutes.

And the other topics are extremely useful anyway. If, for example, we explain to people how we did the evaluations in the Waldorf School, how we tried not to simply write "almost satisfactory," "barely sufficient" (you really cannot tell the difference, anyway, between whether someone has done something in a "barely" or "hardly" sufficient manner), but rather wrote something like a short biography of each child, along with a personal adage or saying for life. People do not need to think very much about how hard that is, which is to say they can see very easily how hard it is to find an adage appropriate to every child; but if you just tell them the results, then it is quite easy and painless for them to receive that. And in the same way, we can also tell people something about the founding of the Waldorf School, how the building slowly proved to be too small, how we had to build sheds because we did not have the money to build a proper building. It is useful for people to hear sometimes that we did not have enough money; this could have fortunate results. If we introduce such things into our considerations, it will first of all be necessarily material, for these are all relevant things; their presence will be clearly justified. But this is also a way in which we can create a pleasant break and diversion for the audience.

Then we can tell them about the college level courses in Dornach, in Stuttgart. We can weave in the fact that all of that currently must be led by overworked Waldorf teachers; that very few people have so far gathered together who are able to lead something out of anthroposophical spiritual science. The fact that the Waldorf teachers are working three times as much as they should—this is something that people can understand pretty easily, can they not? Each of them then fancies that he or she is also working too much. In this way, by speaking about something that is already out there in the world, we can show people something that they will perhaps be happy to hear about, while at the same time communicating something that they should know, that they need to know.

And then we can talk to them also about the Kommende Tag. We should try to give them a picture of how this Kommende Tag is organized. You can see this organization clearly in the leaflets that have been distributed. We should introduce people to the concept behind the Kommende Tag with these leaflets, and say to them, "Of course, you will find that this Kommende Tag does not yet conform fully to the idea of an association" (we will talk more about associations tomorrow) "that it is still formed on the basis of the present economy." But we should say to people at the same time, "Even though we know this, it shows us even more how necessary it is that this economy change, because even with the best intentions it is not possible to form an ideal association on the basis of present-day economic life."

It is also necessary for you to grasp our movement as a whole in your lectures. You should not feel embarrassed about presenting one side, the spiritual side, the anthroposophical orientation of our work, then going into the practical matters of the Kommende Tag and presenting all of that to people. In the lectures that you give, you need not go straight to asking for money. I say this to you parenthetically, but that can be done by another person, who comes along and approaches people for the first time after the lecture; it goes better that way. And although I say this to you parenthetically, that is nevertheless how it should happen. As I said, you need not directly advertise for our movement in your lecture. But you can indicate that in order to meet the demands and intentions of threefolding, without there being any self-serving interests in the background, what is needed is first: money; second: money; and third: money. And whenever one or the other of you finds the right situation in which to say this, you might, when repeating that word "money" three times, emphasize the first iteration more, and then speak with a falling or rising tone on the second iteration. This is something that can, in some way, bring something beneficial to the inner formation of it.

I say that to you only as a way of indicating that you must pay attention to the way in which you say something. In a certain sense, every time you go into a lecture hall, you feel it out to understand whether you should speak in one way or another. You can still sort of feel this out, even when you are in a room full of people you do not know. And so, you must always pay attention to such things. If you want to achieve precisely what must be achieved at present, you will not do so by stepping before a group of people with a finished concept; rather, you must always orient yourself toward relationships between people. You will be able to do this only by having the kind of bearing toward the form and experience of your lectures that I described to you yesterday. At the same time, you should not forget to point out again and again the things that we have already managed to accomplish in the founding of the school and our practical institutions. Right now, this is precisely what people need. And you do them good, when describing the threefold social organism, to use the development of the Waldorf School as an illustration of it. The same is true when you are describing economic life; you should use the example of what we are trying to accomplish with the Kommende Tag. I absolutely do not want you to forget that the world must be made aware of our various institutions through your lectures.

And behind all of this must lie the consciousness that in every corner of the world (I have already said this multiple times in these lectures) there is a force of opposition that will only continue to grow, and that we do not have a very long time to bring about all that we want to bring about and all that must be brought about; we must tackle these things in the near future.

We cannot follow the example of how the anthroposophical movement has progressed thus far. I am saying this now for those who have been in the anthroposophical movement for a while; for at least in part, it has progressed in such a way that its members have far too little interest in what is actually happening in the world around them. Now we are living in a time in which a keen interest in everything happening in the world must be developed. And we have to exemplify what we are bringing, as well as take a critical stance toward everything occurring on a day-to-day basis in the world. This is why we have to interest ourselves in these occurrences. We must seek to demonstrate the necessity of our movement on their basis. We must stress over and over that these events are likely to lead modern civilization toward its downfall. People must understand that if they continue to move forward on the present course, the downfall of modern civilization will most certainly result. The European countries, at the very least, will experience terrible times if we do not lay the foundation for a new society out of a truly active spiritual life and an actively understood political and economic life.

We also have to take away certain phrases from people, ones that always go something like this: "Yes, that might be well and good with the threefold social organism and all, but in order to bring something like that about, you would need decades, if not centuries." This is a frequent objection. There is, however, no more ridiculous objection than this one. The things that are to come about in humanity, particularly when it comes to social institutions, are entirely dependent upon what human beings want, and how much strength and courage they set behind their will toward it. And institutions that might last for centuries due to carelessness and inaction can be overturned in a moment by the use of active powers. But this is exactly why it is necessary for us to bring to people what comes out of our spiritual science, and that can arise through the examination of our present institutions. Do not forget to tell them about the kinds of things that are to come into being here in Stuttgart; for example, the Medical Therapeutic Institute.[†] It might be the case that some people will learn best about the fruits of spiritual science, at least at first, from such institutions.

When working at making something like this plausible for other people, we must also take into consideration the fact that it will not further humanity's development to establish amidst the perspectives of old Catholicism or Evangelicalism or Judaism or the Turkish religions—to establish amidst these sectarian views an anthroposophical worldview. This would certainly be significant for those people who would get together once or twice every week to discuss the questions of that worldview. It would have a subjective significance for these people. But it would have no meaning for the world at large. Only a worldview and an understanding of life that takes hold of eminently practical questions will have any significance for the world as a whole. We will find all too often these days that people are very happy to talk about the eternal in human nature, or about life after death. You can even talk with a large number of people now about reincarnation and karmic law—and not see them fall asleep in boredom. But it is more useful and also more important to make people understand that anthroposophical spiritual science can bring something to medicine, for example, or to therapy; so that people can really see how the things that we take hold of in the spiritual world have a unique significance for the material world. It is not simply a matter of elevating oneself to the plane of spirit in abstraction; rather, it is a matter of elevating oneself in such a way that the spiritual world comes alive and has sufficient strength and power to move into the material world.

This thought: this interpolation of the spiritual into the material world in a multitude of different ways, you should lay this out before people over and over again. Spirit wants to govern matter, not flee from it. This is why it is blasphemous, in a certain sense, when someone like Bruhn, in his little book *Theosophy and Anthroposophy*,† admonishes anthroposophy for wanting to bring all the things supposedly floating about in the heights of heaven above reality—things that are not supposed to be part of material reality—to bring these things into everyday life. It is hard to think of worse corrupters of human life than those teachers who stand at lecterns in universities and teach people nonsense like this. But this happens every day, in a wide variety of ways.

And it is in keeping with the order of the day that people then come forward and say, "Well, anthroposophy might be an attempt to deepen the individual branches of science, but anthroposophy has nothing to do with religion, with Christianity." And then people step up and try to prove that anthroposophy has nothing to do with Christianity or religion. They come and they present totally arbitrary ideas that they have about religion and Christianity. And they make it clear that no one is allowed to shake up these concepts that they have about religion and Christianity!

If only people could be truthful! Then it might actually be possible to be somewhat charitable toward them. If they were to come forward and say, "Now anthroposophy has come on the scene; it is speaking out of different sources than the ones that I have been speaking out of at the theological lectern or the pulpit. I have to choose between giving up my job (but then I have nothing to eat, which would be terrible), and continuing to do my job while denying anthroposophy!" You would not be able to take people like this particularly seriously when it came to our cultural life. But they would be speaking truthfully, just like the law teacher in Graz† spoke truthfully when he proved the existence of human free will to his students by saying, "Human beings have free will! Because if they did not have free will, then they would not have any responsibility for their actions. And if they did not have any responsibility for their actions, then there would be no punishment and penal code. But I am the teacher of penal code. If there were no free will, then I would not be holding a lecture on the penal code. But that is precisely what I have to do. And since there must be someone like me at this university, then there must be a penal code, which means that there must be punishments, which means that people must be responsible for their actions, which means that human beings must have free will." This is more or less how this law teacher in Graz proved the existence of human free will to his students for years. That is basically what he said.

And theologians, among others, would say something similar, if they were being truthful. They too could present the other side of the issue, and then we might be more charitable toward them. They might say, "I could possibly take on the uncomfortable task of founding religion and Christianity anew." For university professors, it could happen that if the theology faculty was large enough some of them might have to move over into the philosophy department. If they were already professors, this would be easier than if they were coming to a university for the first time. But keeping up a living would still be difficult. And they do not want to take on the uncomfortable task and the work of founding these things anew. If, however, they would only say this out loud, then they would be honest, at the very least. Instead, they say all manner of things that do not actually speak to reality, but rather serve a purely decorative function, covering up reality and hiding it. In these matters, we may not allow ourselves to be indulgent or charitable; when it comes to these matters, we must seek out untruthfulness and corruption in all the dark corners of the world, and show it relentlessly to the world.

And we must also not forget to point out the slipshod thought that some people exhibit when they refuse to face up to certain claims in all of their moral complexity and depth. It was not long ago that someone heard how I publicly described the baseless lies of Frohnmeyer,[†] who quite simply described something in Dornach in a lying, biased manner, something that actually looks much different than the biased way in which he characterized it. And this Someone said,[†] "Well, Frohnmeyer really believed that it looked that way." For me it is not simply a matter of pointing out that Frohnmeyer said something untrue in this case; my concern is rather that Frohnmeyer is demonstrating that he makes claims about something in Dornach that fly in the face of reality. What he does in one instance, he does in every other. He is a theologian. He lectures at Basel University. This theologian draws from sources claimed to be sources of truth. Those who bear witness like Frohnmeyer did, those who describe the statue of Christ as he did, show that they have no understanding of how one discovers the truth in these sources. If Napoleon's birth and death dates were not written down in history books, Frohnmeyer would speak falsehoods about these facts too, if he had to discover them himself. This is my concern: to portray all of the corrupting effects of such people on this historical moment; to demonstrate that they are not fit for the positions given to them by the chaotic circumstances of the present. We may not be charitable when it comes to such things.

These are things that will be part of the development of your work in the coming weeks.

Lecture 8

Stuttgart, February 16, 1921 (afternoon)

DURING this hour, I would like to talk about certain colorations that your spoken work will have to take in regard to present-day spiritual life. In particular, you should not limit yourselves by basing your talks solely on the intellectual understanding of social questions; rather, you must work to make the world aware of the fact that we must begin to feel differently toward certain things than is felt in the supposedly dominant circles of the present. What is living in institutions, what occurs in people's external social dealings, is all dependent on what is found in the thinking, feeling, and willing of human beings. This is why I have so strongly stressed that the human being as human being must be shifted into the center of social life, as well as world considerations. But we must develop a feeling ourselves for how the feeling life of the present has erred and now finds itself on a precipitous path downward. We must feel keenly how the civilized world has arrived at its present situation precisely because of this often perverse feeling life. By looking at specific examples, we must make such things clear to ourselves. And we should make them clear to the world through examples. It is easy to find such examples if we simply look objectively at the treatment that our anthroposophical movement has received among our contemporaries.

When speaking about social questions, it is important always to call up the moral moment that was defined by how the leading individuals of the recent past allowed the course of events to run so irresponsibly. Is it not the case that within the leading circles the only concern in world history was how modern technology and the recently developed forms of materialism were going to carry the world forward, and how world history would be borne out by these forces? And it is quite clear that no one cared about what sort of influence this course of world history would have to win over the countless people who developed, because of history's course, into the proletariat class. They simply allowed this to come about with a carelessness that has proven to be tragic, and that must now be brought sharply to their attention if any sort of improvement is to result.

A crude example of this carelessness is something that I have often mentioned in the past. At the end of the 1860s in Austria, there was a minister of police named Giskra.[†] At the time, there were also individuals who were indicating that an important social question was looming on the horizon for modern civilization. And that minister of police, responding to individuals who posed this social question, gave the answer, "Austria knows of no such social question. That question stops at Bodenbach!"

Now this head-in-the-sand approach, this kind of ostrich politicking, is rampantly widespread in the leading circles of recent history. And this, my dear friends, is something that we must see through; we must make the present strongly aware of this. You could say that this lack of consciousness is gradually moving more and more from the external world into the thinking realm; and, sadly, without the awareness of many people, it is taking hold there. This leads directly to a certain crudeness of thinking, and this crudeness of thinking is for the most part denied by contemporary intellectuals. I would like to demonstrate what I have just said to you with an example that has only just come to light.

You see, there is a certain infiltrator from the leading circles that have worked with such carelessness and lack of regard for the course of world events—Count Hermann Keyserling[†]—who has founded in Darmstadt a so-called "School of Wisdom," a truly hideous cultural product of our present culture. His publishing firm is advertising for this School of Wisdom. And a little volume has only just appeared bearing the truly sophisticated title (as you will have to admit): *The Road to Perfection.*[†] This volume needed an endorsement from the publisher. So for this endorsement, on the so-called "cigar band" on the outside of the book, they wrote this: "The position of Count Keyserling toward Theosophy in general, and toward Steiner's Theosophy in particular, is put forward in Chapter 14 of his last book *Philosophy as Art*† under the title 'For and Against Theosophy.' Rudolf Steiner saw the need to respond to this truthful, factually-supported document with personal attacks." This is the advertisement that the publisher wrote for this School of Wisdom! Now, if social salvation is to come about, it is truly necessary to keep a sharp eye on people such as this Count Hermann Keyserling, and to speak frankly and freely to the world about what you discover in your keen observations of them. The vermin of current civilization must be exposed.

Count Keyserling's inner lack of conscience, his intellectual lack of conscience, will now be presented to you as it presents itself in the text, which has the following beautiful sentence, for example, on page 59: "Outside of the general gatherings, all of the participants of the society have a student's right to longer, personal conversations with Count Keyserling. He is available, with prior appointment, and with the exception of Saturdays and Sundays, unless he is travelling, for such conversations every afternoon between three and five o'clock in the rooms of the school, Paradeplatz 2, at the entrance to the Zeughausstraße. Should anyone who is not a student desire to call upon the teacher's time for the purpose of asking questions of wisdom, the business office reserves the right in such cases to charge a consultation rate, for the betterment of the school."

My dear friends, you are quite right to laugh at such things, but really, this is no laughing matter. Precisely in such places lie the most basic faults of our social life. You find then on page 47 the following sentence—you know that I have already talked in a public lecture,† and with a certain recklessness (but that is necessary in such cases, and it was deliberate), about the untruthfulness of Count Hermann Keyserling regarding his claim that I rely heavily on Haeckel.†—Keyserling there writes the following sentence regarding that characterization: "...and instead of correcting a possible error on my part, which I would gladly put up with, for I have had no time for a special research in Steiner's sources... Steiner accuses me of a flat-out lie..." So, this man actually had the nerve to present the possibility that someone would write down any old lie, and then receive merely a rap on the knuckles for it when someone else is able to correct him! Think about the intellectual ruin that this will bring about: a person can write down whatever he or she likes, and the other is obligated to correct it. If we were to work in this manner, we would sink into a social swamp. And then to write something like, "...I have had no time for a special research into Steiner's sources...." What is that saying in reality? In reality, it says, "I have not taken time for an exact examination of the things that I am writing down." And such a man has claimed this as his right!

My dear friends, we must have a feeling for the perverse intellectualist feelings of the present moment. And if we do not, if we are not able to come forward with the revelation of this social swamp, then everything else that we say is in vain. Therefore, I must say it again: simply defending yourself helps nothing. We must consider all of the attacks that come toward us as symptoms, in order to then be able to characterize the intellectual ruin that exists. People must know how they are actually being led today in their spiritual lives.

A university professor from Basel who is always springing out like a little poltergeist, or *Heinzelmann*, in the night with these things (maybe that is where the name Heinzelmann comes from[†]) has been working recently on a response to an impressive denunciation. Dr. Boos[†] has indeed struck back in a particularly strong manner with an answer to certain attacks. There was a claim in the newspapers in Switzerland that anthroposophy is just stolen from various old texts; there was some quote from the Indian Veda and Vedanta literature, the Bhagavad Gita was cited, and among those things that were cited, the Akashic Record[†] also appeared! Now, you see, Dr. Boos then said quite rightly, "To make such a claim simply means that you have proven that you speak falsehoods consciously; for the person who says something like that has to know that if he went to the bookshelves, he could not take down a few of the books of the Veda, the Bhagavad Gita, and then the Akashic Record. This is, however, the way it is being described. Therefore, they must know that they are writing down falsehoods." Now Heinzelmann (that little Puck) in Basel writes, since I have described the matter in the same way, that my description is a "wholly new definition of conscious falsehood";[†] that I had, on page such and such, forwarded the definition that an objective falsehood exists whenever someone falsely claims something that the person must, in actuality, know; this contradicts the formerly common definition of "conscious falsehood," which defines it as something that someone claims "in contradiction to better knowledge."

So this university professor claims that on that page there is a definition. However, there is absolutely no definition there! I only said that what he claimed about the Akashic Record is a claim made in contradiction to better knowledge. So it is simply a lie that any definition is to be found on that page. Smoke is being blown in everyone's eyes insofar as this turns them away from the actual facts: the heart of the matter is that a claim was made in contradiction to better knowledge.

You see, this is all apparently pedantic. In reality, however, it is not; rather, it belongs among today's most urgent matters in regard to moral relationships: we must assert to the leading figures our views on how morally swamp-like thinking has actually become. And this moral swampiness has, at a basic level, spread over all of spiritual life.

Now, it is of course true that this swamp stems from two sources: first, from economic life itself; and second, from the world of journalism. But this cannot stop us from seeking out these things in the areas where they have asserted themselves, and bringing them over and over again into the awareness of humanity.

And if we want to make clear to people at present—who are so hard-pressed for any understanding whatsoever—how necessary it is for the spiritual life to become independent, then we can do so by pointing out what has become of spiritual life under the direction of political and economic life. It is entirely self-evident; we must simply present these things through pure description, without being any more polemical than that, and, I would suggest, with the same tone that we would strive for when describing any other objective fact. This, of course, assumes that we pay attention to such things in the first place. And this is something that we absolutely must be able to have: a free, open view of what is happening, of what is occurring around us. I have already stressed this in other ways.

It would not be at all difficult, I would say, to present the various things that appear in this brochure from Count Keyserling in all of their perniciousness. Is it not the case that in this brochure, in a section where they speak of the beneficial atmosphere of the School of Wisdom in Darmstadt, sentences of this caliber appear: "This"—that is, the atmosphere—"will soon exert such power that a mere sojourn in its rooms will be enough to allow the receptive neophyte to grasp intuitively what is being striven for there."† It goes on: "Yet the creation of a certain elevated cultural atmosphere is not the primary intention behind the School of Wisdom. The atmosphere is the fundamental precondition for striving after something more important. The more important thing we are striving after is assisting competent individuals in intensive private sessions, rather than leaving them alone to be guided by the arbitrary, unconscious influence of a particular lifestyle or reached by leading personalities." And then it goes on: "Whatever worldview one ascribes to, whatever political program one follows, whatever religion one confesses to, whatever interests one pursues; whether young or old, man or woman, in the School of Wisdom, you will learn to relate an arbitrary sort of 'existence' back to a deeper level of 'Being.'" In another passage, it is emphasized further how wonderful the School of Wisdom is because there it does not matter, for example, whether the people who speak about *Freigeld* [demurrage] are right or wrong, or whether other similar movements are right or wrong; the School of Wisdom in Darmstadt considers it to be just a silly detail whether someone who is part of this or that movement is right or wrong. Instead, all of these movements are supposed to come together on the parquet floor of Darmstadt! All of these various interests, these arbitrary systems of belief, these different human constitutions will there be induced "to relate an arbitrary sort of 'existence' back to a deeper level of 'Being.'"

You see, at its root, this is only the shadow side of something that actually cannot get any better unless spiritual life is established on a completely new, and totally free, foundation. If you want to speak of the healing of social relationships today, you must absolutely be aware of the fact that we stand in the midst of an important world-historical moment of human evolution; that certain things are being striven for because they work out of the deepest parts of the human soul life. And one of the most important impulses working out of these deep parts of human soul life is the impulse to overcome the old arrangements of compulsion in human relationships.

Pay close attention to this phrase: "the overcoming of the old arrangements of compulsion in human relationships." We look back into the social relationships of humanity. We find that in ancient times, there was an arrangement that organized social levels purely on the basis of blood relations; based on birth into one lineage or another, into one family or another, one man was made into a lord while the other became a farm hand; one an indentured servant, another a slave. The farther we go back into the evolution of humanity, the more we find that social life had been built upon such blood and hereditary relationships. They even took hold, at least in part, in human consciousness. What remains of the class consciousness of the aristocratic classes to this day is based in those ancient times and is essentially a continuation of those social claims that were based upon blood in older periods.

Now, in the more recent times, a different stratification has been inserted into this social ordering. And this one is based on economic power. All those who were once recognized as lord or servant on the basis of other criteria, namely on the basis of blood relationships, now find themselves in the midst of everything that modern economic relations have brought about: the stratification of society through economic power. The person with economic power belongs to a different class than the one who has nothing, the one who is economically powerless. This has inserted itself into the old system. At a basic level, much of what takes place in our social relationships today is still based on a continuation of the old compulsory arrangements. Current human consciousness has risen up in opposition to this. And at a fundamental level, a large portion of what we call social questions is based on this democratic opposition to the old compulsory arrangements. Therefore, the question has to arise, "How am I to conduct myself in relation to this movement?"

And right there, you must make it quite clear to yourself that without the separation of the free spiritual life from the other limbs of the social organism, on the foundation that I have just described, a sustainable social condition cannot be created. If spiritual life is really established on its own footing, then within this spiritual life, any sort of compulsory social relationships will not be able to exist; rather, only relationships built on free recognition. And this free recognition will unfold all on its own within social life. To put it plainly: you would never hire someone as a music teacher who had never played a musical instrument; and democratic feeling would never demand that absolute equality should be the dominant principle when choosing who to hire as a music teacher. Instead, someone who knows and can perform what is necessary for the job is hired to be a music teacher, based on an entirely independent, free recognition. And if there were nothing anywhere that was practiced out of compulsion, then this recognition of the person who knows and can perform these things could not fail to occur; it would come about entirely of its own accord.

At the moment, there are many, many things in free spiritual life that are similar to structures built on authority. But there will be structures everywhere built upon independent authority; for what is the basis for the current rebellion of countless people against any sort of authority? This rebellion is based on nothing other than the fact that people can discern the following: economic relations place us under compulsory subordination, and we do not recognize that these systems of compulsory subordination are laid on us by economic relations. Just as little do people recognize that similar systems of compulsory subordination are laid on us by political or blood relations.

Against this feeling rises the historical being, which I described as the democratic feeling that comes out of the deepest parts of humanity and appears now on its surface. And since the broad circles of intellectuals and spiritual leaders have not learned any exact details, but only quips from Keyserling, they look at history and they say to themselves, "They are revolting against authority in economic life." And the third aspect, spiritual life, gets taken along, since it does not appear in all of its unique being before the eyes of the human soul. It can do this only when it actually exists in an unmediated, free, self-managed state. For all of these various, deep-seated reasons, we must make clear to others the necessity of freeing spiritual life.

And we must place great value on the following: there must be an area where people truly feel equal to one another. This does not exist currently because, on the one hand, political life has absorbed spiritual life, and on the other hand, economic life has been pulled in by political life, so that the state, in its being, takes on a position of authority on both sides, and there is consequently no ground upon which responsible people can feel completely equal. If that ground existed, and people who are responsible could feel completely equal, then someone could really experience being a person like any other. And then, when standing somewhere else, where that equality could not be experienced because it was an absurdity, that person would recognize the authority and its judgments.

Something is coming forward once again; it is not an opportune moment to say this to people, but I am saying it to you. Something is coming forward that is similar to something that played a role in older times on the basis of other circumstances. Take a village in olden times. In that village, the church father was, in the fullest sense of the word, a kind of God figure. But there were instances in which the church father appeared simply as a human being among other human beings. They treasured these moments greatly. If we were to have a spiritual life on one side with its recognition, its free recognition of independent authority, and an economic life on the other side with its collective decision-making based on the coming-together of the judgments of the associated individuals, and between the two of them a ground where people could encounter the remaining authorities on equal footing—and this would be the case, if the threefold social organism were to come about—then this would, in fact, effect a very real solution to the social questions we face. But it must be the case, in the deepest sense, that the teacher, the spiritual individual—and here I am speaking symbolically—takes off his or her toga when appearing publicly in political life, and also that the worker can take off his or her work apron when stepping out publicly into political life, so that the people from both sides encounter each other wearing the same uniform—which need not be a uniform in the normal sense of the word—so that they can be equal when they stand there on the floor of the rights-political.

We must place great worth on this so that such, I would suggest, moral impulses, which also live externally, can truly enter again into human society. Wildness and barbarianism will doubtless enter the world if the true Marxist ideal of social order comes to pass. But on the other hand, we can be quite sure that if the wide swath of European populations can, after the experiences that they managed to create in

Europe in the last few months, listen long enough and properly, not swayed by their leadership, to the sense of the threefold social organism, then finally a light will go on for them.

But parallel to this action, the other must occur: that is, bringing to consciousness the moral decline of judgments, which I have only just described to you. We have to demonstrate very plainly all the ways in which human judgments have fallen away from morality, as is the case with Count Hermann Keyserling. For that man is a champion at throwing sand in people's eyes; and we must, in the proper manner, present such an example to the world. Then we will have done something extraordinarily moral.

For you see, after Count Hermann Keyserling had done all that I presented to you, or had it all done through his publishing company, he did the following.† In the book he says: "I touch upon this case only so that through its example I can make quite clear how starkly one must differentiate between 'Being' and 'Ability.' Of Steiner's Being, it is impossible for me to have a good impression; *noblesse oblige*" —by that he means that the *noblesse* obligates him not to call a liar a liar—"...but as someone able to do something I find him now as ever to be worthy of attention, and I advise that every critical mind capable of psychic research take advantage of the unusual situation, wherein such a specialist exists, and learn from him. I am familiar not only with the most important of his accessible writings, but also the lecture cycles; and I have won from them the impression that Steiner is not only extraordinarily gifted, but also that he does, in fact, have access to unusual sources of knowledge. When it comes to 'sense,' he is missing that delicate organ, and for that reason he has to find all wisdom abstract and empty unless it relates to phenomena; but what he brings forth about such things is worthy of serious consideration, however absurd some of it might sound at first, and however little his style as a presenter of his being might engender my trust, which is why I sorely regret that his fully unexpected campaign against me has robbed me of the opportunity of having any direct personal contact with him. What I wrote in his defense against his opponents remains true [in the same essay that called forth Steiner's wrath]; that a man of significance should finally be judged according to his best sides; that interest in his knowledge and abilities cannot be allowed to be limited by his errors and his handicaps. On the very same day that I received Steiner's invective, I recommended to a student of mine that he take up a serious study of Steiner's writing and even consider entering the society, because this seemed to me to be his path, and because in his case, I did not need to consider contact with the questionable aspects of Steiner to be dangerous. We should never forget that finally every being is multifaceted; that no bad quality devalues the good ones; and that the character of any society is entirely dependent upon the spirit of its leading members. Anthroposophy, too, can have a future if it leaves behind dogmatic beliefs and the spirit of sectarianism; if it gives up this messy agitation and truly becomes what, according to its constitution, it should be."

So you see, the opportunity has been more than sufficiently offered to people—and there are unfortunately many of them even within the Anthroposophical Society—to say, "Really, what more does Steiner want? Keyserling praises him to the high heavens!" But it does not matter to me if he praises me; it matters to me whether he is a detriment to civilization or not. In the end, everything that Keyserling says appears to me such that I can only describe it by saying, "This man is trying to hide everything that his superficiality foists upon the world by these—in this case I cannot call it anything else—gushy displays of praise." I say this simply because I am fully convinced that Count Keyserling does not have even the tiniest piece of the organ needed to understand the things that he is praising here.

And this must be much more important to us: to go straight to what is relevant in our lectures, to show simply to the world—I have used Count Keyserling today only as an example of this—the current superficiality and unjustified aspirations that exist. If the world were to see what sort of people are leading the way, it would come to an understanding of the liberation of the spiritual life. It would be impossible, by and large, for such heroes to be at the helm of a free spiritual life. It is certain, my dear friends, that the earthly life we live between birth and death will never manifest a throng of angels. And only a person like Professor Rein in Jena can make the strange claim that anthroposophical morality is actually meant for the angels, as he did once in an article.[†] But even if all sorts of strange old fogies are clearly there in the free spiritual life, they will never make up the majority; the majority of people will, through the inner power and impulses of the spiritual life, develop into someone new. It goes without saying that a person like Count Keyserling can easily offer the world the kind of empty thinking he does if that person has come into a social position through old blood ties, as Count Keyserling did; and also if that person then receives some support from other sides, which need not be named, for the establishing of such "Wisdom Schools." But in a free spiritual life, such foolishness could never come about. There would certainly be a sufficient number of people there to scrap such things.

You see, what I wanted to clearly point out in that lecture† was the emptiness and abstraction of Keyserling's words, and all the unreality that exists. And if you remember well, you will know that I first described this emptiness and abstraction, this lack of substantiality, the slogan-like quality of it; and then I went on to say that anyone who indulges in these empty abstractions and phrases will have to, upon encountering something that has a substantial content, fall into untruthfulness. This was the connecting thread. And we arrived at all of this quite naturally. So now what do we do with it? It would be interesting to see how such a man, who has been accused of suffering from emptiness, from intellectual and spiritual suffocation, to see what he had to say in his defense. The Count has the following to say in his newspaper, *The Road to Perfection: Dispatches from the Society for a Free Philosophy, School of Wisdom.* He says—and he is talking about me—that he finds my wisdom bloodless, abstract, and empty, and claims that he already knows what people of my stripe might be able to bring forward; the heart of my philosophy is, according to him, "a kind of soul suffocation, a struggling for breath"; and when it comes to anthroposophy I "do not have the slightest whiff of it." So you see Count Keyserling makes use of the same set of descriptions that I had previously given of him. But as far as that goes, this is just one example. Everything that exists in the predominant tone of the current spiritual life leads finally back to just this sort of thing.

In fact, it is precisely through the development of abstract spiritual life in the last few centuries that we now come by the possibility of seeing very excellent intellectuals step forward into various fields who are actually completely incapable of forming any proper, content-filled thoughts. A good example of this is the outstanding biologist Oscar Hertwig[†] from the University of Berlin. If you read his book in which he criticizes Darwinism, you will have no choice but to say to yourself, "This is a man who must be recognized as absolutely ground-breaking in his field." And the book, *The Origin of Organisms*, it is called, is a good book. But in order to write such a good book, you do not need to do anything more than get inside the mechanisms of thoughtless experimental research, work hard, move up in the world a little (he has been shoehorned into a certain clique of students of Haeckel); and then, if your connections fall out right, you can be a very significant person. He is so significant in fact that he has even been selected to add a little to the wisdom of the former Kaiser Wilhelm II in Berlin by teaching him a little about particular sensational things from his research into lower life forms! Now, shortly after Hertwig's book appeared in its field, Hertwig also published a book on social questions.[†] This book, however, is nothing less than a collection of absolute nonsense, line after line. Why? Well, you see, writing *The Origin of Organisms* did not require any thinking. In that case, he needed only to live within the mechanism of the modern scientific establishment. When it comes to a healthy assessment in the social arena, however, you need to actually start thinking for yourself. So here it is shown that the great intellectuals actually cannot think in even the most simple, primitive fashion.

From such concrete examples, we must grasp the fact that we are in the midst of a so-called scientific and spiritual life that can basically be led without any sort of truly independent thinking. And the more such a spiritual life predominates, the more actual thinking—actual, content-filled, substantial thinking—will continue to sicken.

And then there is the strange fact that people want to test the capabilities of children through experimental psychology, by having them absorb a set of randomly selected words into their memory, in the interest of assessing it; or by doing some other inane activity that is then put forward as "exact science." This is something that is much more prevalent in America than in Europe, but it is already quite popular in Germany. The fact that this is being taken into educational life can only mean that we have removed people so starkly from social life that teachers no longer have any relationship to the children; that they can no longer determine what the children are capable of themselves, but must assess it through an apparatus. And if Bolshevism in Russia continues to last for a while, perhaps these methods will come to replace the tests there to a very large degree. The children will be tested as though they were machines to determine whether they can do something in life or not. This is already among Lunacharsky's[†] ideals.

We have to describe these things freely and without bias, and perhaps eventually we will thereby call forth a feeling in people for what is so plainly evident: how very much we need a renewal, a fructification of the spiritual life; and how this renewal, this fructification, can come about only through the separation of the spiritual realm from the other limbs of society. We must attempt to effect this illustratively, with these examples of present-day phenomena, which we present as clearly as possible.

Lecture 9

Stuttgart, February 16, 1921 (evening)

JUST as it is necessary, on the one hand, to show people the importance of separating and giving a free form to the spiritual life by discussing the threads of the spiritual life at present; it is also necessary, on the other hand, to bring in all the things that demonstrate how economic life must be established on the basis of a principle of association.

Above all else, we must call up in people the certain judgment that the individual human being is not in a position do anything in economic life that might actually bring something productive into it. In the spiritual life, it is certainly true that, in the end, the judgments must come out of individual human beings; this is why a free spiritual life for each individual person must come into being. The conditions must be created that allow each individual, according to ability, to come fully into being. In economic life, this would serve no purpose. On the contrary, it would be detrimental because the economic judgments of an individual have absolutely no value. They can never truly take root in reality.

You will see this clearly when you stand on an anthroposophical basis. All that is part of the spiritual life flows out from within the human being. As a human being, you must bring out of yourself everything that you have brought along from birth. Of course, you give all of this its form through exchange with the surrounding world. You gain experience, whether it is external, internal, physical, or spiritual. But the process that you go through must come out of your own individual capabilities. Now, if we want to take part in economic life, we have no more effective guide in our humanity than these individual human capabilities.

These individual capabilities generally enrich human life, if a person makes use of them. If someone even merely uses them, the collective life is enriched. In economic life as such (that is to say, whenever you are dealing with exchange and valuation of commodities), the only thing that emerges out of the human being is his or her needs. An individual person knows nothing about economic life and its necessities except by way of individual needs; one knows that one must eat and drink, that one has one's own individual needs. But these individual needs have meaning only for oneself; finally, only for one's own self.

Everything that someone produces spiritually has significance for everyone; everything that someone produces spiritually is, from the start, of social significance. Your needs (and they are why one must, in fact, desire the existence of economic life) have significance only for yourself. Economically, you can know only what you have to do to take care of yourself. This does not, however, produce any sort of social standard, nor any sort of foundation for social judgment. The very thing that should be active in social life is excluded if your only standard is what you need for yourself. This is why a social judgment will never find its basis in the knowledge taken from individual needs. The individual human being has no basis for social judgment. If you conduct business solely as an individual, paying attention only to your own needs, and making use of your own reason and capabilities not to produce something for the collective (as in the case of spiritual life) but rather to satisfy your own needs, then you are working, no matter what the circumstances, as an anti-social being.

This is the same reason that all forms of cleverness do not help anything when it comes to economic judgments. Again and again, I find that I must put forward the example of the defense of the gold standard during the nineteenth century. If you read the Parliamentary reports and other things, for example what some of the pragmatists in various countries wrote in defense of the gold standard, you will actually find everywhere a great display of individual mental keenness. Everything that was said was actually extraordinarily clever, you might say. You gain a lot of respect for human capabilities if you go back and read the speeches that were made about the gold standard. But what the cleverest of these people said always culminated in the idea that the gold standard would necessarily bring about free trade the world over. And the reasons that were presented to solidify this assessment are actually incontrovertible. But precisely the opposite has happened everywhere! Following the move to the gold standard, the need for protective duties and the like has come about everywhere. All over the world, free trade has been limited. And this example demonstrates quite clearly that individual human cleverness is of no help when it comes to economic questions, even when it appears as strongly as it did in the nineteenth century. We err as individuals when we try to conduct ourselves in economic life on the basis of individual judgments.

From this, we can see with apodictic certainty the necessity of associations. Only when people in the most disparate branches and elements of life come together in association; only when they fill out and broaden their knowledge beyond what they know about one area by becoming familiar not only with their own needs, but also the needs of others with whom they are associated; only then will a collective judgment emerge that can move over into economic affairs and lead us toward social healing. There is absolutely no way around the necessity of associations when you simply point out this most basic circumstance. Furthermore, what will become of the economic life as such under the influence of the threefold social organism? What do we actually have in economic life then? We have three factors.

The first is something that comes out of an expertise in the production of one thing or another. We must have experts, no matter whether that expertise is in hauling coal or in harvesting grain or in husbanding cattle or in some other industry altogether; people must be experts at what they do.

The second is that within our current economic life, the exchange of goods, of basic staples, must be conducted properly. Trade must be conducted in the right way. The goods must be brought to a place where they are needed. Only there do they really have any value. Otherwise, they are not commodities, but objects. We must make that distinction. Something, even food, can in some locations be just an object and not a commodity. If there is an enormous amount of food of a certain quality somewhere, but the people there do not need it all, then there are only as many commodities as there are needed objects.

The rest of them are just things, and they will become commodities only if they are taken to a place where they are needed. Without trade, nothing can become a commodity. This is the second important point. But this second factor is connected with human labor. The transformation of natural and non-natural things from object to commodity occurs through human labor. Labor begins with something that we take from the natural world. Thus, it is always possible to trace something created back to its source as an object; and if you trace something back to that state, then you cannot talk about any sort of economic character in that object itself. The thing becomes economic only once it is brought into exchange. Only by doing this does it become something that has significance within the economy. This, however, is connected to the whole process of separating out and unfolding human labor, with the manner and the time, and so forth, of human labor.

The third factor in economic life is that we recognize needs. Only if the needs of a particular territory are known, can production be carried out in a sensible manner. Something that is overproduced will become disproportionately cheap; and something that is underproduced will become disproportionately expensive. The price of something is dependent upon how many people are appointed to the production of a particular item. This is the basic condition of economic life, that the satisfaction of needs, and specifically the free satisfaction of needs, be the starting point. How much should be made available somewhere cannot be determined by statistics, because it is part of a living process and can be determined only by a group of associated people who are personally familiar with the sum of the needs in a particular area through personal connections with individuals who need one thing or another, and who can work out together how many people are needed for the production of a particular article from a purely human, living standpoint, and not on the basis of statistics. So the first thing that you have within an associative life are people who go out into a particular territory constituted on some sort of economic basis in order to learn about what people there need, and who then develop the will to direct negotiations about how many people have to undertake production in a particular branch of the economy so that those needs can be satisfied. All of this must be connected with an understanding of the freedom of those needs. The first people to take up the task I have just described cannot be allowed to maintain some sort of perspective on whether one sort of need is justified or not; rather, there must be a concern finally for the objective statement of needs.

The responsibility for combating senseless needs—luxurious, harmful needs—lies not in associative economic life, but rather with the influence of the spiritual life. Senseless, harmful needs must be driven out of the world by teachings from the spiritual life that lead to the refinement of desires, of feelings. A free spiritual life will necessarily be in the position to do this. Simply put: movie theaters cannot be forbidden by the police, but people must be informed in such a way that they have no taste for them. This is the one healthy way of fighting harmful influences in social life. In the moment when, for the sake of economics or politics, we start to tax our needs as such, then we no longer have a threefold social organism, but instead a chaotic intermingling of spiritual, economic, and other interests. Threefolding must be taken seriously in the deepest fabric of our society. There is no freedom when one or another group of censors exists; when one thing or another can be forbidden that lies within the realm of human needs. You can still fulminate in the same way against movie theaters if you have a fanatical opinion about them; this does not hinder free social life. But in the moment that you call for the police—when you cry out, "This should be forbidden!"—in that moment, you hamper free spiritual life. This must be firmly grasped, and we may not shrink back from that fact out of a certain radicalism.

So, first of all, we are dealing with people who inform themselves about the needs within a particular territory and then lead negotiations, rather than making laws, about the necessary production there.

You see, it is possible to describe the matter somewhat differently, and then it might even be taken as, shall we say, a little more mundane. But finally, you can also say, as a way of illustrating the point, that in associations one needs objective agents who are interested not only in helping the person for whom they are the agent to sell as much as possible, but who also really ask themselves, "What do people here need?"—and who then know enough about the trade to understand how production should be undertaken so that these needs are met.

With that, we have what I would like to call the first branch of the association. The second branch is then made up of the people who tend to the distribution; the ones who are to ship a product once it has been manufactured; who follow the negotiations and ship the product to the place where it is needed. So we find, in effect, experts on consumption, experts on trade, and experts on production. But these come out of a free spiritual life, for it encompasses everything that comes out of the spirit in the form of human capacities for productive life. What I have first named, expertise, flows through teachings that come out of the spiritual life.

You see, in the associations of economic life, representatives of all three limbs of the social organism will be there; but the associations themselves will be limited to the economic limb and will deal only with economic matters: with the consumption, distribution, and production of goods, as well as the resultant determination of price. In the threefold social organism, it is therefore important that there be corporations that are competent simply within the bounds of the appropriate limb. In economic associations, only economic questions are dealt with; but naturally there are people within the associations who have capacities and competencies for dealing with what comes out of the spiritual and the rights-political realms. Thus, it is not a matter of simply setting the three limbs of the social organism beside one another schematically; rather, there must be administrating bodies, corporations that have competence in particular areas. This is what is important.

You will find this presented clearly and in full detail in *Towards Social Renewal.* First of all, it is important that the following appeal be made regarding the relationship of capital to spiritual life: that those who have brought together the means of production through their capacities remain at the task for as long as these capacities are present. Making this decree is an important matter for the spiritual life. Then enough right to judgment should be ascribed to such people that they are then able to elect a successor. This also belongs to free spiritual life. And if they cannot or do not want to elect a successor, then the corporation of spiritual life will decide it. You see, everything that is a function of abstract capitalism becomes the work of free spiritual life within economic life. This is how it is in the human organism. The blood is connected with the circulatory system, but it flows into the head and pulses through it. In the actual social organism, it is exactly the same. This is why it is to a certain extent fatal that, particularly abroad and especially in the northern countries, a very strong tendency has arisen to speak about the "tripartite" social organism, rather than the threefold social organism. This "tripartite" social organism naturally calls up a set of terrible misunderstandings. We are dealing with a division of society into limbs, not separate parts. The individual limbs necessarily work within each other. We must call forth a clear understanding of this.

And we can hope that the rational bourgeois, as well as the proletarian, will eventually arrive at an understanding of the matter. In 1919, we already saw the beginning of precisely that; perhaps a beginning has also been made here or there in other places. But the opposition became so active from all sides that we were temporarily unable to stand firm with the few people we had. This is why we have called upon your potent energies, so that a kind of strengthening of our advocacy for the threefold social organism might come about. It is absolutely necessary, I would like to suggest, that a strong push be made on behalf of everything that comes out of anthroposophical spiritual science and the Threefold Social Organism. For in a certain way, we are dealing with matters of short-term survival. We should not give in to any sort of illusions about this.

But we must work everywhere with great clarity. For that reason I have tried again now to give as clear an imagination as possible of the associative life. If you still want to know more about associations, then I will take care of that this evening by answering your various questions. It must absolutely run all throughout our lectures that we strive for clarity; and that we try to call up an understanding for how a lack of clarity in public conditions, in social conditions, has led to the present state of affairs. I would like to give you an example of that.

When you are asked questions about this or that nowadays, people come to you with schematized questions. They ask, "What is the situation with capital, with small businesses, with property?" and so on. Now, when it comes to healthy social relationships, the question of property is dealt with in *Towards Social Renewal*,[†] although apparently it is only touched on in a dependent clause. But everything that otherwise figures into the discussion is rooted in the fact that, in our social life, property plays an incredibly confusing role.

As the new economic life arose and imprinted upon everything the character of a commodity, including labor, for example, so that everything could suddenly be bought, property also became a commodity. You could buy and sell it. But what is also hidden in this buying and selling of property? If you want to gain insight into this, you have to go back to very primitive relationships, in which the feudal lord had acquired a particular piece of property through conquest or some other means and then divided it among those who worked it; those who then gave back a certain quota in goods or some other kind of due, which amounted effectively to the beginnings of rent. But for what reason did these people pay dues to him, the feudal lord—or to the church, the cloister—why did they pay? Why did it seem reasonable to them that they should turn over such dues?

The only thing that made it reasonable was the fact that while they, the small occupants, worked their property in order to plant it and to harvest, every other second-best person out there might come and drive them off that land. Being able to work a piece of property called for the protection of that property. Most of the feudal lords had their own army, which they supported with the dues they were paid; this was for the protection of property. And the rent was not paid for the right to work the land; rather, for the protection of the land. The right to work the land came out of necessity, since the lord certainly could not work all of that land himself. It had nothing to do with any other sort of relationships. But the property had to be protected. And for that, you paid your dues. People paid dues to the cloisters for the same reason. The cloisters also supported their own armies with which they protected property, or they were bound to a place through some sort of agreement that provided for the protection of the land through some other relationship of power. If you are looking for the origins of property rent, you must understand it as dues paid for the protection of property. If we look closely at this original meaning of property rent, we see that it is related to times when very primitive relationships predominated, when sovereign feudal lords or cloisters that obeyed no one dominated in economic relationships.

These relationships stopped, first in Western Europe and then later in Central Europe, due to the fact that, gradually, certain rights that individuals had—in certain regions of Germany, they stopped being individual rights later than everywhere else—were conferred instead onto individual princes, which then became a political act, rather than an economic one. The rights were conferred. With the conferral of rights, everything that was in place for the protection of property was also conferred to these princes. It then became necessary for the princes to maintain the armies. For that, they naturally had to demand that dues be paid. This led to the gradual development of the system of taxes, now applied so heavily to us. These dues added to the former, but curiously, the former continued to exist! But it lost its meaning, since the people who were now the landowners no longer had to pay anything additional for the protection of their property; the territorial prince and the state were there for that. But property rent remained. And with the new economic life, it crossed over gradually into the everyday circulation of commodities. Because the connection between property rent and property lost its meaning, property was able to become simply an object to be won. It is absolute nonsense, turned into reality. Something exists with the circulating process of value that at the most basic level has completely lost its meaning, but is nevertheless dealt with every day as though it were a commodity.

Such things can be detected everywhere in our economic life. They have come about for some sort of justified reason. These justified reasons have now been replaced by something else; but the old things remain. And thereby, some sort of new process has taken hold and installed senselessness into social life.

If you simply take economic life as it is; if, for example, you are a professor of economics and have thereby the task of thinking as little as possible in the manner that I have just described, then you define property rent exactly as it is says in the books. And it figures into life as something just as senseless. So you can see how much we have to do in order to make people understand that we have nonsense not only in our systems of thought, but also all throughout our economic life. And if somebody sighs at the economic life, it is actually for precisely these underlying reasons. What is important is that we now arrive at a more solid, more unbiased, more comprehensive thinking than the one that can be developed by sitting in contemporary educational institutions.

For in the end, what sort of thinking does one develop there now? You develop the kind of thinking that could perhaps be represented mathematically; but it is developed in such a way that it stands far away from all reality. So you develop thinking that can be learned through experimentation, that can be learned systematically; you develop thinking that, in the case of people like Poincaré,† Mach† and others, has finally become a mere formality, something that they call simply a "recapitulation of external reality." To put it briefly: you develop absolutely no thinking! And because you do not develop any thinking, you cannot really begin to take up the national economy.

Of course, over time a national economic method has been established; Lujo Brentano† wielded it in a particularly clever way. On the basis of understandable conditions, a theory has developed that one should not think about how economic life should be, but rather just observe it properly. Now, just imagine how one is supposed to arrive at a science of economic life merely by observing it! It would be like recommending to educators that they simply watch the children. No real activity can ever come out of that. This is why our national economic theorists are so terribly sterile, because they have this method that demands passivity toward external reality.

And the opposite side of this shows itself when people really begin to join in economic life. On the one hand, they develop a science that only observes. But then when the war came to Central Europe, suddenly one was supposed to get involved in economic life, to the point of influencing price formation. What was the result? The national economist Terhalle† has summarized the results of that, and for this furnishes all sorts of supporting documents in his book on *Free or Bound Price Formation*. First, things are made in such a way that one can see that the people who made then had absolutely no idea what the point of them was. Second, foundational theoretical schemas have been laid that have so little to do with reality that their use results in the ruination of that reality. Third, the influencing of price formation brought only harm, and not help, to individual businesses; and finally, honest craft and business was harmed for the benefit of the profiteers! Think for a moment about what it means that an official national economist working on the basis of national economic investigations must arrive at this judgment of rights-political national economic activity: they benefited the profiteers at the expense of honest business and craft! We must only feel what this actually means. These things must be said to people as clearly as possible so that they see how insensible to reality our civilization is.

If we do not set about making clear the kinds of things that I just said to you in relation to property rent, then we never will be able to demonstrate to people the necessity of associations. Think just for a moment in the most urgent manner, prevalent to associations, and immediately the experience emerges of just how adversely all of the unnatural things that are in economic life affect price formation. Of course, this cannot become evident if we attend to economic life in such a way that various agents go out into the country and create businesses for individual undertakings. In that situation, the connection between production and consumption will never be evident to them. They are not interested in turning their eye toward how much should be produced. For them, only one self-evident "truth" is valid: that their employers be able to produce as much as possible. This interest in maximizing the employers' production must be replaced by the positive knowledge of how many producers are necessary because the need for a particular article is at such a level and must be attended to in such a way that neither too few nor too many people are working on that product in a given area. This kind of fact-based knowledge must replace the interest for the individual businessperson. This is the important point when it comes to associations.

Now we must demonstrate to people how the economic life demands a unification of the separate limbs of life due to the fact that it has so many absurd elements within it—aside from property rent, there are many others as well. The nature of the cartel, with all of its rationing of earnings, deposits, distribution, the mergers, the consolidations—where does this actually come from?—In Europe, this more often takes the form of the cartel; in America, the form of the trust.—It comes from the fact that because of the many absurd elements present in economic life, the individual can no longer produce anything. Think for a moment of how different it is today, where everything demands a large scale undertaking, from how it was when individual producers existed as small scale operations in economic life. What question can a person ask currently, if he wants to put himself forward as a producer? His only question is, "What is the market situation for this article; will there be a demand for it?" An article for which there is a demand looks promising; an article for which there is a lack of demand does not.

In earlier times, when the number of producers was small, this did not matter as much; only when there came to be too many did the individual producer fail. But let us assume for a moment that everything is actually directed toward the establishment of large-scale production whenever it is noticed that a particular article is needed; let us assume that this actually serves a purpose. By establishing the large-scale production, we annihilate the very thing from which we inferred that the large-scale production was needed! Insofar as everything tends toward large-scale production, we no longer follow the same standards that guided the earlier small-scale producers. This is why the necessity for consolidation arises. And so then we have cartels and trusts and so on. But the leading circles were entirely careless in relation to consumption. Because they did not attend to this, the mergers and incorporations are based solely on the interests of the producers. Consumption is not considered.

This is the essence of what is demonstrated: that we will not get anywhere in economic life without associations. Therefore, the one-sided associations of cartels and trusts, which come about solely for the interests of the producers, must be overhauled so that they are instead oriented toward an understanding of consumption and an insight into the needs of a particular territory. This is how the trusts and cartels, in that they are caricatures of what must finally be created, demonstrate how necessary it is to move in a particular direction, in the direction of associations. All that is left to do now is to seek out how these associations should be created.

Wherever we go, we must describe things that come out of real life. Only then will we perhaps be able to make it understandable for people how necessary associations are for economic life. And thus, the important thing will be that you direct the lectures that you will give toward the clearest concepts possible. The guiding assumption for this must necessarily be that everything put forward in *Towards Social Renewal* is at its core a kind of axiom for modern social life. No one will ever have to prove the truth of the Pythagorean Theorem by applying it to every object in existence; but proof of it must be shown in a few individual cases. Similarly, you do not have prove in every possible instance the insights into social relationships as they are won; through their content, they are proven in much the same way as the Pythagorean Theorem. And all that is left then is to show how these things must be incorporated into life. This must attended to.

And I would like to add that we should consider our activity in such a way that it connects to all that has already occurred. This is why I said yesterday that it is necessary for us to consider our movement as a whole and not to feel embarrassed about presenting to people what we have done, or about saying to them that it is out there. It is the case that the following experience happens more and more, and it is actually quite alarming. Whenever I go somewhere and give a lecture, there is always a table full of books at the entrance to each lecture hall. If I do not mention any of the books, this is always seen as very non-materialistic and spiritual. If I mention one of them, then it is purchased, and usually there are not enough of them there. But people just, in a way, non-materialistically overlook the others. Now, I always regret that there are so many books that you cannot mention all of them in the course of one lecture. But we must also move about in the present with a realistic sense of what can be done. Thus, I recommend to you that you take the opportunity to recommend our threefold social organism newsletter when you can, for we must eventually reach the stage where it is distributed daily. But we will not get to that point if we do not make it more popular than it is now. And do not forget, at the same time, to recommend other publications! Otherwise they will be sent back in large numbers, not purchased. It does seem strange to say such things in the midst of serious lectures, but if I do not say them, then most of the time, they do not get done these days. And we have, after all, come together in order to understand the things that should be done. For we want to make something happen in the near future.

Lecture 10

Stuttgart, February 17, 1921 (afternoon)

If you take a look around in some of the more sophisticated literature today, you will nevertheless (at least in many cases) be able to notice that all of the authors somewhere put forward an observation that goes something like this. Economists do not have to concern themselves with how people are educated, or how they will fare regarding their needs; such things must be left to the ethicists, the hygienists, and the like. I have already presented this to you from another perspective.

If you take an observation like this seriously, it is nothing less than a proof of the necessity for the threefold social organism. For what are they really saying? They are saying that when you think economically, nothing results that might lead to ethics or hygiene; rather, what leads to ethics and hygiene must come from elsewhere.

If you think through the practical implications of such an observation, which until now has really been intended only theoretically, it tells you that economic judgments should be truly economic; meaning that the economy should be organized so that only those things that are actually and simply economic play into its judgments (refraining from all ethics, all hygienic concerns, and the like); and meaning also that actual institutions would exist alongside the economy and provide for the hygienic formation of an ethical social life—those things would lie within free spiritual life.

And for you, this will be an important pedagogical and didactic perspective: that you show how the foundations are really everywhere for what will lead to results, when utilized properly, in the threefold social organism. You can say, "If they really are thinking economically, the economists can think only as one must within the associative limb of the social organism. Except that what is thought of in this manner will not be in books; rather, events will occur that will carry economic thought over purely into the economy itself."

Since I want to provide more indications about methodology, I mention this today as precisely an introductory methodological remark, to make you aware that when speaking about the threefold social organism you can always start with what people have already thought of themselves. No one today has the courage to follow through the consequences of these thoughts, but the essential thing for us is to show the necessary consequences of these thoughts for social life.

By the same token, you will have other questions to deal with if you direct yourself toward social life. If you familiarize yourself with the development of economic thought, you will find that in recent times, a plethora of utopian ideas have appeared. As far as these utopian ideas go, we need look back only as far as the eighteenth century—the previous centuries are less significant for the present. But since the eighteenth century, a sizeable number of such utopias have been thought up. Why did these utopian ideas come about? This is important for you to know, so that you can allow that knowledge to flow into the whole bearing of your lectures.

You see, the following is the case for spiritual life. Fundamentally, it all leads back to ancient, primal wisdom and the customs associated with it. Just take for example the kind of totally decadent spiritual life that we have in Europe: Catholicism, on the one hand, and on the other, the incredibly watered-down modern life of *Bildung*,† which is still flavored by old religious concepts; they are everywhere within it. You can follow those traces even into the materialistic parts of modern medicine; and in philology they are there, these offshoots of theocratic or theological thinking.

So when you really confront just how much all of modern thinking is infused with this element that leads back to ancient, primal wisdom, you will understand the whole way in which spiritual life, I must now say it this way, governs itself, for it has become downright anarchic, at least when it has not been bound up tightly in the political life. You will notice that, within this kind of governance, traces can be seen of things that were part of the constitutions of the territories in which this ancient, primal wisdom dominated. In the church, you see it in the structure of the hierarchies. This can be traced back to the perspectives of that ancient, primal wisdom. In the area of jurisprudence, you can perhaps see it only in the fight that manifests externally as the battle between materialism and the life of the spirit. In the fight being carried out now by lawyers and judges against wearing robes during judicial processes, those who support wearing the robe act out the remainder of the old thinking; those who argue against wearing the robe display modern, materialistic thinking. And this has a much greater significance than people think. And if you consider the formalities that are attached to getting a doctorate in some of our universities, you will very easily detect the traces of the old theocratic element. In all of it, we have something that has been lost to people, but that points backward to previous time, recalling a period when people actually knew how spiritual life was to be governed. Though we no longer have this spiritual life as something living in the present, we still have its forms everywhere; and even the discarded clothing, I would like to suggest, is still around. We need new forms, and we need them everywhere. They will be found in a free spiritual life.

Another thing is this. In England, for example, the political-democratic element developed out of the democratic element in the church. This came about in England simply through a process of stripping down the church-centered past, and building up the democratic form from that. The result is that everywhere, the rights-political has been born out of the theocratic-religious element. One simply does not notice it as much in other places. For example, there is a secret connection in the whole bureaucratic existence, at whose head one can think of the absolute leader being appointed "by the grace of God." This clearly betrays its origins in theocratic-religious element, for an appointment "by the grace of God" occurred only through an appointment by spiritual authorities. The whole body of the bureaucracy is simply the secular version of church hierarchy. The other aspect that also fundamentally developed out of the theocratic-religious element is the army. People today will find this paradoxical. But the army is also nothing more than a result of the whole organization of the political entity, like a shadow that results from an illuminated object.

And so, I would like to suggest, during the separation of the secular element from the theocratic-religious, a certain administrating quality gradually developed within the political. This can be proved in full detail when you consider the transition of the forms of governance; how they showed themselves quite clearly in their theocratic-hierarchical form when Charlemagne† placed such great value on being crowned by the pope in Rome. One can see how church life then transitioned into the secular; how certain latecomers in this transition remained; in France, for example, high political positions were occupied by cardinals. If you think this through, you will be able to grasp quite clearly the gradual development of administrative independence in the rights-political realm and the roots of this administrative element in the theocratic-religious realm. You can grasp these things on your own.

Now modern economic life is moving in, and has brought with it certain instinctive trading customs, but until now nothing has been so deeply and inwardly enmeshed as the ancient hierarchical-religious or political-militaristic elements. These two elements have bound up the world in tight uniformity. It was in opposition to this that the impulse has recently come about to interpenetrate everything and fill it consciously with complicated economic life. That was not needed in ancient times because people were drawing on inexhaustible sources; it has now crowded into modern life completely. The necessity has now arisen to find a certain means of administrating this economic life. But this administration has not yet been found.

At the most basic level, the associative principle is the first attempt to bring something into economic life that can be drawn in parallel to the political and the religious. For the first time, there is an attempt to found something truly organically in economic life. Until now, this has not happened. All of the various theoretical attempts today to achieve a way of thinking, to organize economic life as such, have been based on utopian theories, which are always infiltrated by carry-overs from the past. So people have continued to think, "if you organize something, then you have to organize it as in the church hierarchy or the political realm"; but people were not aware of this as they were doing it.

And the practical, external expression of this is the appearance of economic liberalism in the first half of the nineteenth century. Why did this economic liberalism suddenly crop up? What is it really? It is an appeal to individual virtue within economics. It was the same in the theocratic-hierarchical element. Before you founded an organization, you had to appeal to each of the leading individuals. The same was true in the political element. Before you went over into parliamentarianism, you had to appeal to those who had the necessary capabilities to administer the political realm. Economic liberalism is nothing other than this appeal to the individual virtue of people in the economic arena. But because things in the world developed more quickly, it became more quickly necessary to find the practices that are currently paralyzing the harmful effects of absolutist individuals.

You need only to study the constitution of the Catholic Church, and you will find everywhere within the church—which simply preserves an older administration of the spiritual life—that the administration, the institution, is based on binding and controlling the faults of individuality. In a certain sense, it is precisely because of this that individuality can be actualized.

I once took part in a conversation in Vienna in which a professor of the Viennese theological faculty who had somewhat liberal tendencies (which he indulged only in the most careful manner) complained that they made him keep his mouth shut about Rome, and never allowed him to express his opinion from the lectern. The topic was discussed in detail, as was the fact that in Innsbruck, where a Jesuit was the head of the same department, this Jesuit had been allowed to speak quite openly about the same topic. And those who had some experience in such things said to themselves, "Yes, for the Catholic Church, it is not important that, for example, exegesis be delivered freely at the university; but rather that the individuals who stand within the church present the absolutely certain sense that they stand firm within the organization, despite their liberal perspectives. And this, of course, was something that this Jesuit achieved to a large degree." As a result, he is allowed certain freedoms. For the organization does not destroy individuality. It is not destroyed at all. Within the church hierarchy of Catholicism, each individual is free, to a large degree. But those who take things up in a way similar to Protestantism, those who make a serious affair of the dogma, they are made to keep their mouths shut; Catholicism makes a serious affair only of symbolism. There is always the danger that these questionable individuals will throw away their robes. But this cannot happen. Everything can occur within the boundaries of the church; but no one is allowed to stand outside of it.

Naturally, something like this cannot be imitated. But it can lead us to discover something characteristic of the other side: older times appealed to the individual, but had an organization such that the individual could never be "harmful" to the organization. In political life, the time has already passed in which people are aware that both aspects need to be present.

In economic life, it is a matter of finding the transition from economic liberalism to the associative principle. We thereby put ourselves right into the midst of what has to happen. In regard to these matters, this is precisely what the being of this world-historical moment contains for us: the associative principle in economic life is nothing other than what must necessarily follow the degeneration of economic liberalism. And in modern times, because thinking is in a certain sense inactive, people have not found the courage to move into activity, to transition from liberalistic thinking to active thinking. But everywhere the attempt is being made. If you pay attention, you will have interesting experiences of this.

Recently I picked up the little economic pamphlet from the Göschen collection.[†] It addresses economic liberalism, and says that the necessity arose to transition from individualistic economic forms to a form of social economic organization. And it was thereby necessary for the individual institutions to move ever more into the hands of state administration: state socialism! So not even the slightest understanding of the necessity of the associative principle, but rather: state socialism! And in a different passage of this Göschen pamphlet (this one also comes from a sly devil, but not such a bad one) we find a sentence telling us that the World War has shown us that this line of thinking was correct; he means the line of thinking that said we should gradually take everything that had previously been undertaken by individuals and give it over to the state. I said to myself, "Now I've got to take a look at the title page. In what year would it be possible for someone to write something like that?" I found: 1918! It was the last moment in which someone could write something like that without being called a fool. [Interruption: "Excuse me, Herr Doctor: 1920!" Herr Blume shows the newest edition]. You have to wonder whether it says that in the newest edition. Here it says: "New Edition."

If it is still there, it is because these things have simply remained there in 1920 in all of their stupidity. Yes, indeed! He did not feel it was necessary to correct these things after two years! They are not clever, these sly foxes. I opened to the title page—1918—and said to myself, "Could things have been such that anyone believed that having national economics, or even city-based economics, take over the world economics of the old system was absolutely the right thing?" I remember that at that moment the communes were teetering at the brink of ruin, and would all collapse in the near future.

What I want to point out is that modern thinking has not found the real, proper transition from liberalistic economy to associative economy.

It would perhaps be altogether impossible to really grasp the associative principle if one did not simultaneously come to know the principle of threefolding in the fullest sense. For, what will work properly within the threefold social organism would have a detrimental effect within a unified state. And this must be strongly emphasized, at the very least in the nuance that you give to your lectures. For example, a person has nothing to do with threefolding who says, "Well, we will just leave spiritual life to the state. We do not want a threefold social organism. But a twofold social order (something similar was even suggested in the Weimar National Assembly)—yes, a twofold order is good! That is good: separate out economic life!" But this will never do, for the simple reason that a separate economic life, associatively organized, would necessarily have associations that are entirely dependent upon the state, and not upon people who have developed with a free spiritual life; and so economic life would always be influenced by the political. The whole of economic life would be taken over by the mentality of the political realm.

By the same token, we will never, in reality, establish free schools like the Waldorf School if we allow the teachers to be taken from political institutions, so that we are always forced to have political approbation for teachers when we hire them. If someone says that we can establish a free school, but can do this only if we find state-approved teachers, this demonstrates that people have no real understanding of the situation. For this means nothing less than standing by the old, but making it look like the new; it throws sand in people's eyes. The moment is too serious for such things. What should come about in the true sense of the threefold social organism is precisely what true threefolding contains within itself, despite the danger that the resulting practical institutions might not immediately achieve success because of people's resistance to them. The most important thing today is that the idea of threefolding enters into as many people's heads as possible. Only in this way will we arrive at the quickest practical actualization of it.

And now to say something about the method behind this. You cannot lecture on the idea of threefolding without laying a foundation of anthroposophical spiritual science, presented of course in a tactful way that is didactically and pedagogically proper. This follows necessarily from how thinking has developed in social life recently.

Is it not the case that all sorts of utopias have cropped up, and that a certain system has developed which has gained widespread popularity among the proletariat: the Marxist system? To be sure, this Marxist system has taken a number of different forms. Revisionism on the one hand; Leninism on the other. This is a kind of radicalism that says, "We know well that Marxism does not answer the social question, but it does result in the radical destruction of all that is extant; and after that will come a different humanity that will build anew." But at the base of all this lies the Marxist system. Karl Marx understood well how to find a way into the souls of the modern proletariat. In a certain sense, we must even admit that this Marxism—not so much in the theory as it lived in Karl Marx, but much more in the form that it has taken on in the perspectives of the proletariat—as far as its worldview is concerned, is the most modern form of conceiving the social life. All of the others, whether they are supported by practitioners or university professors, are always somewhat backward-looking.

Precisely because Marxism is the most modern form, all those who really want to do something that penetrates into society must consider it closely. It goes without saying that you cannot speak to the mass of humanity today unless you have a clear understanding, or at the very least emotionally intuitive understanding, of Marxism's significance. The core of the matter is nothing less than the fact that Marxism is the worldview and life concept that best speaks to the whole social position of the modern proletariat. And if you fight Marxism on a purely theoretical level, then you are doing something ill-suited to reality. You end up fighting Marxism without considering that everything has been allowed to get to a place in reality where the proletariat has become what it is. This can be traced back to the carelessness of the rest of the population. But as it got to the point where the proletariat became what it is today, the proletariat could do nothing other than take up Marxism as its worldview and life concept. Marxism necessarily contains within it the threefolding of human social life for the proletariat concept. By becoming a Marxist, the worker takes from Marxism the perspective on threefolding social life that is appropriate to that class. This idea is contained within it.

For you see, in modern times it is becoming increasingly customary to turn away from consumption, and the ability to see through it, and to turn one's sights toward mere acquisition. With that, the only necessity that one has is to leave behind enough from these acquisitions to allow for the administration of the social organism. Regardless of whether one was an aristocrat or a bourgeois, the acquirer was interested only in the yield of the acquisition as it related to what was received, and to how much one had to give up so that the whole could be kept together. What form did this take for people who stood in midst of the real social organism because of old privileges or other such circumstances? They tried as much as possible always to act out of the principle of acquisition. Consumption was disregarded, and taxes were agreed to, albeit with grumblings, for the sake of all that was necessary for maintaining the whole.

What did the modern proletarians do? They merely stood at their machines, outside of capitalism. They disagreed with certain taxes on principle, provided they did not collapse. For they had no interest in the reality of the old social organism. They were also interested only in what was left over after acquisitions. Because they did not stand within the administration of capital, this leftover became for them merely an object of criticism, what they call surplus. The relationship of the proletariat to surplus—criticizing it—is the same one that the bourgeoise has to taxes, which is allowed under protest. When the bourgeoise allows taxes, it does not penetrate into what lies behind them. The proletariat does not either. But it practices criticism. It took one look at surplus and then practiced criticism. This shows nicely that it is simply a matter of adding something positive to this criticism. This would be, of course, the associative principle. But in the theory of surplus there is something that embodies for the proletariat the economic element within a worldview and life concept.

The second thing that lives in Marxist theory, insofar as it is the life concept and worldview of the proletariat, is class struggle, which according to the views of the proletariat, must exist. This is the rights-political element. By way of class conflict, the proletariat endeavors to fight for its rights, to organize its labor, and so on. And so the second limb of social life is there within it. It is simply the other side of what we find in the bourgeois and the aristocratic class. They do not extend beyond their class. They do not have the talent for overcoming the standards of their class and moving into what is generally human. The workers do this consciously; but of course they also take on their class. And so within Marxism we also have something that has taken the form of the rights-political element in modern life, an element that has not yet found a way to transition to the truly democratic; indeed, one that has not yet found its way to the place it must go: where all human beings who have come to maturity stand beside one another as equals in the rights-political realm.

This is more or less what all of the classes believe, which I have mentioned until now. When there was still an aristocratic class (let us say, sometime before the French Revolution), this class was internally democratic; but anyone below that class ceased to be a human being; was no longer human in the full sense of the word. Then came the bourgeoisie. Again, within that class, everything was very democratic. But once again, everyone who was beneath that class ceased to be human. Everything in modern times is tending toward universal democracy. All of those who stand outside of the social organism, such as the proletariat, constitute their own class, opposing the others at the site of the universally human, which can be defined as the place where all people, no matter what they believe, all people who have reached maturity, conduct their affairs with each other as equals in everything that should be the concern of democratic parliamentarianism. And so, in the phenomenon of class conflict, we have something that I would like to suggest must be characterized as follows: the proletariat knows that it must, insofar as it is modern, must arrive at something other than what has been there until now. But it has not learned universal humanity. Thus, it takes its own class, instead of universal humanity, as its basis.

And the Marxist worldview and life concept of the proletariat also have something for the spiritual element. This is precisely the materialistic understanding of history. In the materialistic age and in the whole education of the modern proletariat, which deals only with the mechanics of life and not with the psyche or the spirit, it is quite understandable that spiritual life, from the perspective of the proletariat, became the materialistic understanding of history. But this understanding illustrates the spiritual element in accordance with its worldview and life concept.

So in proletarian Marixsm you have the most radical living expression of what modern humanity actually wants, and also why it does not know how to help itself. And you have to present something as an alternative to this that seems just as well-grounded for the proletariat as proletarian Marxism. What is the core of this proletarian Marxism as a worldview? Its core as a worldview is skepticism toward human beings.

In the era of humanity's ancient wisdom, this skepticism toward humans was justified; for back then godly forces resided within human beings and directed human actions. People knew that what came unconsciously out of the depths of their souls could be recognized as the revelations of the gods as the directive forces for their lives. Back then, you had skepticism toward human beings and faith in the gods. When the political-administrative, the bureaucratic-militaristic elements were assembled from the older theocratic-religious element, this skepticism toward human beings continued to exist. For what came about was the belief that the human being as such cannot be responsible for directing fortune; that must be done by the state. The state became a false god, an idol. And this led the individual human being, who was now bound up in that system, to skepticism toward humans and faith in the external idol. Naturally, as the concept of God continued to decline, it became more and more idolized.

Proletarian Marxism is the third and final stage of the skepticism toward the human being. The proletariat, in its materialistic philosophy of history, says, "It is not the human being who directs fortune, but rather the 'forces of production' do it. As human beings, we stand in history with our ideologies, powerless. The development of the processes of production determines the course of history. And what human beings are within these forces of production is also only the result of those forces of production."

Skepticism toward humans and true faith in tangible totems! There is no fundamental difference between the African native who has moved into decadence by other means and prays to an actual chunk of wood, makes it a fetish, and the European proletariat who sees the means and processes of production as what directs the course of history. There is absolutely no logical or principle difference—it is our fantastical superstition! And we must really see this. Human beings have moved into decadence in various ways. In Africa there was also an original, ancient wisdom. Then this came under the auspices of administration; we can see this in Egypt. Then it decayed. Fetishism is not something that exists from the start, but rather something that appears in decadence. At the start, pure faith in the gods exists, and only in degeneration does fetishism come about. Within civilized regions, instead of praying to physical chunks of wood, the "forces of production" are worshipped. Of course, the worship of them takes on different forms. But the "forces of production" and the "process of production" are made into false gods. It is the last phase of skepticism toward human beings, the phase of an economically superstitious way of thinking. There is also principally no difference between an African native worshipping an idol with an incantation, and someone participating in a gathering of the modern proletariat and ranting with Marxist phrases. The prayers sound different, but we must be clear about the inner core of the matter.

What must oppose this now is not skepticism toward human beings, but rather faith in them. And in the end, it is all a matter of finding this faith in people, the faith that within human beings the directive forces for life are revealed. As human beings, we must come fully to ourselves, to full self-consciousness. We must find the ability to say to ourselves, "Everything external is superstition. The one and only thing that exists within us is the directive forces that must take hold in life!"

For this, it is necessary to have the courage to overcome merely passive prayer and to actively pray for taking hold of the godly in our will. This transition to active prayer, to any sort of inner activity; this transition from skepticism toward human beings to faith in human beings, this is the zeal that must lie within your hearts and souls. We must feel that we are the ones who stand at the historical turning point when people will be led from skepticism toward human beings to faith in human beings.

You do not need to say this to people, but you must step up to the podium with full consciousness of this, with the awareness that, "I have to communicate to humanity that the directive forces of life must be actively grasped in our interiority; that life in the future must be so administered that people say to themselves, 'I must be the one who does things.'"

It was the final superstition of civilization that people did not have faith in themselves, but rather that they believed that the "forces of production" directed life. And out of this superstition came about the terrible sort of false religious ceremony in the East, where an attempt was made to take what is not governed by the soul and nevertheless to have the soul absorb it. The individual who unified most completely two things that do not go together (inner passivity in convictions and activity in business) is Lenin. Lenin is the person who most purely crystallized in modern times everything from the past. He crystallized, most purely, actualized incapacity; an actualized drive toward destruction, toward downfall.

What will lead us to develop, what will lead toward a reinfusion of social life with true life forces, is finding the ability to create in people a faith in humanity out of the current skepticism toward it; a faith that finally expresses itself as follows: "What I will experience as good fortune or bad, or as a social institution, or as something in external life—all these things I will do myself!"

You cannot bring this to people without simultaneously strengthening them with your words. You have to bring people to a place where they have trust, where they have belief in their own being. And this is precisely what you must strive for in your hearts at the most basic level. How you do this at the moment will perhaps depend on your own capacities. But if you devote yourself with good will to these matters, then soon it will no longer depend on these capacities; instead, your capacities will be seized by the necessity of these times. And you will outgrow yourself precisely by bringing this faith to people; so that faith in humanity will have to replace skepticism toward humanity.

This is what I wanted to say to you before you go off to give your lectures. Feel the strength that lies within when you say to yourself, "My task is to effect the transition in others from the final superstition, the final skepticism toward humanity to faith in humanity, faith in the inner activity of the human being!" When this is your guide, you are striving toward true advancement. Everything else will lead only to a furthering of the state of decadence. There, you say to yourself, "Everything in a state of decline should no longer be supported and held upright." Instead, as far as I am concerned, look to Nietzsche:[†] "You push it forward so that it will collapse all the more quickly. But you love not what comes from yesterday and today, but rather comes with tomorrow!"

My dear friends, I would like you to go out into the world as people of tomorrow and to imprint your words with the consciousness of people of tomorrow.

II

Training Course for Upper Silesians

Lecture 1

Stuttgart, January 1, 1921

THE inspiration for our congress here is connected with an idea that has been discussed for a long time by the Association for the Threefold Social Organism.† Actually it would be necessary for us to prepare comprehensively, meaning in a longer period of instruction and discussion, for activism on behalf of the threefold social organism. From April, 1919, onward, the threefolding movement was supposed to have an effect more quickly than it has proved to do. And therefore, at the beginning of the year recently past, I was already emphasizing the necessity of taking up activism on behalf of the Association for Threefolding, not through some sort of formal examination of the art of speaking or the like, but through a deeply felt understanding of the urgency with which something like the threefolding movement must be handled in this, our most dire and fevered moment.

All around us, of course, we see all manner of political, social, or other kinds of activism happening, and everywhere you look you see how the whole way in which these actions are conducted is essentially a kind of dying out. In the most recent period, we have had the most gloomy experiences of this in the way that people, whenever something is to be communicated from the perspective of present-day life, are thinking about and staging things that are necessary for the further development of one relationship or another. We saw it at the League of Nations meeting in Geneva,† where everything that is important today was merely talked about in passing; where people did not actually go into any of the issues in question; and about which you could say that the only ones who actually managed things in such a way that their actions had legs were the ones who left—the Argentineans.

Now, I said that our threefolding movement had been predicted to make greater progress than it actually has. This, of course, is connected with the fact that in our current era, in which there is never enough time, it is not possible to conduct such a movement with a slow tempo, because otherwise the possibility of bringing about something that will lead to healing within Europe and Central Europe in particular will disappear. It is therefore necessary that we be clear that we are heading with great alacrity toward downfall, even if sometimes one or two find a way of slipping out of it.

And so, above all, we must come to understand what the necessary conditions are for an agitation, or whatever one wants to call it; and we will do this now by way of a concrete question. You see, I said that our discussions have emerged from an idea. The idea was that around fifty individuals would gather here[†] with the purpose of gaining an understanding of the methods and more especially the foundations of such an agitation. For unless agitations are conducted in a drastic and widespread manner, and soon, we will never get anywhere with something as comprehensive as the threefolding of society must be.

Standing before you right now is a vote that will affect the fate of Upper Silesia. We can discuss something of what actually must happen with all intensity in the near future; we can discuss this only generally in the few days that are granted to us for this particular question.

First, what is necessary now is the conviction that we cannot link any of the things that will actually bring civilization to salvation to the old configurations of public life. You cannot, if you hope to be effective, say this to the public in the words that I will speak now, but you must have this in the background when choosing your words, when choosing the materials that you will present. You must be convinced of the fact that the question—"Could we perhaps make a compromise with this political party, with this professional organization or something like that, by allowing them to continue with their usual way of thinking?"—that all such questions should be answered with a definitive "No." When the Anthroposophical Society was beginning its work, I would always hear things like this from all sides. "Well, this is how people in Munich are, and you have to deal with things a certain way; in Berlin, people are this way, and you have to do everything like this; in Hannover and other places, you have to handle things differently." All of this is nonsense, it really is meaningless; the only thing that has any meaning is that we be clear about what must be newly created and formed; and that we have the will to bring these newly formed things to people, that we make ourselves understand how possible it is to achieve these new forms, not only in our intellectual understanding, but also in our feelings.

I would like to characterize the second condition as follows: we need to have substance in our agitation, true content. During the last several centuries, when people did political or social or other forms of work, what did they work with? They worked with catch-phrases, with turns of phrases; and the name that they invented for this kind of speech was "ideals." In their heads, they were working with ideals. Now, with ideals—if what is hidden there in that word is precisely what was meant by it in the nineteenth and twentieth centuries—with ideals it is possible to make a momentary impression on people's feelings and perceptions, to excite them, to make them jump around and make all sorts of crazy gestures, but you cannot achieve any sort of real results with this excitement that is built on empty words. And achieving results is really what is important now. We can achieve results only if we say, "We are living today in a kind of societal ordering wherein our downfall itself is threefolded."

The downfall is threefolded, and the disorganized division (I cannot say organized) of this downfall shows itself in the most crucial places. We are witnessing a downfall of our spiritual life that expresses itself finally within the various religious confessions, on the one hand, and in our schools on the other, which do not even know where to blow their smoke as they burn. These two things in our spiritual life, the church and the schools, are one aspect of our downfall. They are connected in the most intimate way with a further aspect of the downfall, which essentially feeds the life of the churches and schools; they are connected with the principle of nationalism. Everywhere those things that people are trying to bring into our schools, those things that live in the schools, reach up from the foundations of the nation. And on the other hand, all of the various confessions, in the most diverse territories of the world, even if they try to be international, direct themselves specifically toward the nation.

A further aspect is the rights-political realm, which is everywhere sailing toward its downfall. The important thing there is that people are finally leaving behind, we might already say, every damaging cover-up of the relationships that, at least in the central regions of Europe, have continued on out of old customs. But such a situation must be seen at least distinctly enough that something clear emerges from it. Today people do not have any idea of how corrupt the political life of modern civilization had actually become before it brought about the catastrophe of 1914. You see, many examples of this can be offered. Let us look at one of them. Within Germany and the bordering territories there are still today a number of people who, as you may perhaps know, do not see that a certain individual with the name of Helfferich[†] was a destructive vermin in every place that he ever did anything. For example, you need only to remember that shortly before the outbreak of war this individual, Helfferich, gave a speech in which he said, "What some people are claiming, that Germany could starve if a war came, that seems to me little more than a theory. For if such a war were to break out, then so many different powers would be involved that you would have to have a pretty big distrust of German diplomacy to believe that everyone would be against us. But such distrust is beyond my ability to comprehend." This is more or less what Helfferich said shortly before the outbreak of war in 1914. Now, there is so much intellectual ignominy in this—I say "ignominy" because it is simultaneously intellectual and moral—that it is precisely things like this that must, when we look hard at them, make clear to us the level of corruption at which modern civilization finds itself.

Just think of all that is really said in these words from Helfferich: "If the thing that so many people are predicting comes about, that Germany would be blockaded from all sides if a war were to come, then one can have no trust in German diplomacy. But we must have precisely that trust!" Just think, a man like him says that we must have this trust; this means that sand must be thrown in people's eyes, because he was aware that this trust is impossible. Today you must be clear with yourself that if you intend to go on working with unreality, you cannot make any sort of progress. Even words like "radical" or "not radical" have more or less lost their value because it is now a matter of speaking about certain things more radically than was done before. Above all, it is important that you present to people concretely what leads to the detriment of humanity. We must arrive at very keen characterizations, not only of the currently existing relations, but also of the individuals; only then can we really have any sort of lasting effect. And if we then consider such a question as the question of the Upper Silesian vote from this perspective, then we will have to be seized by an idea, by the thought: "How should one relate to the vote itself: German or Polish?" This is the first question that presents itself: German or Polish?

In this time, we must actually bring ourselves to consider such questions also from a certain objective, human-oriented perspective, not from a perspective that simply comes out of old ways of thinking (even if they are those that we call nationalistic); such questions must be considered from an objective, human-oriented standpoint. And within the masses wherein this happens, within those masses we will make progress.

And to that end, as much as it is possible in this short period of time that can be dedicated to our understanding, I would like to demonstrate to you particular things from which one can call up the reasons for the conviction that from an objective human standpoint both answers—German and Polish—result in an equally great misfortune: a great misfortune for the population of Upper Silesia, a great misfortune for Poland, a great misfortune for Germany, a great misfortune for Europe, a great misfortune for the entire world. I would like to show you that, objectively, the question, "German or Polish?" cannot actually exist for the Upper Silesian population; and that it is a matter of seeing that for this small population complex we are actually dealing with a life question that requires us to arrive at a means of judgment such as the one provided by the threefold social organism. That is, to rise above everything that up until now has been offered up as a means of assessment.

You see, when such questions are posed, we must be able to have a deep-seated feeling that in every undertaking, socially, politically, and economically, laws are at work; and that these things are not ruled by arbitrariness, but that these laws in turn become actualized, so that in a vote we can go about things only in a way allowed to us by law. We can discuss and vote on whether a furnace door should be affixed to this or that side of an oven—and we would do well, when it comes to such questions, to consult with people who know something about it—but we cannot have a vote once we have put wood into the furnace on whether that wood can be lit only with a match, or rather with a piece of ice. You see, questions of the application of will must be brought into a proper relationship with the demands of life. This is why you cannot just speak from the separate realm of the will, from nebulousness and indeterminacy; and also why you cannot arrange to have a small population exposed in the world to vote on its own fate. Now, when everything still comes from old systems of thinking, we might shy away from saying publicly that this will lead most certainly toward downfall. We might be afraid to say precisely what is right to people, because it would seem to be absurd to them. But this is exactly what is important; saying to people what is right. If you want to speak about this question, then you must truly speak from a starting point that also affords a view of the powers that really have an effect.

In the study of the Polish character, you can observe very well how utterly impossible it would be to simply declare that such an exposed territory be incorporated into the Polish region. And if you consider the relationship of the Upper Silesian territory to the Polish region, than already the other relationship crops up, the relationship to the Prussian German region.

It does not suffice to judge the character of the Polish population and its place within European politics on the basis of a very few observations that you have made of this or that Pole; nor will it work to consider things on the basis of how one or another series of events coming out of Poland has been taken up in history. None of that suffices; instead, you must make clear to yourself what sort of special role the Polish population has played within an ever-expanding European territory. This role that the Polish population has played is, at a basic level, very characteristic for the development of other political relationships within Europe, and the Polish factor plays very, very heavily into European political relationships.

If you consider Poland, you see that from a cultural-political perspective it is so fundamentally exposed to both Western and Eastern influences; and it shows such inner peculiarities, this Polish population, that you can really say, "What the disposition was of people elsewhere since the fifteenth and sixteenth centuries has found clear expression in the Polish population." We cannot consider Poland except to see how, on the one hand, the cultural-political and spiritual traditions of the East can be found in the Eastern regions; and how now, even though Poland has experienced all manner of fates, the modern Russian character has gradually moved in. We cannot assess Poland without taking into consideration the way that, in its southern regions, coming out of relationships from the Middle Ages, the Austrian Empire—now on the brink of collapse—is preparing for its own disintegration; and also the way that finally, in the West, the German Empire formed—though destined for a short existence.

You see, what lives within the European life of Poland is actually connected with all of these things. If you look at the end of the fifteenth century and the beginning of the sixteenth century, relationships appear in the German regions that actually did not find any sort of direct continuation. You need only to remember names like Götz von Berlichingen,† Franz von Sickingen,† Ulrich von Hutten† and so on, and you can see certain relationships that existed then but then did not find any sort of continuation. What were these relationships built on? There was a feudal caste there; a feudal caste that understandably was able to produce such strong, and in a certain sense, remarkable people as the ones I have named. But this feudal caste was built upon an ignorant, more or less uncivilized mass of peasants. And the fact that this feudal caste worked in such a way that the great lords always lived among the others, who were ignorant peasants, and that these lords also were the active practitioners of the administration, and also fundamentally ruled over the spiritual life; this is what gave the social life in Central Europe its structure. But right around the end of the fifteenth and beginning of the sixteenth century, this structure was abolished in Central Europe. It was abolished in such a way that one can say that within the German-speaking regions the underlying sense of this structure had rotted through and through. And in place of this structure stepped something that had been initially worked through in the territorial princedoms, now gathered together into the German Empire; that is, the military and bureaucratic organization of the social organism. And so, out of the feudal-aristocratic element, which could be built up only on the broad foundations of an uncivilized peasantry, territorial princedoms expanded with militaristic and bureaucratic foundations. Within this Central Europe, most especially in Prussia, this became the ethos. It did not become something that was merely imposed upon the social order; it became the ethos.

Here, is it not the case that we can perhaps think about two opposites? One would be a man positioned within the old, knightly Götz-von-Berlichingen-society, who keeps himself busy with something or another. How does he busy himself? He busies himself, for example, by using his knowledge to arrange things; by setting up schools on the basis of what his religious world-pictures provide; by thinking about how one speaks of proper human understanding to a particular parish that is not so large. Into the sixteenth century, this is how things were organized in regions that spoke German; then such things were reorganized, then came bureaucracy and the military. And if we think of the one person who could not have existed in the Götz-von-Berlichingen-society, we would think of the lieutenant of the Prussian Reserve. So, the possibility for the existence of such a soul is created only after the start of the sixteenth century. And is it not the case that the reserve lieutenant is a combination of bureaucratic and military existence? This came into being in Central Europe, not only in the regions where it could be understood, but also in regions where it could not be understood. Our history, for example, is written in such a way that this ethos is alive within it; and our history is taught in school in such a way that this ethos lies within it. But because of the fact that due to the character of the German population this transformation could not take hold in the deepest, the most inner parts of the soul; because of this fact, territorial princedoms came into being, and not a full kaiserdom. That was attempted for the first time in the nineteenth century during the war, the war in the 1870s, but was not able to succeed.

Because of the most disparate historical relationships, the full elaboration of which would be too much for this occasion, a great wave swept everything toward the state, toward the rights-political, and led to the imprisonment of the economic life within the political element. A great wave swept over Central Europe, and it is because of this that Central Europe is the way it is.

Now, if you take a look at Russia, there you have in the social structure what was suddenly created in Central Europe at the beginning of the sixteenth century. You have a widespread, uneducated, uncivilized peasantry that is somehow supposed to be regulated, that is somehow supposed to be incorporated into a social organism. The situation at hand is just the same as it was in Central Europe when it moved into the sixteenth century, but in Russia the solution in individualism was not to be found. In Russia, everything was being very quickly incorporated into czarist centralization, so that the middle point that existed in Europe between kaiserdom and the uncivilized masses was not there. Everything was moving in a direction wherein each person, regardless of whether suited to it or not, was being made into a bureaucrat or a military person, with the central authority giving the directives. In various ways, in Germany on the one hand, in Russia on the other, what was being annihilated was any sort of true *Volksorganization*, any sort of organization of common humanity. On the one hand, it was being driven into kaiserdom, and on the other hand, into territorial princedoms.

And a third, then, is Austria. Austria, which grew up entirely out of patriarchal relationships that lived on as a kind of family tradition within the lineage of princes. This Austria was being gradually compelled to bring together the most diverse populations under the auspices of Roman centralization, which wants to govern. It takes on a kind of democratic allure, but nevertheless wants to rule the populace in the manner of the Spanish Middle Ages.

In the midst of these three streams you find the Polish factor, which is bracing itself fundamentally against all three of them; and which, I would like to suggest, has determined itself, in a rather strange manner, against all three streams out of a sort of inner position. The Polish factor does indeed take on all of those misleading elements from the West: parliamentarianism, the school system, and so on. I would say that it takes on all of those things that become a certain analytical aspect of life; all that develops into the element of judgment, of discernment. From the East, it takes the element of synthesis, life in the form of big concepts and ideas. But, you see, within the Polish factor, analysis becomes sloppiness, and the Eastern impulse toward synthesis turns toward fantasizing. These two elements are always definitely there: sloppiness from the Western stream, from ordered analysis, and from the Eastern stream, the fantasizing and also the lack of truthfulness. This lack of truthfulness is just the shadow side of Eastern synthesis, and the sloppiness is just the shadow side of becoming pedantic. If pedantry goes so far that it becomes impossible to follow it, then it collapses into its opposite, into sloppiness. In Austria there was never a lack of penetrating regulations on all aspects of life; the essential point is that no single one of them could be followed. First of all, they all contradict each other, and second, there are so many that no one can really pay attention to all of them at once.

How did it happen that this Polish being came about in Europe, when all around it was something entirely different? How did it happen that Poland continued tenaciously to develop its own nature? This happened because, as the great Russian wave with its inherent plans for conquest came crashing over Europe, it was necessary for the others who also came under consideration (I cannot describe all of this in detail now, but one could do so) to react to this Russian being in the way described. Above all, it was necessary for the Prussian and the Austrian Empire in the eighteenth century to react to this Russian element. From a certain standpoint, it is easy to reproach the Prussians and the Austrians for dividing Poland[†] with Russia; but when we do this, we forget that if they had not divided it, Russia would have simply taken it all for itself. You see, these things have to be considered objectively. Prussia and Austria took part in the division of Poland because they could not allow Russia to take over all of Poland itself, which surely would have happened otherwise. And so, Poland was divided up.

But within this divided population, that from which there had been a break in Europe in the German element at the beginning of the sixteenth century, the feudal nobility continued to live on, with its broad foundation in the uncivilized peasantry. That from which a similar break had been made, at least outwardly, in Russia—all of that continued to live on in Poland. The Polish being essentially preserved what had lived within the European social structure of the fifteenth century, which always had a kind of antique element in it, a Greek element within it. We marvel at Greece; but the greatness of Greece is due to the fact that it was the most highly developed of what we say was taken over by Europe in the fifteenth century. If we are to be clear about it, we must realize that we marvel at Greece rightly when looking at what history has made of it. And on the other hand, we can also realize that we took a tremendous step forward when the effort was made to overcome gradually what could only be built on the basis of a rural proletariat. The evolution of Europe into the fifteenth century was still oriented toward Greece; we can say of this "Greek Europe" that it is something that does not provide for any truly human state of being. A certain upper class, the one that was dominant in Poland, this upper class retained this Greek ethos; that is, the ethos of living within an upper class of nobility with a simple, uncivilized peasantry beneath it, and not one differentiated into bourgeoisie and proletariat. And such was its disposition, this Polish population, when it was divided up. For is it not the case that those within this upper class were the only ones doing any thinking, any true thinking, in Poland? They began to hate Russia, Prussia, and Austria. But then, within this Polish aspect, there were these people upon whom nothing really depended, precisely this whole uncivilized lower class with no political or other kind of intelligence. And you see, some of them went to Russia, some to Austria; in Russia, they went where the Polish element was within Russian relationships; and in Austria, wherever the Polish element was within Galicia. And some of them came to Prussia, where the Polish element was in Silesia and Posen. The Polish class did not change, but simply acquitted itself within the existing relationships as well as it could, considering that it was completely ill-suited to them, particularly the political ones.

In response to this, the lower class integrated itself in a most unusual manner. Of course, what has risen up from that lower class must be sought these days as a new fermentation, precisely as what has risen up from the lower class that was beneath the top layer of the Polish nobility. You see, it is curious that this lower class has actually retained a particular structure within the context of the relationships that emerged from the division of Poland. Because of the structure that existed in Russian Poland, this lower class has taken on a spiritual element in the most eminent sense; a spiritual element directed toward a deepening of thinking and a deepening of the sciences through a certain religious element. Up until the revolution, one did not distinguish between religious life and the scientific in Russia. Allowing spiritual thoughts, the perceptions of the sensory life to run freely through big, comprehensive, synthetic ideas, is what has been brought over into the Polish element from the East by the Russian element. Without the influence of the spiritual side of social life, people like Slowacki[†] and

Dunajewski[†] are, I believe, unimaginable. In contrast, the section of the Polish being that went over to Austria, there this lower class took from Austria the state-rights-political. And this is why the most refined political minds and speakers, such as Hausner[†] and Wolski,[†] have come out of Austrian Galicia, essentially out of Poland. This people could never have come out of the Polish being if it had not been absorbed by the neighboring areas, where comprehensive, synthetic ideas could be learned from Russia, and the necessary standpoint for constitutional, political thinking from Austria. Such a man as Hausner, who played such a large role in the 1870s and 1880s, was an assemblyman in a Polish-Galician city. Such a figure and his parliamentary colleague Wolski, they are what we might call "political minds," through and through; not people who can necessarily rule, but who can see through these relationships in a wonderful manner.

You see, this is what is being said everywhere now about political relationships, without there being any substance to the words. We must concern ourselves with what has happened. When considering the course for activists, I did not think that individuals would be instructed how to speak, but rather I thought that materials on activism should be distributed, and it is from this perspective that I am speaking now.

Everything that happened in the year 1918, that has happened throughout the events since 1914, you could find prophesized in the previous century at the end of the 1870s, within the Austrian Parliament. It is true that at that time, such people as Hausner and Wolski spoke about the downfall of Austria, about the inability to really confront the proletarian question, and other questions; in short, everything that had to be said was spoken about in the Austrian Parliament. The people then had just about all of it right, except for two things: the timing of it all and the possibilities that exist in the present. As far as the timing goes, they saw things in all sorts of warped, fantastical ways. Take a man like Hausner. He once said very grandiosely in a speech that in the moment Austria marches into Bosnia the ground is laid for collapse. The things that came about for others later, Hausner had already brought up in the 1870s. But he got the timing wrong. He thought that it would happen within ten years. This is due to the influence of the Eastern element; it existed even in level-headed Hausner—

the fantastic. He sees what is true, but his view on the timing is blurred. What still needed two, three, or four more decades to come about, he predicted would come in the next decade. And then, Hausner once offered a critique of the Germans, with a complete misunderstanding at that time. You can read in the speech that he gave around 1880 that it was not suited to the relationships of that moment at all; but with a certain, sensitive sort of grimness, he does describe the situation of our present moment. So these people make mistakes, but it is nevertheless the case that one can say that Poland has been particularly pushed by the East toward big, comprehensive thinking; and pushed by Austria toward the political-state life, which was largely dominated by such people as Hausner and Wolski.

And therefore, we must also believe—this is absolutely true and shows itself to be so in reality—that the parts of Poland that came over into Prussia have received their particular stimulus toward a development of the economic life, and that this must become the fulcrum point for the dealings of those parts of civilization that came to Prussia from Poland: the handling of the economic life. Poland has been particularly endowed with economic life from Prussia, political life from Austria, and religious-spiritual life from Russia.

We have here a threefolding that demonstrates that the Polish people have been endowed by Russia with a gift for great spiritual ideas. If you study what is called Polish Messianism,[†] the writings of Slowacki, or even what it is that the Polish people talk about from day to day, you find that impulse comes out of the East. If, on the other hand, you study what lives in the Polish people, what they make of their politicians, leaving them basically alone in the plotting of conspiracies and the like, you will find that they get this from Austria. And you will find that they have their economic life from Prussia.

But with all of this, it is not possible to build any sort of Poland, any sort of Polish state. Europe must also divide in such a way that a particular population takes something different than the Polish take from Austria, namely the spiritual; and from Austria something different than the Polish take from Prussia, namely the political; and from Prussia, the economic; this must come about through a great process of splitting up. The capacities for these three areas can certainly be achieved, but no unified state can come out of this. It might be constructed, but it will always collapse again. There will never in reality be a Poland for any extended period of time, because there can never be one. In the decisive moment Poland must be divided so that the Polish people can fully develop their abilities. But, there will never be a Poland, and to speak of Poland now is an illusion. We must do everything we can to bring to popular awareness such ideas, the seed of which I have just indicated to you in regard to the impossibility of such national structures, sought after in an attempt to construct a unified state. We have to bring into people's thinking and feeling the knowledge that we go barreling toward misfortune every time we speak about "being Polish." We have to get away from "Polish" and move toward the universally human, for only the things that have developed historically into this threefolding will come to fruition. Take a look at these matters from the opposite side: the Poles received great, comprehensive ideas from Russia; the Russians gave them these ideas. But Russia no longer has these ideas itself, for it has drifted into Bolshevism. The Russians were not strong enough to construct a social organism. They are living within a social organism that is moving completely toward devastation.

Look at what was especially characteristic of Austria in the most notable parliament in the world during the 1870s, when there were men such as Hausner, Dunajewski, Dzieduszycki,† and others like them. For example, the old Czechs Rieger† and Grégr,† as well. Not to mention other people like Herbst,† Plener,† Carneri,† who were Germans. Back then you had the most eminent Czechs, the most eminent Poles, and the most eminent Germans. Regarding the Germans, you had the same sort of situation as you did with the Poles. We see again how in the lower class among the Czechs such men were formed into the most refined politicians by living within the context of Austrian relationships. And in Austria, people became fine politicians, arriving at a subtle understanding of political relationships. But this started with the Germans in Austria. And a person like Otto Hausner, with his subtle grasp of politics, with his accurate predictions of Austria's downfall, once said, "If we continue to conduct our economics as we are currently, then in five years there will no longer be an Austrian parliament." (He overstated this, of course.) Only later did what he said come true, but it was an accurate prediction. People like this were made possible solely by the Germans in Austria, who actually took this form of parliamentarianism from the West and transplanted it in Central Europe through the schools. But the Germans in Austria are the ones from whom the others became familiar with this refined, subtle concept of political life. They themselves, however, conducted themselves within this concept as clumsily as possible. This is characteristic: that they should act clumsily; this is what others learn from them and what becomes important to the others. In the moment that it crosses over into the minds of the others, it becomes significant for European life as ferment. As a result, the Germans depended upon maintaining their hold on the territory in which they resided. They could not do this. The Poles did not have to maintain their hold on anything, because they did not have anything. They were thus able to develop the ideas as such. The Germans could not do anything with the ideas; they gave them to the others, and in so doing, buried their own social organism.

Now we come to the third element: in Germany, an economic life has truly developed. You could say that the economic life in Central European Germany has surpassed all the other developments of economic life in the world. Tremendous economic relationships have developed there. But they are growing up into thin air; they cannot support themselves. Poland could again learn a lot from them, but the Germans themselves cannot continue to practice economics in this way. They are steering themselves toward catastrophe. This would have been the case even if the war had not come.

So again, we see a threefolding of the European downfall: from the spiritual side in Russia, from the rights-political in Austria, from the economic in Germany. The only way to oppose this is through a threefolded ascent, which is to say, having a fully conscious grasp on the idea of threefolding.

And now we have to imagine that there is a territory that has to decide whether it wants to belong to those who are unable to really form a state (to Poland), or whether it should become a limb of that threefolded Europe that has brought together all the elements directing it toward downfall—Austria, Prussian Germany, and Russia. In other words, it has to decide whether it will belong to one of these three limbs, in this case to Germany. Such a decision must induce us to think about wherein the healing lies when we say, "We are not concerned with what has come about in Europe, but we want to put into these moments of development precisely what must come anew." It might be possible to speak cleverly and to show that everything that I have presented here today is not clever, but the conclusions that one would draw from this sort of talk will never lead us to a rational Europe. Therefore, it is necessary that we base ourselves on positive, real relationships. This is what I wanted to say to you today.

Lecture 2

Stuttgart, January 2, 1921

I AM sorry that we do not have more time to talk. Right now, I can only present to you certain suggestions regarding our particular problem. This afternoon, I will turn to the questions that you, friends, wish to pose.

Yesterday, I attempted, in the context of a certain historical sequence, to make clear to you the hopelessness that exists in regard to the question of Upper Silesia in the context of present-day relationships. But this hopelessness can also appear to us from various other sides. It is the case now that people who continue to think with old presuppositions give themselves over to terrible illusions about the future of European life. Indeed, such people live exclusively on illusions. And those friends of ours who have resolved to work truly for the betterment of world relationships must make clear to themselves that within the masses we can make progress only insofar as we are able to bring about enlightenment, and relatively quickly. And not only enlightenment about local affairs, but enlightenment also about world relationships in general, which actually are playing into the relationships of the smallest territories now. We will not be able simply to build on the institutions that already exist. We must first have recourse only to those people who are inclined to take up our ideas, so that we have an ever greater number of such people; and then, with these people we can really start something. And we must try to make it clear to these people that even within the context of present-day relationships they must act in a way that is in keeping with the sense of our ideas. For you see, yesterday we established that from both the German and the Polish side, there is essentially no future either in the old or the newly hoped-for relationships. We can also make it clear to ourselves that, on the other hand, this hopelessness also has other foundations. Obviously, Upper Silesia is integrated into all of European relations. What is unique about its position is that it has to make a decision about its fate in a particular manner. This must be considered. Wherever decisions are to be made at this time, the larger perspective must be factored in.

Let us look for a moment at European relationships from a different perspective than we did yesterday. You see, economic relations in Europe are such that in Central and Eastern Europe, in regard to everything that has developed out of the old relationships, things are headed toward a rapid decline. We in Europe no longer work on the old economic foundations that are there; even less so when it comes to the political and spiritual foundations. The people who are concerning themselves now with public affairs have some picture of the terrible threat of this downfall, but their images of it are illusory. The main illusion that we see in the people of Central Europe—and in Eastern Europe the same is true—is that they believe an understanding with the Anglo-Saxon element, or with the West in general, is possible under the standards of the old relationships. But such an understanding is actually not possible, and a vote like this one on the question of Upper Silesia will always stumble on precisely the impossibility of such an understanding. It has to stumble upon this possibility. One cannot simply cast a ballot in these relationships currently being created by the statesmen and economists. What kind of imagination can someone have, who even half-thinks—and hardly anyone thinks even that much—what imagination can someone have for a possible rehabilitation of European economic conditions, among other things? It could be said that the first thing that would be possible would be a big loan of currency,[†] a big advance that would come through America. You know, of course, such things are being talked about now; major advances, credit, which could come only out of America, would be given to the Europeans, perhaps guaranteed by the independent states that want to consolidate themselves, and economic life could then be elevated by such a loan of currency. Europe could then buy raw materials and food; and perhaps in the course of thirty, forty, or fifty years, European economic relationships would be improved. This imagination bespeaks a kind of half-thinking. There will never be any sort of administration in America that would be in a position to simply do away with the oppositions that exist within European relations. The nations of Europe are not in a position to offer sufficient guarantees, even if there were only small measures attached—and such small measures could never be under these conditions. Guarantees cannot be given that would really lead to a successful bettering of European economic relationships through a currency loan; this also shows the impossibility of furthering economic life because of currency differences. This is why the possibility is closed of achieving something in this manner. One could nevertheless go on thinking that it would be possible to approach individual people in the neutral countries, or the Allied countries, or America, about extending credit, in good faith, to individual economic figures in the European nations. This action alone, within the context of current relationships, could move only within a very small frame; for the people in the neutral countries or among the Allied Powers who could be asked to extend that credit are so few in number that we cannot actually imagine any sort of improvement of European relations by this means. Thus do people fall into all kinds of illusions. They skip over any sort of middle step, and think immediately about some sort of world economic organization, which is somehow to develop out of the idea of folk economics. They think about how, in some sort of world state, all of economic life could be put under a political purview, so that the particular liabilities of the besieged countries would not come under consideration. Now, this is of course a terrible sort of utopia; but it is precisely this that has now cropped up in the world, as evidenced by the gathering in Geneva. And to place your hopes in such an association of the people, oriented as it is toward the economic side, is necessarily utopian at present. What is truly important now is that we look more deeply into the evolutionary forces of humanity, and that the attempt is then made to arrive at regulations that will really be able and required to help. Such regulations are to be won only through threefolding. As soon as you give yourself over to the illusion that something can be done without threefolding, then you are simply participating in the downfall. Just think for a moment about what it would mean if, for example, the Upper Silesians were to vote in favor of annexation by Germany. This would amount to nothing less than the Upper Silesian population's consigning its small territory to a larger territory that, if it continues to handle things as it has been doing, must soon fall into barbarianism. It cannot be a matter of allowing annexation by a territory that has not already shown itself to have overcome the old relationships. This has not been demonstrated by the decisive crises in Prussian Germany; in fact, quite the opposite has been shown. And so we regard the facts of the matter in a simply objective manner: annexation by Prussian Germany means consigning oneself to impossible circumstances.

For you see, now we arrive at the other illusion (and we shall go into this further), which the best people on the side of the Allied powers allow themselves. There are people like Keynes,† who has a certain following, and Norman Angell,† who also has quite a large following. How do these people think? These people think that the Versailles Treaty must absolutely be revised, that we cannot get anywhere on the basis of the current treaty. But why do they think that? They think, "Europe was, before now, in economic exchange with the entire world. If Europe falls into barbarianism, then its economic life collapses. And with that"—this is how these people think, particularly Norman Angell—"and with that, the economic life not only of the Allied Powers will collapse"—it goes without saying that that will collapse—"but also the American economic life, because the places for export to Europe will no longer be there. We need the economic countries for both sides of the Allied Powers and America in order to be able to enter into fruitful economic exchange." You see, on this basis, the best people of the Allied Powers make their judgments. You could say that actually, in the last few months, several very significant things have been said along these lines, and that the number of people is steadily growing who are convinced of the non-viability of the Versaille Treaty and all that results from it. But they are wrong, and live in an illusion; they make their judgments out of the existing habits of thought and feeling. We must not retreat fearfully from gruesome realities. It is simply untrue that the Anglo-Saxon world is dependent upon being in economic exchange with Central and Eastern Europe. At the very most, they would have to reorganize their whole economic life and turn it into a closed and contained economic body. They could then go on existing, even if a great number of people died of hunger in Europe. What people are saying is well-intentioned, but not true. It would take perhaps fifteen to thirty years before the economic life in countries outside of Central and Eastern Europe could be reorganized so that it was entirely self-sufficient, but the real possibility for such a reorganization is there. If one were actually in a position to carry out what these people imagine, then whatever was done out of the old preconditions in Central and Eastern Europe would have to lead ultimately to the enhancement of the West via a detour through barbarianism. On the basis of old preconditions, nothing else can be imagined.

It is possible to imagine that a majority might exist, namely in America, who would simply work to leave Europe to its fasting, and make the Western regions of the world into a self-contained economic area. But voting to join with the current conditions in Central Europe would be the same as running toward this condition. By joining with Poland, you would be doing no less. All that has just been said takes away any hope. You would also be doing no less than giving yourself over to the Allied Powers' way of thinking. Poland is the little fosterling of the Allied Powers, but in all of the instances where it matters this will do nothing to help it; it will either be delivered to the ruins of European relationships or it will be thrust into the catastrophic experiences that I will soon describe.

So a vote in either direction is a patent absurdity. We must hold this matter up clearly before our souls: a vote like this is an absurdity. Still, we will speak about the conditions under which it might go in one direction or the other. We must nevertheless be clear that the world cannot be preserved with thoughts that were thought in the past. This can be shown most clearly in what I tried to describe yesterday. Poland, I said, has maintained what the rest of Europe has overcome, to a certain degree: a form of noble class. Beneath this noble class, a lower class has developed that has gained its impulse toward sanity and activism, I would suggest, through a threefolding. That is, it took from Russia the spiritual, from Prussian Germany the economic, and from Austria (via Galicia) the rights-political. This lower class has lived mostly within the bourgeois stream that has had the upper hand in Europe for a while now, so the things that have formed in Poland through a combination of the lower class and what came from the rest of Europe have now worked their way in the bourgeoisie. But its effectiveness is currently lackluster, just as the bourgeoisie in general is lackluster.

Now there is simply this broad foundation, and this broad foundation comes toward us as a true *simulacrum*, as a likeness of the real. In the West, it comes out more as a worker movement gone bourgeois; in Central Europe as a more or less nuanced form of social democracy; and the farther east we go, the more it presents itself as a form of Bolshevism. The life conditions of Bolshevism in Russia—we must make these clear to ourselves. After all, the Silesian region currently in question lies very close to the life conditions of Bolshevism, and we must bring a real and full clarity about these Bolshevist living conditions.

You see, the basis of Bolshevism is that the upper class, whether it be the aristocracy or the bourgeoise, has found no possibility in recent times of extending its thinking beyond the same regions into which labor and, above all, human will have extended themselves. People have continued working with the old way of thinking; have built up the commercial, the economic element; have drawn upon a whole mass of the population. But no steps have been taken to attend to this mass of the population by any means other than the old state relationships. And, unfortunately, it must be said that this still is not happening today, because the one way in which it could actually happen, is not happening. This must be our primary concern. For it is a characteristic example of how leaders were brought to bear upon a situation when things were actually moving and stirring within the masses of the population. It was not done well. Ludendorff[†] explains in his recollections that he was the one who called up the Bolshevist leaders in Russia; he says that it was a military necessity for him, and the politicians were consequently obligated to ward off the terrible results of this necessity. So he does not deny that he gave Bolshevism in Russia its leaders; he merely says that the politicians were not clever enough to repair the tremendously foolish thing that he had done. Such things are possible these days, and they are tolerated. So out of the very oldest forms of state relationships, which was how Ludendorff thought, the leading individuals were appointed to Bolshevism, not out of a sensible cooperation between people who know something about the course of humanity, nor those who would actually want to lead toward new relationships and not just lead with the old relationships. This is something that must be recognized at the most fundamental level. Since the World War, it is no longer true that the broad lower class is made up only of the old proletariat. All members of previous classes belong to this wide-reaching lower class. And people are not reckoning with this fact, either. People are not yet reckoning with the idea that, above all else, rational ideas must be brought to those who have retained some intelligence from the time prior to the war, so that a leading intelligence comes ever more into the world in a reasonable manner. This is the most important issue for this time: that the people who have maintained something of their intelligence have their eyes opened so that they can become the true leaders. Without this, we will not move forward. For you see what stands before us. As I have already mentioned: the reconstruction of Central and Eastern Europe is not possible except on a foundation of threefolding; it cannot be done by the people of Central and Eastern Europe, nor by the people of the Allied Powers. The people from the Allied Powers and America could do something under only one condition, whether we are talking about the extension of a large-scale loan or small-scale credit. They can do this under only one condition, namely, that a significant wage push take place in Europe, over and against America. The American proletariat would be immediately against this, and the English proletariat also might not allow it. Any measure taken in this direction would lead to revolution in the Western regions. And this is precisely what must be made a part of humanity's outlook, that the Bolshevist Revolution has also gripped the Western world, not yet from without, but from within the broad lower class. The leading individuals in the West can construct as many barriers as they like against the Bolshevist contamination of the West, but the transmission of Bolshevism from the East is not the main issue for the West; rather, its main concern, the core of the matter, is what is coming up from below.

Now, there are already a number of people (and this number will quickly grow) who see that it is entirely impossible to avoid revolution if one continues to work out of an ethos. And just as people who were thinking in that old way said, "We must have a war in order to conquer the revolution in our own country." This means nothing less than that among the people in the West who are still thinking in an old way, work must be being done toward a second World War. There is no other way to turn away from the inner Bolshevism of the West except to work toward a second World War. The approach of this second World War is made all the more certain by the fact that in the East, as soon as things came to a head, an understanding could never be won for the economic standards of the West. The way of thinking that has come forward now in Russia is even connected in the East with Eastern religious imaginations; and so an ethos has developed in Asia to whose direction the Japanese population and its leaders are unusually well-suited, so that the division between East and West will soon fall into the economic confusions of the future. A second World War, which must develop between Asia and America and what lies between them, will doubtless develop entirely out of an economic underpinning. You all hear the cry that rises up from the lower class: "World revolution!" It will be possible to disguise these thoughts of world revolution only by unleashing the storm of a second World War. It is otherwise unthinkable.

We now find ourselves living in a time in which the conflict between America and Asia is growing ever starker. It goes without saying that the people who lie in the middle will be pulled into this conflict. You can be quite sure that Asia, with the Japanese at the head, will be in the same position over and against the West that Central Europe was against the Allied Powers. In the East, they will perhaps give themselves over to a feeling of confidence about their victory for a time; but just as America was a deciding factor in Europe, so will it also be a deciding factor in Asia. But there will be a Ludendorff in the East who will send the necessary leaders to the West in order to contaminate it with a Bolshevist, or in this case Asian, element. There will be one among the Japanese as well. And then you will have the very thing toward which everyone's sentiments are directed right now; you will have brought it about through a second World War. We must imagine an America in which a Lenin is practicing economics, just as Lenin is doing in Russia right now. We must not close ourselves off from this perspective. We must be clear that the causes of the present urgency lie in economic downfall; that the effects lie in the barbarization of humanity. To this, we can only present one single counterbalancing fact, which may perhaps be said here in connection to these things. It must also penetrate throughout all of our work, while also not being made into material for an agitation, for in the moment that it is made into something like that, it will immediately be destroyed within this world-historical moment.

You see, all over the world there are people who, because they have reached an end with the present-day economic, political, and spiritual thought, have simply begun to consider this idea of threefolding. The things that have arisen in reaction to the translation of *Towards Social Renewal* into English[†] are an indication of a fully legitimate proof of this. If we are able to make use of the fact that *Towards Social Renewal* is being discussed in English newspapers; if we could be strong enough to make an appropriate impact, then we will, for as long as the trail is warm, be able to develop a very effective agitation. But the place where we fail is having a sufficient number of individuals who can work effectively for our cause. This led to my indicating back in the spring of 1920 that we would need to have fifty people here in Stuttgart who could discuss with me and with each other what is necessary in order for this to be brought to people.[†] So here we are today. There is no other way than to enlighten a great number of people. But for this, a sufficient number of enlightened people are necessary who speak from the foundations of the matter. For you can be sure: if you present the things that we have discussed today and yesterday, they will have an effect; it need only be brought to a sufficient number of people. It will not be enough for us to spread out with just ten people; rather we must fan out into the world with hundreds of activists. This is necessary: that we always have more and more individuals involved.

So, as I said, from out of the lower class rises an understanding in opposition to barbarianism the world over; but leaders must be there, leaders who can understand what lies within the threefold social organism by way of their inner qualities. These leaders can exist only in Central Europe. This is the paradox that stands before humanity now, that in those regions that are the most opposed, the most besieged, nevertheless live the people who are most able to understand the way out from the confusions of humanity. In this regard, we in Central Europe have been tested well enough. Just think, since the first half of the nineteenth century, the thought of an organization of the German people built primarily on ideals has emanated from the best qualities of that German populace.

What manifested itself as a striving for unity, particularly since 1848,[†] came out of the most beautiful qualities of the German population in Central Europe; it was essentially a precious stone in the cultural evolution of humanity. And it has a particular quality about it that must be called upon: it has the quality that will not allow it to be held in contempt, not be hated by any population on Earth, but rather accepted by everyone. Even the Poles would accept it, if it were to appear with the quality that it once did as a political idea in Germany.

Among those people who later, in so-called Realist Germany, were mocked as the "Idealists of '48," there were basically a few who best brought certain qualities to expression. Everything that has come onto the scene in the last few decades in Central Europe, in Austria as well as Germany, has been in opposition to that. It was later that things developed that at the most basic level contradict the German being; and these are the things that are hated by the whole world, that the whole world is complaining about. As long as Central Europe does not see that it has to work out of foundations that are in the spiritual realm, that it cannot base its historical mission entirely on power relationships but only on the spiritual, then there will not be an impulse for any sort of evolved Central Europe, but ultimately only an impulse toward the downfall of the whole civilized world.

In this regard, we can actually look back to Fichte.[†] I will draw attention to only two points in Fichte, to the last words that he said in his "Speech to the German Nation" in which he called upon the Germans to remember their own qualities, to work out of what lies within them, because this will allow them to look from a higher point of view at the world. And on the other hand, he admonished them to relinquish their claim on sea power. Go and read in the "Speech to the German Nation" how strongly Fichte advised against striving after any sort of sea power. Fichte mocked the so-called freedom of the seas. This came out of a deep-seated instinct.

And you see, the moment we touch upon these things, we must simultaneously be made aware that here is the lever that can reverse things. Go and read the important section, which was not understood at the time, just as the whole book was not understood, the important section that I tried to offer in my *Thoughts during the Time of War*,[†] that is, that the German populace is not guilty of the war. Read that section, and then read the caption on the cover, which says that the book is intended for Germans and for those people who do not believe that they must hate them; for I knew well that this could be understood only by certain people. But there were no people like that at the time, even though I was asked to put out a second edition of the book. I refrained from doing so because basically the only people who were taking it were the ones who believed that they had to hate the Germans. In Germany, people neatly kept silent about these matters. The book could really have meant something only if someone had taken it up fully in all of its factual foundation. And so it had to be taken out of bookstores. Within the circles of people who were German, or who did not think it was required to hate the Germans, I wanted to call forth a certain feeling that existed in their depths of soul. If this feeling, as it was intended at that time, had really come out into the open, it would have established an atmosphere; that means that if people had been able to see externally that such a feeling existed, then it would have led to something good. If people were to perceive such a sentiment now, it would still lead to something positive.

Allow me now to say the following; I ask you to consider the words that I will now read to you precisely in connection with what we are currently discussing. "The German people did not compel their government into the war. They knew nothing about it in advance and did not agree with it. We do not want to attach responsibility to the German people, who have also suffered sorrows in this war for which they were not the cause."

So now I ask you, does this not accord perfectly with what I expressed during the war in that little book, *Thoughts During the Time of War?* But who, under the influence of certain other people, said these words on June 14, 1917? It was Woodrow Wilson.[†] If this matter is properly conceived, then the possibility for an understanding throughout the world lies within it. We must think about this turn of phrase; even today we must think that in the moment when something was actualized in Europe that proved to be dealing solely with the genuine evolution of humanity, and proved not to be dealing at all with a collection of old things, we must realize that in that moment a common understanding with the world can be found coming out of Central Europe. In the moment when, even if only on a limited scale, an appeal can be made at some point to the self-determination of people in Central Europe, it must be shown that the German being, when it truly comes out of itself, does not want to have any connection to the old forms of power. This is regardless of whether the old forms are old statesmen or industrialists, and regardless of whether they stand on the side of Helfferich† or Erzberger,† or on the side of German democracy. Everything that has a connection with what came to the surface for the first time in the Wilhelmine period† must be discarded. And we must find what can be said within the true foundations of the German being, to which the Austrian being also belongs. For then, what is said will be in accord with what is said by others the world over who still have some sense of reality. It would make an enormous impression upon the world if some small group were to say, "We want nothing to do with Prussia in the form that it has taken on; we want nothing to do with everything that stands under the protection of the Allied Powers. We know that wholly other forces can come forth from our foundations; we want to orient ourselves toward threefolding. We do not want to have only a pseudo-autonomy as it has come forward; we want a genuine, a true autonomy, and will establish ourselves provisionally within this true and genuine autonomy. We will transform the vote into a protest against the fact of the vote." This is the necessary consequence that results from the facts of history, as well as those of present-day international affairs.

Certainly, one can respond by saying, "The result of something like this today would be that you place yourself on the Earth between two chairs." This will not be the result, if it can popularized sufficiently, and fast enough, that it becomes at the very least something clearly perceptible in the case of the vote in Upper Silesia. Only by way of such things can we make progress in our movement. The one thing that stands against us is that we are not in a position to get far enough before the day of the vote to actually realize the kind of protest that should stand against the fact of the vote as such. Then any work in this region will become especially complicated. For those who promulgate our ideas will not find a foothold in Prussian Germany any more easily than they did in Poland. And so, they actually have nothing to lose that they would not lose anyway, regardless of whether one result or the other comes about. The only possibility for any success in this matter is if a sufficiently large number of people launch this protest out into the world. Even today, this protest would be as effective as if Kühlmann[†] had simply stood up at the proper time before the German Reichstag and presented the whole threefolding prospectus against the ideas of Wilson. For in the future, it will not be a matter of achieving compromised victories, but rather of standing stalwartly for something of meaning that you have taken from the matter for yourself. And if it would only happen, fostered by the fact of this vote, that a relatively small number of people—it really needs to be, of course, thousands—cried out into the world, "We, as Upper Silesians, see that it is absurd to annex to one side or the other," people would hear that throughout the world. It would become a factor throughout the world because it would have been generated by the fact that it was connected to this vote. We must strive to publish what we have to say week after week in something like the journal *The Threefold Social Organism,*[†] where it can be as full of spirit as possible; however, it will be circulated only through decreasing, inward-flowing waves. We must also see to it that wherever something important is happening in the world the threefolding movement has a voice; that it does not simply stand on the sidelines of world events, but rather seeks the moments in which something can really be done, because humanity is simply hypnotized by the other things that are happening. Do you believe the Allied Powers will take notice of the threefold movement if we do nothing but circulate threefolding here in theory? No, their eyes are hypnotized by things like the Upper Silesia vote. What thousands of people say in connection to such things will help the others see what they would otherwise overlook.

These are the things that we must pay particular attention to in the present moment here. Of course, should it not be possible to win over a sufficiently large number of people, then under the present circumstances there is nothing left but for our friends to say, "Someday, the threefold movement will indeed move beyond its birth pangs into reality, and within the German population perhaps, of necessity, an understanding for threefolding will develop; and so we will vote provisionally for annexation by Prussian Germany in the hope, however, that this Prussia will fall away." But this is only a surrogate solution, and to it we would then append the conditions under which we suffer. What we must look toward is winning people to our cause who can be active within our movement, who can be active in the sense of our threefold movement. And in this regard (and we cannot keep silent about this), we have not been working with enough force or effectiveness. Currently, we are lacking supporters who can do work in every region where we need them. The people that we do have are certainly energetic workers, but actually, there must be such people everywhere. They would perhaps need a thirty-six-hour day, if not a sixty-four-hour day, or more. The few people within our ranks who do effective work are aware of this. We need more and more people; and if we succeed in getting more and more people, then we will indeed arrive at an advancement of the threefold movement in Central Europe, one with which something can really be done. But we should not let such an auspicious moment pass by unutilized, in which we could really show the world what threefolding is all about. The world would concern itself with threefolding if we could make use of it. If the things that the Upper Silesian task signifies for us were known, the world would concern itself to an unprecedented degree with the threefold movement; and we must bring this about, for without it we will not get anywhere in the future.

This is what must be especially emphasized by those who have now taken it upon themselves to campaign for our concerns within the Upper Silesian population; this is what they must inscribe upon their hearts. We cannot say that the threefold movement should, in general, be expanded, because this is impossible right at the beginning. You see, with the threefold movement in the background, I had once, during the so-called World War, brought things about in such a way that someone was campaigning heavily for the establishment of an organized news service in Zurich during the war.† I was able to make it clear to someone that nothing could be accomplished on the basis of the old press relationships. The matter had progressed so far that, on a Tuesday (I have had to relate this story again and again), I was told, "It appears to be very likely that in the next few days you will be able to relocate to Zurich to set up the news service." But on the next day, the refusal came from the headquarters, which was indeed all-powerful, advising me that so many people in Germany were waiting on such a post that it could not really be earmarked for an Austrian. Now, we need only to think about such things in order to get a feeling for how all of the words that were once spoken out of the idealism of our time no longer have any meaning, for how we must look at things when they become clear to us in the light of the threefold movement. If only the call could someday sound in the way I have described, then things would happen.

You see, you must be clear about the fact that until now the hindrance to a furthering of humanity that is now going forward consisted of the fact that the actual spiritual movement was for many long centuries bound up in external power relationships, in external constellations. Just think about the fact that the whole step forward of the bourgeoise, and along with this, everything that we achieve in our arts and sciences; that all this was basically connected with the formation of the nation-states. That is, it was because the states were leading that the whole upsurge of the last centuries took place. Finally, people are in a position to no longer take what comes from the states as the directive force. They turn toward the old state, which is now supposed to lead. This old state will fail, regardless of whether it is undercut by social democracy, Bolshevism, or some intellectual group or another, it will always fail the peasants of the world. Very interesting studies of this can be made in Switzerland, for example. In Switzerland, when the people were very near to a revolution,[†] it was the peasants who fought against it. The Swiss have only the peasants to thank for the fact that the impending revolution did not break out. Here we have quite clearly the opposition between the general peasantry and what arises in individual cultural classes: these were the states, this was the state, and so forth. Only in Russia did the matter turn out differently. The 600,000 people who are now in the throes of the Bolshevist birth pains in Russia are not the ones who brought this about; what has arranged for this situation is that the whole mass of the peasantry dotes upon Lenin, and that this mass believes that they have some hope of receiving land. This peasantry believes that only if Lenin stays will things be completed in such a manner. If Lenin falls, then they will not get their land.

What is the one single solution within this great cultural question lying in humanity's future? Naturally, this culture is dependent on there being spiritual leaders present. We can formulate it thus: until now these spiritual leaders had to look back to particular power constellations, back to the villages, back then to the cities, had to look back to the being of the state because there was no sentiment present for creating a kind of organization that by way of its very recognition would be directive in and of itself. And this is the possibility for allowing the sources of high culture to realize themselves: creating such an organization, independent from all other social constitutions. And between this spiritual organism and the broad economic organism, the rights-political organism would stand, just as the rhythmic circulatory system stands between the nervous system and the metabolic system. The only solution to the question of the future is the establishment of a spiritual life that will work directly through itself. You can see work that has been done on this in my book *Towards Social Renewal*.[†] Only the creation of this spiritual organism will lead us forward. In the moment that we allow ourselves to fall backward by pleading for the creation of a spiritual aristocracy, we do not understand the matter at hand. The Catholic Church when it is commensurate with the old relationships is finally just such an organization. It is independent from the state organization, and so on, but it no longer has a mission; its mission is done. The fact that it can be organized into such a large pseudo-power lies in the independence of the institution from external power relationships. To that end, such a spiritual organization, independent of everything except itself, must be created. Understanding of this must be awakened in people. And if we find the right way of doing it, this understanding can be awakened, for it is no longer the pre-war proletariat alone that makes up the wide-reaching lower class; rather, other classes have already been forced down into it, and our present task is to win them over, paying no regard to their class standing. But not by preaching our ideas; instead, when there are concrete matters to attend to, we must handle them in accordance with those ideas.

Question and Answer Session

Stuttgart, January 2, 1921

Several questions have already been presented to me, and I think that you may also, in the course of our discussion, bring forward what lies in your hearts. First of all, we have some of the important questions posed already:

How should activists relate to the Catholic Church?

Well, it is really a matter, first of all, for as long as you can, you will find it necessary not to relate to the Catholic Church at all, but rather, for as long as you can, to remain as close to the matter as possible and avoid stepping onto the field that will cause you to touch upon the Catholic Church at all. This question naturally amounts to something different in the areas that you are reckoning with here than in other areas of Europe. To that end, you will of course not be able to maintain the same attitude toward the Catholic Church that people have in the regions that could be brought into some sort of relationship to the Polish being. You must consider that for the evolution of Poland, the Roman Catholic Church has had an unusually large significance. The Polish being has taken up the Western Catholic religion and melded it very strongly with all of Polish culture. Whereas the rest of Europe has freed itself altogether from the religious confessions in many branches of human life, namely the spiritual life, the Catholic confession continues to play a very significant role in Polish life. Is it not the case that the life of *Bildung* in Europe in the last century took place under the sign of the emancipation from church life? You must of course consider that this life of *Bildung* was able to keep itself free of the influence of the Catholic Church to a certain extent, because of the fact that the upper class simultaneously ignored it in order to win influence over the lower classes of the population, which just yesterday I had to present to you as particularly unfortunate.

You see, we must take up something other than just the region currently under consideration so that, by way of comparison, we can better understand what we are really dealing with. I would like to start with a concrete phenomenon. You see, for those who, like I, recently came over into Germany from Austria, (so around the end of the 1880s, and the start of the 1890s), for us the German *Gymnasium*† seemed, in its inner division, particularly regarding the material taught, to be fundamentally backward when compared to the Austrian school system. The Austrian upper school system (not the elementary school system, but the *Gymnasium* and the *Realschule*†) was actually established in the 1850s under the leadership of Leo Thun.† He was Minister of Religion and Education, who would most happily have left the whole of Austrian administration to the church. As he went about the *Gymnasium* reforms, he created an objectively founded but also church-approved constitution that was then ruined by the pseudo-liberal regime. When I opposed the pseudo-liberal regime of Herr von Gautsch† at the end of the 1880s, people always responded to me with the fear that this protest might lead us back to clericalism. This same phenomenon expresses itself by other means as well, namely that the school books used during my youth, especially those used for the more scientific and mathematical subjects, were all written by Benedictine monks. And when other people began to write books, the books became abstract, bureaucratized, whereas the books written by the Benedictine monks were actually very good textbooks. In connection with the political, the liberalism in Austria has to be connected back to the emancipation from the Catholic Church. It came about as a branching off from the Catholic Church. A certain process of freeing the spiritual life was hindered in Europe by the founding of Protestantism. Protestantism did not have a liberating effect on the spiritual life; rather it effected a step backward. Protestantism became popular to a certain degree. As a result, it made an impact on *Bildung*, which was then obligated always to take the apparently progressive Protestant religion into account; while already at the start of Protestantism, one was so removed from Catholicism that one had the feeling that one had to get away from it. If Protestantism had not been founded, people would have eventually gotten away from the Catholic principle. But then you know that Protestantism brought about a consolidation of the Catholic Church, through the Counter-Reformation, for example. The Jesuits were created as a reaction, as a counter to Protestantism. Now Protestantism has been incorporated into the life of the worldly educated to a very high degree. Take for example those individuals who worked as philosophers in Austria. For the most part, these were people who basically were not forced to recognize any sort of influence from the dogma of the Catholic Church and the like. You could prove, on the other hand, that Kantianism is really nothing other than Protestantism transformed into philosophy. This can be confirmed, that every single passage wherein Kant takes up the question of faith and knowledge, it is nothing other than the Protestant principle carried over into philosophy. This proves to us that Catholicism was on the road to dissolution, and that Protestantism then brought about its consolidation.

All of this continues to play a role in all of the phenomena that I described in my book *The Riddle of the Human Being*† in regard to Austrian spiritual life. This Austrian spiritual life was enabled solely by the fact that the church took no notice of it. A matter that would have been impossible in Protestant circles, where everything circulates through the church. I do not mean that the church literally plays a role in everything, but the whole way of thinking is circulated through the church. Even the school system in Protestant countries took on a pietistic, sanctimonious course, whereas the schools in Austria, for example, were free of this pietistic edge apart from the times when the appointed Fathers would conduct the hollow religion lessons. For example, the Austrians who are here would not be able to say, even though the younger of them have grown up under the liberal regime, that they noticed as much of the pure Christian confession in their history lessons or their geography lessons as one can notice in the German school system. This must all be noted of necessity. You see, at a certain point even the Benedictines laid great value on making things liberal; and the grasp of concepts, which had a great influence on human education in general, the formation of concepts went better under the formal Catholic influence than the subtle process of concept formation (which often, however, did not really grasp the matter at hand) within Protestantism.

Now, this all is true regarding Catholicism in areas that have nothing to do with Poland. Poland, on the other hand, took on Catholicism at a time when it was very strong, and thus its own unique *Bildung* melded strongly with Catholicism. But it created something different, and this is what first creates the strength of the Polish being within Catholicism and also fundamentally strengthened the Polish national being: the Poles understood to nationalize the clergy. The Polish clergy is also Polish-national, and it thinks, feels, and senses as such. But now we find ourselves standing before the fact that the Catholic Church is thinking about increasing its power by all means available to it. Protestantism as such is on its last breath. I mean that you should not give in to any confusion about this: world-historically, it is in its final stages; it has dogmatized itself as a religion of confession; has degenerated into a workplace for preachers. A church will never be able to survive if it bases itself solely on the preaching of dogma. Churches can exist only as ritual, as that which abandons dogma. The Catholic Church does not fundamentally lay itself upon dogma in its own constitution, and here I am drawing your attention to something that absolutely must be kept in mind.

Among anthroposophists there are always well-intentioned people who nevertheless place a certain value on thinking past the facts. Sometimes, it is even a kind of compulsion to think past the facts. And in the area that interests us right now, this expresses itself in that anthroposophists like to emphasize that we will befriend some religious confession, the community attached to some confession, by getting as close to them as possible. In the case of the Catholic, you can actually greatly increase your enmity with them when you try to get close to their dogma. The Catholic Church will only hate another community more when they find some similarity with them, or if they find at all that Christian truth is being sought. For the Catholic Church has as its goal the careful avoidance of Christian truth and the maximal increase of its own power. This is the goal of the Catholic Church. You will not move them by becoming more Christian. You can only reconcile yourself to them by simply being a man who, like a Roman, can swear by the Catholic Church. There is no other way to reconcile yourself to them.

Now, the church feels that in the face of current events, that they believe they can fundamentally increase their power. It knew well that building upon the dynasties would not be able to help it much, because it is typically more well-informed than others. It also knows that those dynasties which still have the crown on their heads are dying out. So they do not want to connect themselves to things that are on the decline. On the other hand, the church will use the upward striving of the broad masses to increase its own power. And the Catholic Church makes use of everything that might be at their disposal, and so it is now utilizing, in its great world politicking (which sometimes has a kind of genius about it; genius in the sense that it manages to bind humanity ever tighter in the chains of Rome). It is utilizing something like the nationalization of the Polish clergy; and Poland will become a major player in the actions of the Catholic Church. In other words, the Catholic Church will see, in my opinion, something in the process of nationalization that they will then want to incorporate into their games with world politics. So above all, it is important to always be aware of the things that are coming out of the church, but to go against the church as little as possible, unless you are obligated to go on the defensive. For example, in Switzerland, we had to go on the defensive.† But what is important is that we work on the basis of the matter at hand and ignore the church, let it alone, as long as it does not attack us. It will of course, because its task is get rid of everything in the world that is not Catholic—it will attack us; but we should avoid having contact with it for as long as we can. But then, when it is no longer to possible to relate to the Church in such a way that we can simply ignore it, then it is important that we not engage in any sort of discussion of dogma. In the moment that we engage with dogma, we will actually be playing a losing game; because the heart of matter is not that we somehow prove the dogma of the Catholic Church to be false. If you just take the foundational dogma, ignoring all of the things that have come about due to political circumstances, you find that all of it leads back into a very gray antiquity. And if you start to understand these foundational principles, you come to respect them. The detriments of the Catholic Church are not to be found in its dogma, but rather in the fact that this dogma is misused. And in any case, by way of the unusually large tradition that it has, it is able to defend its dogma more sagely, by way of an incredibly precise logic (of the sort that we might wish for the German philosophers, who do not have it), it can defend itself better than one is able to attack it. The only thing that can be done then is to present to the wider world the Catholic Church in all of its moral weakness. For example, in Switzerland, we limited ourselves to proving that the members of the Catholic Church spread lies about us. Members of Protestant confessions do this to the same extent, of course. They all rely entirely on lies and a false presentation of the matter. Now, what is important is that you always find opportunities to expose these people as liars. Nowhere will you find so many lies as you will within the members of the religious confessions, and therefore it is necessary for us to seize upon this point and to see how we can go about proving their deceitfulness to others.

Is it not the case that there is a certain stratification when it comes to lies? In the first position are the Churches, in the second is the press, and in the third are the politicians. This is a totally objective description and does not come out of any sort of emotion. The enthusiasm for lying is called upon by those things that one can receive only through a church upbringing. The enthusiasm for lying in the press is called up by social relationships; and in politics, I would suggest that lying is actually just a continuation into civilian life of something that is quite understandable within the military (and politics is intimately connected with the military). If you want to conquer an opponent, you have to deceive him. The whole strategy depends on it; you have to learn to deceive others. That is how the system works. Through the relationship between the military and politics, this is carried over into civilian life. But in the military it is a method; and in the other classes (in the press and in the members of the religious confessions) it is an enthusiasm for lying. Describing these things in this way is not radicalism; it is simply an objective fact. The harmful thing is that a large part of humanity has not come to recognize, through human judgment, that it is actually impossible to be within a religious confession and speak the truth. You see, one can become a tragic individual within a religious confession; but one cannot hold an office within a confession and speak the truth. Nowadays, this is altogether impossible, and so I would like to suggest that our attitude toward the Catholic Church can be expressed as follows: ignore the aspirations of the Catholic Church as much as possible, and concern ourselves with revealing deceitfulness in individual instances. Then we will at the very least clear the way for a path offered by the facts.

QUESTION: The first thing that was considered was making the appeal to the people in German; but advertisements were given to the Polish newspapers. Would it be advisable to distribute the appeal in Polish?

RUDOLF STEINER: I would think that it would be good, even if the appeal could be distributed only in a very limited way, to also have it in Polish and to distribute it in Polish as well, as much as possible. It seems absolutely necessary to me that we emphasize the international quality of this whole action in that way.

HERR M. BARTSCH:† The Upper Silesians are fighting like cats and dogs, and if we turn first of all to the big cities, where almost seventy percent of the population is German, we believe that these people will have some prejudice against us if they hear that the appeal has also been published in Polish. We want to win them to our side and then go public with the appeal in Polish. But we can go along with the other recommendations made here in the last few hours.

RUDOLF STEINER: When it comes to a second and third advance, it will not depend exclusively on a German majority. In the country, we will most likely be dealing with an outspoken Polish majority, and it will be necessary that we also succeed in working out this question with those people in the country. In that case, we will have to have a Polish language appeal.

RESPONSE: The Silesian Pole unfortunately cannot read standard Polish, and only understands the so-called *Wasserpolak*.† So we can only turn toward the leading circles.

RUDOLF STEINER: Naturally, it is not necessary to have a version of the appeal in Polish if, during the agitation, you find yourselves in the company of people who all understand German, including the Poles. But in any case, we must have a Polish version so that when it is needed, we have it on hand. You should also have a version that the people in the country can read.

RESPONSE: They cannot read Polish at all, not even the *Wasserpolak*. The speakers even speak German to them, because they cannot make themselves understood with their standard Polish.

RUDOLF STEINER: But in principle, there must also be a version of the appeal in Polish. Care could be taken in its distribution. There is a certain delicateness about this. We got a very good idea of this in Austria where people abominated the others, and then it was impossible to get anywhere. The Czechs, for example, mostly understood the German language. In Bohemia, we had the same situation that you are now confronting in Poland. But in that case, the most harmful thing that was done was that the Czechs were not taken enough into consideration.

QUESTION: How can it be expressed to the Poles that they have received economic stimulus from the Germans?

RUDOLF STEINER: I think that this is something that our friends must know from life experience. For a certain mercantile stream is dominant precisely in those individuals who have gradually found their way into the Polish being and into the German being, and who, precisely by way of this turn, have acquired an economic sensibility. The easy mobility of the Polish soul life effected this change, and I believe that one could simply prove, by studying the mercantile life, how strongly the Polish element has affected it in the areas where both Polish and German is spoken, so much so that we can see that those Poles who have learned German are more savvy businessmen than the Germans themselves. This is something that you could prove. And these people are the sort of businessmen that you would not be able to find within Polish society itself. Just compare them with how non-business-oriented a Pole is, for as long as he remains just a Pole. Then think about what will become of him when he receives a German influence. This must naturally be proved out of direct life experience, but it can be proved.

QUESTION: Would it be advisable to set down a unified resolution from this gathering, wherein the threefold social organism is presented to the public as a new possibility, or to send such a resolution over to the Entente commission?

RUDOLF STEINER: As far as something like that goes, it would be best if something were to arise spontaneously from the congress itself, rather than being developed artificially. That would be best, if it were not necessary to artificially write up some resolution, but rather if such a resolution were to arise from the gathering. I do not know if you have noticed whether people there are leaning in that direction or not. I do not believe that it would be such a bad thing if a resolution were not set down word-for-word. On the other hand, it could be very significant if someone were to arrange things, with no concern for the results, such that people could express their opinions in a sort of vote about what is really important here. Something like, if someone could bring it about in as careful a manner as possible, allowing people to say that they would like to take into consideration the idea of a protest against the vote. Then, of course, what must follow, in the case that the action would be brought about by succeeding in finding a sufficient number of people, is that a registry of the protesters be made up. This must be made up only after the vote.

QUESTION: Should news of this be brought to the Telegraph Union?†

RUDOLF STEINER: I do not believe there is any reason not to. That should certainly be done. But perhaps someone else knows better.

RESPONSE: It has recently come to our attention that the Telegraph Union has close ties with Stinnes,† and reservations have been expressed about having any sort of relationship with the Telegraph Union.

RUDOLF STEINER: The Telegraph Union will perhaps refuse us. It must be disposed to finding a means of launching these things into the daily press.

RESPONSE: No doubt about that.

RUDOLF STEINER: Granted, and even if a relationship exists between the Telegraph Union and the Stinnes venture, I do not see why there should be any reservations about turning our news, which we have decided should be passed along, over to the Telegraph Union. If, for example, a Jesuit institution were to stoop to bearing our news out into the world, would we have any reason not to give our news to the Jesuits?

RESPONSE: Stinnes himself once spoke about an organization that was more or less tantamount to the associations you mentioned, and this is well-known in proletarian circles. If the thoughts of threefolding were now to appear in this press, they would perhaps be filled with distrust.

RUDOLF STEINER: If you pay attention to such things nowadays, then you barely will be able to do anything in the world. You can have reservations about any action if you take issue with making use of a usance (it is a usance, plain and simple, if you turn toward the Telegraph Union) in one way or another. I do not see any way of avoiding a distrusting response from some people. You would have to set up your own telegraph service. There is barely any connection between the Telegraph Union and what we want from it, or what its connections are to the Stinnes group.

QUESTION: How should one relate in general to the Entente commission?

RUDOLF STEINER: In that case, the matter is such that one can say that however one relates to it, this direct relationship to it will have no great significance. For this commission has every reason, at the moment, to remain entirely neutral; and for the time being it will not deal with anything that opposes its intentions. In fact, it is naïve to think that you can really achieve anything at all with the Entente commission. The only thing that we could do would be, as we have already said, to simply communicate the matter to the Entente commission, if we felt like doing so; meaning we simply say: this is what we are presenting. This is the only thing that could be considered, but counting on the

Entente commission in any way is impossible. Should one go before them? In what form? When? I say that if you simply want to inform them about this, then you could go before them. If someone were to be so strong as to be capable of negotiating with them, then let there be a conversation about it. However, we will not be able to bring it to much more than a demonstration that would perhaps strike deep into the will of humanity. And we must be satisfied with that. But we cannot ever wish that the Entente commission will gain a real influence. We must remain independent from it.

QUESTION: Where can one find some basic information in the published literature for what was said in the first lecture.

RUDOLF STEINER: This is the general question that can be related to everything in history. It is possible nowadays to gain enlightenment about the true course of European history only by attempting to seek things out without consideration for any corresponding presentation of history. So I have to say that if you are looking for the literature that relates to what I spoke about, almost everything which literature offers is a proof of what I said; you just have to read between the lines. There is no specific literature for it, but all historical literature points toward it. You need only to see the matter in the proper light. If you limit yourself to taking a person like Lamprecht[†] or the like at his word, then you will have not material for proof. But if you look at what is written between the lines, then you will find the supporting documents everywhere. Pointing toward any specific literature is unnecessary.

QUESTION: What form should the promotion in the region outside of Upper Silesia take? Special issues of the newspaper? Brochures and so on?

RUDOLF STEINER: Exceptional care must be taken, of course. Naturally, people could somehow take a position from outside on how the question of Upper Silesia should be decided. Still, I think that a definitive intervention from outside the movement itself could be incredibly disruptive. Some sort of intervention in the threefolding newspaper, a direct agitating intervention could, under certain circumstances, disrupt the movement considerably. On the other hand, I would consider it useful, once our friends have begun to work energetically on this, to make the world aware of what is happening, and in such a way that they do not believe that the movement was transported in from the outside; for that would be a great detriment, if people were to believe that this matter was brought into Silesia from without. The Silesians would not tolerate this, and the world would say, "People from outside should not get involved in internal affairs."

Question: Silesia plays a large role in economic relations. Would it be possible to achieve a reciprocal relationship, by way of a proper report of everything happening in Upper Silesia?

Rudolf Steiner: We can try our best. In a news report, we could bring in the economic consequences for the world; and indeed this is something that unfortunately, due to a lack of time, we could not discuss in detail. It is also true that one would be able to show what sort of economic consequences it would have for the world if Upper Silesia, as we suggested, refused to be annexed to either Poland or Prussia. This would allow the economic life of Upper Silesia to be freed. It is my opinion that this would win over the sympathies of the world, and as regards the economic realm would also be heavily endorsed by the world. But apart from that, the direct economic consequences are still to be expressed. Only through the realization of what we want will economic freedom come about. Otherwise, politics will weigh heavily on Upper Silesian economics. In this regard, articles could also be written to show what the world stands to gain from the liberation of Upper Silesian economics. But I would think that one should not write with the direct tone that one thing or another should be done. If you start now, if the protest in Upper Silesia begins, then it must proceed step by step, otherwise there is no point. As such, it will naturally be the case that articles can quickly be published that express the questions upon which you base your protest, taking the protest as its starting place. If people reproach us for the fact that this whole thing comes out of the organization for the threefold social organism, we should not try to get around this. But in the moment that people recognize (and the world must be given an insight into this), that the threefold movement is not something that belongs to Stuttgart, but rather something that is just as applicable to somewhere else; that it is, in fact, a human impulse; in that moment, no one can say that the people who are demonstrating in Upper Silesia did not arrive at the insight themselves. Threefolding is not something you import; it is a universal human matter.

RESPONSE: Perhaps in Germany one could, if one were to handle the vote with the utmost care, one could use the question of the vote as an object lesson?

RUDOLF STEINER: This is already stated in the appeal. This side of the question can be discussed everywhere, of course, for it is not limited to Upper Silesia. Someone who was properly initiated into these matters could also treat Czechoslovakia from this vantage point, for example, but not Alsace. During the war, Alsace offered a useful object lesson; but now it cannot, since it has come about that the Alsatians will not take a position on it at the moment. In this case, this perspective is held only outwardly. In Alsace, there is absolutely no discussion. The Alsatians are content to belong to France, just as they were content to belong to Germany. Before the war, the matter had to be described; there the possibility existed, the Alsace problem offered an object lesson. Nowadays, it is Czechoslovakia; it is Yugoslavia; it would also be the so-called Russian border countries, and above all Russia itself. Russia is the great object lesson of the present. If threefolding were known there, a very strong movement would be started. But nobody there knows about threefolding.

QUESTION: We had intended to mention the Kommende Tag[†] in the lectures.

RUDOLF STEINER: If you did that, it would of course be a good thing; that is something entirely different. You are free to say out of yourselves, "We want to see the question decided in this way and are going to mention it." It is important only that you not end up hearing the reproach that might be leveled against you because of this, that the rest of the world is deciding the question of Upper Silesia. In a certain sense, if we do not manage to achieve anything, it will be determined from without, even if there is a vote. For the vote is really just a decorative thing. For if the vote goes toward Prussian Germany, it is not at all clear what the Entente will say to that; on the other hand, should what I earlier described to you come to pass, and the vote goes in the direction of Poland, which is the less likely of the two possibilities for you, then the fate of Upper Silesians is clearly decided from without.

QUESTION: Can we give lectures in other places in Germany with titles like "Threefolding and the Question of Upper Silesia?"

RUDOLF STEINER: If you conduct them with the attitude that we have introduced here. If the lectures are corroborated by the example of Upper Silesia.

QUESTION: There is an organization called the "Society for Loyalist Upper Silesians." That Society should perhaps be informed of this; they would probably be very interested in the matter.

RUDOLF STEINER: This could probably happen by having the committee that has formed in Upper Silesia initiate something with them. The threefold movement can take over from there.

RESPONSE: A number of presentations regarding the question of Upper Silesia have been made by German national associations.

RUDOLF STEINER: The sorts of things that Herr Molt[†] gave me are not from the Silesians themselves. They are not something that is connected to any sort of inner truth. "A burning torch has been cast into the house of Germany, the fire teams are riding, their alarms sound through the Empire," and so on. Things like this are, of course, nothing more than a false front thrown up by the Germans. In that case, we are dealing with a conquest of the Upper Silesian ideals.

RESPONSE: The Upper Silesian populace has already become immune to this sort of false front. You do not see it at any of the gatherings anymore and we hope that thoughts are arising to which it can adhere.

RESPONSE: From the circles that are sending out those fliers, attacks against the threefold movement in general will result, and this could provide an opportunity to discuss threefolding.

RUDOLF STEINER: In that case, we are already thrown on the defensive. We cannot show up with any sort of conciliatory tone, but must be as energetic as possible. For the people from which things like that appeal come, the fight with the threefold movement is sure to happen. They will fight everything that comes from the threefold movement; for it already has a wide scope. These people are really overrated when it comes to their sense of the truth. A terrible strain of deceptiveness is what rules there.

HERR BARTSCH SENIOR: We would be grateful for support from other speakers from the rest of Germany.

RUDOLF STEINER: That can happen. If you call for them yourself, then we will do our best to see that speakers are there. The important thing to know is that our speakers have the task of interpreting threefolding. This can happen at any time. That could happen tomorrow, if you liked.

QUESTION: What is being done in Dornach about this? What is the outlook there?

RUDOLF STEINER: I believe that everything that comes directly from Dornach now (for as long as we do not have an obvious agitation within Upper Silesia itself), will only hurt the situation. Nothing can come from us in Dornach; it has to happen out of some sort of neutral side or from the Entente. In order to win people over, something can be done only once there is an agitation under direction in Silesia, one that has become publicly visible. I can neither tell you that something is already happening in Dornach (I cannot imagine what might happen, even); nor could I advise that something happen there before the agitation in Upper Silesia has begun. Once it has, then Dornach can undertake the things that need to happen in Germany.

QUESTION: Is it not advisable to really put the largest emphasis on the presentation of the big, encompassing ideas themselves, including in Silesia?

RUDOLF STEINER: These things must be allowed to flow into the matter at hand. But we cannot pass up any opportunity that presents itself to place the idea of threefolding in the proper light, for everything depends on the popularization of the threefolding idea. And as crucial as it is to address concrete relationships, it is just as urgent to bring forward the idea of threefolding in as many forms as possible; thus, we should never suppress it.

RESPONSE: What I mean is, not go into the details of everything, but focus on the big picture. I can imagine that if one were to speak about the question of wages, for example, this would not really have an impact; rather, one has to set up the whole historical backdrop. That is what I meant.

RUDOLF STEINER: This depends on whether threefolding lives in you in a very active way. The misstep that we so often make happens because as soon as people start to address threefolding, it takes on a utopian character. The threefold social organism is not utopian! But the discussion often takes on a terribly utopian character. There is no point in talking about what will happen to the seamstress or the painter in the threefold social organism. All of these things take on a necessarily utopian character. And if you want to campaign in Upper Silesia today and you start talking in this utopian style, then people will say to you, "Well, we really have other things to think about right now than what a future State might look like." Something does not become utopian by being fantastical and foolish; rather, it is utopian as soon as it cannot rationally be a part of the current agenda. This is why I have always used these things only as examples, and why I would not like to see them utilized further. The main thing is to understand the threefold social organism through and through. I organized my lecture yesterday in such a way as to show how threefolding makes it understandable that the Poles have become the way that they are. This penetration of the idea of threefolding into all the relationships of life is what is important; this is how an understanding of it will be called up. It is not a matter of details that one can sink one's teeth into. If you are asked about it, you cannot avoid it; but it would be false to speak of just those sorts of details in such a connection.

QUESTION: Would it not be good for the perspectives that have been offered to us during these two days to be disseminated in a brochure?

RUDOLF STEINER: If the brochures were distributed in Upper Silesia, that could be very useful. There are certainly perspectives that have been discussed here that could be distributed. Someone should make it quickly and send me one!

QUESTION: I feel always that the idea of threefolding is born out of the deepest and purest impulses that live in human nature. Now it is becoming clear that a counter-impulse is arising that leads to the development of an instinctive opposition. How should one deal with these sorts of controversies?

RUDOLF STEINER: You have to handle this question on a case-by-case basis. In general, much depends on whether we succeed in popularizing the idea of threefolding as such, independent of all sentimentality. You see, when it comes to well-meaning, sentimental thoughts of reform, the world is not lacking. If you could really better the world with only the kinds of things that appeal to that which is most noble in human nature, then someone would have succeeded in making the world a better place long ago. I can only respond with the same the thing that I have been saying to people for decades: with abstract ethical principles, you will accomplish about as much as when you speak to a stove with the categorical imperative, "You must make the room warm." That does not help. You can garnish your sermon beautifully with ethical words, but that accomplishes nothing. But it does help when you light the fire and stoke the stove, when you do what the thing as such calls for. The same is true of the threefold social organism. You have to make a case for it as best you can, and the people nowadays who have an inner opposition to the threefold social organism—as you say, out of an anti-ethical sense…

Question: Thus embracing the anthroposophical way of considering things in the same moment, I would say…

Rudolf Steiner: Well, indeed, then as soon as the spiritual-scientific foundations as such are attacked, you can do nothing more than defend them. What I am saying is true also of the foundations of anthroposophical spiritual science. Without those, we will not get anywhere, for the one means the other. A threefold social organism with the free spiritual life it calls for is imaginable only on anthroposophical preconditions. So just as the spiritual life will never be free without threefolding, so too will the threefold social organism be empty without the fructification of anthroposophy. We must always be bringing this into reality. Thus, we must not hesitate to defend anthroposophy as resolutely as we do the threefold social organism. We must stand fully on an anthroposophical foundation and bring about everything needed to realize it fully. There are people among us who say, "Anthroposophy is dead; threefolding lives!" Yes, that has been said to me several times. This, in my opinion, is the most baseless thing that one can say. The Threefold Social Order is just floating in the air without anthroposophy.

Response: I wanted to point out that I am hearing from many different sides that a particular need for anthroposophy exists right now.

Rudolf Steiner: There is a very strong need for anthroposophy, but over and against this need we must also emphasize the practical side of anthroposophy. For as soon as this need starts to tends toward a retreat from the world, we do great harm in emphasizing that need too strongly. The need to retreat from the world, which tends toward sectarianism, is something that we must not hesitate to fight. We must show that anthroposophy is both the way into the highest spiritual regions, and the way toward managing the physical world. We must emphasize this sharply, for otherwise it would be very easy to speak too much to the passivity of present day humanity. You see, people want to have anthroposophy because of a certain sentimental streak, because they would rather take a reproachful attitude toward the external world.

RESPONSE: I thought that the oppositional movement, this negative impulse, is often, practically speaking, far more active than the anthroposophical impulse in many people.

RUDOLF STEINER: That has to move in the direction that we have indicated.

QUESTION: I do not know how much the question has been discussed in the interim of how this action should proceed after the trial period of approximately eight days. It would be good if we were already considering how the matter might eventually proceed, depending on its success.

HERR BARTSCH SENIOR: If there is a need for further public discussions and lectures, then we will organize more gatherings. We will make contact immediately with the gentlemen so that this action might be further supported. We will see to it that talks are made in smaller localities, and in the larger ones perhaps again. It would be very good if we were to have speakers from outside come in and speak.

RUDOLF STEINER: It is important that the agitation be set in motion both through public lectures and through more private work in smaller circles. I imagine that you can only hope to try various things and eventually be able to glean from that the best method for proceeding. I also imagine that your valiant and courageous work will not stop before the vote is over. We are dealing with an either-or here: either you plunge in with the intention of taking this to the public, or you give up the whole thing. A tremendous amount depends on this matter. For example the question, "How do we bring the threefold movement out into the country, which until now has been a sort of riddle for us; for it is not so easy to get out there, because you have to have cause to do so." *This* question—for the Upper Silesians this question will be, if it succeeds, this question will be decisive. Because if you go out into the country to campaign about the vote, you will be able to win over some portion of the rural population. Then you are in, and have gained ground for the future. We are always looking for ways to penetrate into particular circles. We tried this to a large extent with the question of the workers' council.[†] It is only because we were flanked so strongly by the social Democrats on the one hand, and because we made some practical mistakes ourselves on the other, that the matter had to be buried; but the attempt must be made to gain a foothold, and we will only get it when we are able to come with concrete questions, because those can always be discussed.

QUESTION: What should be the guiding perspectives when dealing with the magnates and tycoons that are strongly allied with the Catholic Church?

RUDOLF STEINER: This is something that each individual must decide on a case-by-case, magnate-by-magnate basis. It would of course be desirable if they were to take up an action like this. But it is really a question of the utilization of personal influence and circumspection, so any sort of directive in regard to this matter can hardly be given. Because with the magnates, you always have to look for the right moment to address the proper thing. In this case, it will be a matter of seeing whether they are oriented more toward the Polish or the German. The two groups are fundamentally different from one another. Just as the lower classes are divided, so too (and to an even greater degree) are the Polish aristocracy divided from the German aristocracy. They understand each other far less than the lower classes, because they have very different habits and customs. And for those who are standing outside and considering the matter from without, for them, the Polish magnates and moguls have rubbed off on all of the rest of the aristocracy in a very strange way. I do not know what our friends in Silesia would say about that. But in my opinion there is a particular streak in the Silesian magnates where you can see how the Polish being has rubbed off on them. This aspect of that class, which differs so greatly between the Pomeranian and the Silesian magnates, can by and large be traced back to the proximity of the Polish element. So you see, sometimes selection plays a role; but you can be quite sure (and you need not take this personally), an aristocrat in economic life like Count Keyserling is possible in Silesia, but would not be among the Pomeranian aristocracy. This rubs off on the rest immediately. Because the Poles take up economic life so fully, it rubs off immediately. This terribly resilient, absolutely certain conviction about their own being exists in the Poles, and this has a suggestive effect on all the surroundings. Who could have succeeded, for example, in doing what the Poles managed to do in the Austrian parliament? A reactionary movement came about in the schools. The whole set of prior public school regulations was to be rewritten with reactionary intent. This under the minister that the parody comics wrote up as "Ta-affe."† So a reactionary school regulation came forward, and it was matter of making some sort of majority for the rewriting of these regulations out of this impossible conglomeration of parties who were sitting in the Austrian parliament. The Polish delegates were crucial for this majority. They agreed to this reactionary school regulation, but took Galicia out of it; they left that region to the old ways. Think about that: deciding on a reactionary school regulation for every region of Austria except Galicia, leaving Galicia out. This was their way of demonstrating that they recognized something very terrible in these regulations and were imposing it on the rest of Austria. This sort of thing is possible only in Poland. Of course, the same sort of thing is true when it comes to the good things as well.

QUESTION: What are we to make of the Pope's decree that priests should not take part in the vote in Upper Silesia?

RUDOLF STEINER: This is ultimately a question that can only be posed to Rome, for the Catholic Church possesses precisely that thing that I was stressing earlier. Nowadays, it has a pronounced world political orientation, and so every individual fact plays a marked role in it. But you can be sure that if the Catholic Church has issued such a decree, then in the Church's mind it has great significance. Exactly what they are hoping to achieve by this is a question that only Rome can answer. But for us it is of no consequence, because in this case, we are in agreement with the Catholic Church. What I mean is, it is inconsequential for us in the sense that we cannot change our position on the matter just because the Catholic Church has proposed the same thing for their clergy.

It would be going far too far to construe some sort of cohesive picture on the part of the Catholic Church. It has an entirely different set of intentions, and the Church makes decisions simply on the basis of probabilities. What the Church wants is by and large easy to see. It wants to gain influence in Silesia, regardless of how the vote turns out; if it is abstaining from the vote, that means that it knows the result is uncertain. If the vote was definitely going to be in favor of Poland, then the clergy would definitely side with that. This is the only thing that is interesting to us about this matter. Otherwise, however, the results can just take their natural course. So the Catholic Church might, when it sees that the supporters of the threefold movement are also staying neutral, put on a friendly face. I ask you to remember that this is not genuine friendliness. You will fall into a terrible pitfall if you take it seriously.

Well, my dear friends, we are reaching the end of our considerations, and I would like to stress once more that for our movement for the threefold social organism, much depends on what you will do in regard to this question; not so much on what you might achieve, but rather on the actions that you take. In other words, whether you are able to make visible to the world what we are striving after. It could of course make a difference for the energy behind the implementation of the threefold social organism if one thing or another is done in a particular region. But when such a question as this one hangs in the balance, then what is important to emphasize is that very much depends on what you have before you to do for our entire threefolding movement. And we all will certainly have good cause to exert ourselves on behalf of the threefold social organism with the most lively, energetic thoughts, as well as (I hope) cause to follow with active offers of help everything that you will be undertaking in the coming weeks, in this most exceptionally important corner of the world. We need only to think of the significance it would have if the matter in Upper Silesia were to develop in the way indicated by our appeal. We can hardly dare to allow ourselves this thought; but if it were to come about that a genuine attempt was made, even once, to move toward a threefold social organism in some area, even provisionally—this would be an enormous step forward, because it would affect the threefold movement in such an intensive way to have a model present somewhere. You must remember that we are always extremely limited when it comes to presenting threefolding in all of its practicality. We can agitate on its behalf—and indeed, this is the most important thing, the most absolutely critical thing that we can do. Because only when the idea of threefolding is there in as many human minds as possible will something truly comprehensive occur; but we must start by developing something practical. Until now, the only thing that exists with a purely threefolded culture is the Waldorf School.[†] That is really something that, by the fact of its very constitution, works pedagogically in the spirit of the threefold social organism, because we stand vigilant watch at the doors to keep out all external pedagogy and didacticism.

We cannot point to something like the Kommende Tag as an example of a purely threefold culture. The Kommende Tag is there to generate promotion for the threefold movement in such a way that people can see that those of us who are in the threefold movement are people who can manage things well financially. But how little the world is inclined to turn toward the idea of threefolding, particularly in the practical realm, has been shown to us from the start, in the fact that every time the possibility has existed to establish the threefold social organism, the most severe opposition has appeared. Very practical advice could have been given to the ministers in Württemberg. Since the spring of 1919, when the parliament would have been very easy to convince, it would have been very easy for them to do something. They would have been able to carry out what I recommended: dissolve the spiritual life on the left, the economic side on the right, and hang on to what is left over. Then it all would have happened with absolute simplicity, for this is the thing: that spiritual life seek self-regulation, and that economic life aspire to self-regulation. The economic life at the time would have taken up the cause with unusual enthusiasm. The participants in German spiritual life (that is, the official German spiritual life) my dear friends, carry out actions like making Hindenburg† the honorary doctor of all departments of the German academy; but deeds of real consequence, we must expect these less and less, the higher we climb in the hierarchy of earthly spiritual life. It is no different in Switzerland. The public school teachers in Switzerland have taken up our cause well. As soon as you go into the higher schools—we might say that the principles go down the more you go up—there is a marked increase in the idiocy of people's concepts. It is already quite severe in the *Gymnasium* teachers, and it is immeasurable in the University professors. I mean the concepts that people use to understand the matter at hand. So we are necessarily limited in what would be the most crucial thing for us: in the proof of how this works in practical life.

You will do an unbelievable amount for the threefold movement, the more you bring it into the relationships that already exist in the world. If you can only bring it about that a very large number of people—so large that it would be demonstrable to the world—have it in their heads that Upper Silesia must strive provisionally for threefolding and if you have the possibility of leading people to remain true to the sign of the threefold social organism and to look with enormous regret at the fate of Upper Silesia, whether it annexes to Poland or to Prussian German, then you will perhaps have given to these people something of tremendous usefulness from the threefold movement. We absolutely need people who understand that the matter is entirely different when one is sympathetic to the threefold movement; we need people who say, "The fate of the future depends upon the threefold social organism." We stand now before an either-or scenario: either the world grasps the idea of threefolding, or the world goes the way that Spengler† predicted. The world hangs in the balance between these two poles.

My friends, go now to Upper Silesia, work upon people's hearts with the thoughts that I have presented to you, and rest assured: on the basis of these thoughts, we will accompany your actions. We extend our hands to you faithfully as you undertake these actions, and as we disperse now to understand so important a matter, we are conscious of the fact that we have spoken about and resolved upon something that is of incredible importance to our threefold movement and to the future of humanity. With this in mind, we should disperse now to undertake our next actions.

Appendix

Newspaper Appeal for the Rescue of Upper Silesia

Rudolf Steiner's Notes on the Training Course for Speakers

NEWSPAPER APPEAL

Appeal for the Rescue of Upper Silesia

Upper Silesians! People of Europe!

Should—to the torment of the populace, the detriment of the economy, the obliteration of all culture—the strife in Upper Silesia, the hidden public internal battle become a lasting condition? Shall Upper Silesia remain the center of a constant threat to Europe?

No! But how can this be prevented?

The question of Upper Silesia is a question for Europe. The thoughts and wishes of the whole of Europe turn on the economic thriving of industry, and particularly on the coal reserves in Upper Silesia. Upper Silesia is a decisive factor for the course of Europe's economic crisis. The spiritual-cultural problems and tasks of this region, as a middle ground between Eastern and Central Europe, have great weight. The spirituality of the Upper Silesian populace can only have the proper effect once a real solution to the question of nationality is found. Were that solution found, it would be a decisive victory for the inception of a whole new age of relations between populations.

The healing of political and state relations is also an absolute necessity for European interests if Upper Silesia is not to become an unsettling threat that constantly calls the status of European peace into question.

So the problem of Upper Silesia is a question of economic, rights-political, and spiritual-cultural healing for all of Europe. Versailles, St. Germain, and Spaa brought about nothing less than a solution for the European problem and social questions. But since the question of Upper Silesia can be solved only in a connection with a truly timely and complete reformation of European relationships, **no current solution to this question that is truly based in reality can be anything other than a temporary one. Therefore, just such a transitory condition must be consciously created in Upper Silesia.** Neither Wilson's well-known (but ungrounded) 14 points, whose application is a complete impossibility, particularly in the East, nor the violent methods of a prior epoch can lead to a reconstruction of European life. We can arrive at this new construction only when we are clear about the fact that we are dealing with **three different areas:**

Economic Life
Rights-Political Life
Spiritual-Cultural Life

Until now, these three areas have been amalgamated in the State, and it is from this confusion that the chaotic conditions of the present ultimately emerged. The only realistic form of social life must thereby consist in the liberation and independence of these three regions. The path to this is pointed out by the threefold social organism.

The threefold social organism demands that the state release from its power the economic life on one side and the spiritual life on the other.

The only things that belong in economic life therefore are the production of goods, the distribution of goods, and the use of goods—all of which are to be carried out by experts working on an "associational foundation." Uninhibited by state and political powers, the producers and consumers working together in various countries would see to it that all needs are being met.

The spiritual limb in the threefold social organism encompasses science, art, religion, and the whole of the educational and judicial system. All of these spiritual-cultural factors can carry out their task and properly fructify the social life only in full independence from state influence. The spiritual life, the culture, must take form out of the free cooperation of all spiritual-creative individuals and establish its own administrative body.

To the middle limb of the social organism, the rights-political part, is left first and foremost the police and administrative activities, carried out on a foundation of rights; it is regulated by a democratically-elected parliament. Since this parliament takes up only purely state or political questions, it cannot disturb the economic or the spiritual life.

(All details about the threefold social organism can be found in the book *Towards Social Renewal* by Dr. Rudolf Steiner, the journal *The*

Coming Day from A. G. Press, Stuttgart, Champignystraße 17, as well as the weekly newspaper from the same press, *The Threefold Social Order,* and the rest of the recommended literature.)

Only by way of such a threefolding of the social organism in Europe will the progress of the economic be able to occur independent of political state borders, crossing them according to its own regulations. By the same token, the spiritual exchange across borders between peoples divided by political borders is made possible in freedom, in a state independent of state powers.

Until such a healthy threefolding of the social organism is carried out in the whole of Europe, the question of Upper Silesia cannot be realistically brought to a final solution.

Precisely in Upper Silesia, the state of affairs cries out in a particularly strong way for such a threefolding.

Here, two cultures, two independent and individual populations, interpenetrated with one another, are fighting for the possibility of surviving. Education and the judicial system are the two most important points that lead to friction. Only through the liberation of the spiritual life can these two burning questions be solved in Upper Silesia. Then the two cultures, the German and the Polish, will be able to develop their life forces appropriately, without having to fear oppression by the other and without the political state grasping at one party or another. Not only individual academies, but also individual administrating bodies for cultural life will be able to erect a kind of nationality that does away with friction. And if the economic system in Upper Silesia were to be liberated from the state and political life, then the questions of Upper Silesia will allow themselves to integrate in the whole European economy, and to be solved only through the agreement of the economic experts of the separate countries.

At present then, the following is the only thing that makes any sense in reality, the only thing that makes life possible:

The Upper Silesian region temporarily refuses annexation to any bordering country until an understanding for the threefold social organism has awakened there. It constitutes itself in such a way that its economic factors administrate themselves, as do its spiritual factors. It shall create an agreement between both through a provisional

rights-political organization that extends only to the borders of this region and remain in this state until the clarification of the whole of European relations.

Although this situation is a temporary one, if it is brought about, it will serve as an example for the regulations that all of Europe must strive for in order to heal its relationships.

Believing that this appeal does not lie within the German spirit can only be the result of short-sightedness. True German sensibility has always thought in this manner.

And so, citizens of Upper Silesia, gather all the branches of your economic life together in free associations independent of the state! Declare your schools and your courts independent of the state and let them administer themselves! Establish a temporary, parliamentarian state for policing and administration until the European affairs establish a healthier foundation! The only thing that will help you is what you can press upon the Entente Commission with these demands. Everything else is worthless to you.

Association for the Threefold Social Organism.

Breslau Chapter

Speakers on threefolding and Upper Silesia from the Breslau chapter of the Association for the Threefold Social Organism can be reached at 16 Kaiser Wilhelm-Strasse, Breslau.

Published in *The Coming Day,* A.G. Press, Printed in Stuttgart

RUDOLF STEINER'S NOTES ON THE TRAINING COURSE FOR SPEAKERS

From Notebook, Archive No. 50, pages 269–299

I (2/12/21): Skepticism cannot be spoken in these lectures. It is assumed that in the impulse of threefolding the most urgent demand of the present is fulfilled. 1) One must speak out of love for the issue and out of love for humanity.—Imponderables—2) One must see through the false belief that the economic question can solve itself. 3.) One must have insight in the present for: 1) the insufficient understanding of spiritual productivity. 2) the insufficient interest for the *needs* of others. (p. 269)

A weak, merely observatory intellectualism is present. —Effect for as long as one speaks / the speaking cutout man. Discussion participants; thinking and acting—connected with each other / You can only speak: out of love of the issue—out of love for humanity / Difference of key interests of others. (p. 270)

Sameness of world-interests. Practical psychology in Germany!—Understanding out of foundational insight.—It is a matter of recognizing: 1) that the understanding of spiritual productivity has been lost. 2) that an interest in the needs of *other* people has vanished from economic life. One must be clear about this: if people suffer from cause, then they cause this lack. How this is carried out. (p. 271)

February 13th, 1921: Stuttgart: 1) The political-democratic element in England is disentangling itself from the religious-democratic element—but still the economic element is stuck there = private property and economic freedom—2) In Russia, the bourgeois element is being inserted into the hereditary system—3) Capital—Work—Nature / Administration—Parliament—Human being. / economic foundations—collective understanding—ability (p. 272)

It is necessary to only engage in economic relationships with these states.—All relationships with the East must be built upon the spiritual: the Russians have taken up the German spiritual life—but turned against the economic life— (p. 273)

In Europe, one has "solved" only those questions that were objectively "solved:" 1) the national [questions] decided since 1721 = absolutist 2) the economic-social [questions]: decided since 1763—anarchistic. Europe: no longer productive in spiritual life—In economic life the "rug has been ripped out from under its feet." (p. 274)

(p. 275) [blank]

1721 Asian-ism from the East: it is flooding Europe—1763 European-ism: it gives itself over to the West—then in the nineteenth century: in Europe, the theocratic element and economic danger. Oppositions West-East / spiritual: *technology* de-spiritualization in spirit. Spirituality of the *common man* / economic: human de-naturalization of nature / natural aspects of nature: the *abstract* man / For Europe, these great questions arise: 1) How does one arrive at a spiritual content 2) How should one organize political life. 3) How does practice economics so as not to do away with that which is human. (p. 276)

(p. 277) [blank]

Carried over from the religious in the political life—William III of Orange / transplanted to North America—Prussian: Great Elector. Army of civil servants—Russia: Europe: imitation. But such that something primitive remains: the theocratic. England: sea and trade power. Opposed to France, under Colbert—*then*: in the Seven Years' War against England and Prussia—1763: decree in America. (p. 278)

1721: Nordic War ends: Russia at the Baltic Sea. *Peace at Nystadt*: Sweden Russia / Sweden gives up: Livonia, Estonia, Swedish Ingria, Karelian Finland given up—bureaucratic aristocracy / *Treaty of Paris*: France gives up Louisiana, Canada— (p. 279)

Saving work: to displace someone in work (p. 280)

England: classes: right to approve unusual expenditures. *centralized / France / Germany* classes centrifugal / *England*: Sea power. Protestantism. Jacob I: 1603-1625 catholic political tendencies / independent parliament / Oliver Cromwell 1653-1658 / 1651 navigation papers of the Puritans (independents) / *Idea for a State*: Economic treatment of the idea for a state *Democratic Idea*: church-religious *then extricated* (p. 281)

The great questions of the present: 1) *The spiritual question*: Insufficient attempts from the old. Newmann in Rome. The independent spiritual life. In connection with technology. 2) *The rights-political question*: Everything that figures into the social life as work belongs here also. — 3) The *economic life* must externally encompass only commodities because this is all that it encompass inwardly. (p. 282)

Capitalism demands this independence—means of production. The modern era has made the labor force into a commodity because the dominant economic life can only tolerate commodities. Price: the correct price is there when the proper number of people are involved in the production of a product in the case of natural production. If consumption can be satisfied. (p. 283)

2nd *Theme*: The free educational life and the school system in its relationship to the state and the economy. 3rd *Theme*: 1) The economic system of associations and its relationship to the state and to the free spiritual life. 2) The *state* as protector. It has to carry out what the free spiritual life brings forward and gives form to. It stands in direct connection with the human aspect of people working spiritually. E.g. all appointments are matters of the free spiritual life. That the (p. 284)

appointees are accorded human rights is a matter of the state. Thus, everything is built finally on what people are capable of. — (p. 285)

3.) Constant trade as a part of the nature of trade. Commodities: need—attainable for a cost. Object of trade. Reciprocity—object of production: expertise / 1) Need 2) Human collectivity 3. Expertise (p. 286)

The economic question cannot be solved without the emancipation of the economic life—The political question necessitates the relationship between people — the spiritual question necessitates a productive spiritual life — the idea behind of spiritual production (p. 287)

The church—the states—the economic collectives. 1) Describe the being of the Waldorf School rooted in free spiritual life — draw attention to the opposing tendencies at present— (p. 288)

Beginning of the end — well worked through and then after recommendations — beginning with the obvious—every lecture should be new to the lecturer / Always paying attention to the object and the feeling of responsibility (p. 289)

Excess of births in Russia—debt to France—private economy—they work—public economy: they grow—*Grain*: Worth something when consumed—moves over into the substance of muscles, nerves, and brain — *Consumption*—? *Use* creates economic value (p. 290)

Commodities—as object of consumption—as object of trade / as object of production *Work*: (p. 291)

(p. 292)
North America South America—In South America: *fewer needs* / *Art*—created according to *demand.*—physical goods: in circulation / spiritual goods:

According to different kind: *spiritual*—it is need that should be generated—and the fulfillment is then present of its own accord—*physical*—it is the fulfillment that should be generated—the need is present of its own accord.— (p. 293)

(p. 294)
The world must know now what the works of the anthroposophic movement are. Schools—the movement in their being opposed to distortion.—Practical implementations = etc.—There is no view towards productive work—e.g. the teacher who makes his students more skillful—his *being* flows into the process—all of that must however be *assessed*: but "unemployment" wages?

(p. 295)
scientifically-oriented institutions

(p. 296)
Stuttgart, February 16, 1921: 1.) We cannot move forward unless the compulsory relationships are resolved into those of *free recognition.* 2.) *Associations*: they can originate in consumption. Their task is to recognize needs. 3.) Leadership in these matters comes out of the spiritual world. From the rights-political, the relationships between human beings. From the economic, the impulse for price determination.

(p. 297)
An individual should not assess his or her *own* spiritual significance.

(p. 298)
Property rent originally designated payment for the protection of a piece of land that was being used; was thus [crossed-out: *rights-political*] spiritual in origin—Then land and property became a *commodity*—The effect of the spiritual life on the question of need. The proletarian stands there with *only* an entirely general sense of need. He has no spiritual life generating specific needs—Life of associations: Need—labor is regulated—and also the question of capital.

(p. 299)
Land and property cannot never be allowed to move over into capital—if this capital does not circulate—Wage: detached from the individual—as is *capital—Newspaper for the Threefold Social Organism*

EDITORIAL AND REFERENCE NOTES

I
WORKING ON BEHALF OF THE THREEFOLD SOCIAL ORGANISM

A training course for speakers

Lecture 1

Page 6, "Take my book *Towards Social Renewal*"
Die Kernpunkte der socialen Frage in den Lebensnotwendigkeiten der Gegenwart und Zukunft (1919), GA 23. In English: *Towards Social Renewal: Rethinking the Basis of Society,* trans. M. Barton, Rudolf Steiner Press, 1999.

Page 6, "I recently discussed the content ..."
By invitation from the Economic Society of the Canton in Bern, Rudolf Steiner gave a lecture on February 4, 1921, in Bern, "The Form of Economic Life under the Influence of the Threefold Social Organism." A transcript of this lecture does not exist.

Page 10, "All over, in those Schwätzanstalten"
Translator's note: Steiner claims that *Schwätzanstalt* is a literal German translation of "Parliament," but this is not entirely true. Parliament is derived from the verb *parlar*—"to speak"—the closet equivalent of which might be *reden* or *sprechen* in German. Instead, Steiner uses the verb *schwätzen,* which means something much closer to "gossip" or "chinwag," with all of the same negative connotations. "Parliament"—or literally, "an institution of speaking"—becomes here *Schwätzanstalt*—"an institution of gossip and chinwagging." For reasons of clarity, and because Steiner emphasizes that this is a "literal" German translation, I have left *Schwätzanstalt* in the original German when Steiner uses it, and translated as "Parliament" the German cognate *Parlament.*

Page 11, "I wrote about this in the series of articles"
The article series appeared in 1905/06 under the title "Theosophy and Social Questions" ("Theosophie und soziale Frage") in the journal *Lucifer-Gnosis (Luzifer-Gnosis),* edited by Rudolf Steiner. In Steiner's Collected Works, they can be found in the volume *Lucifer-Gnosis: Foundational Essays on Anthroposophy and Reports from the Journal "Lucifer" and "Lucifer-Gnosis" 1903-1908, (Lucifer-Gnosis; Grundlegende Aufsätze zur Anthroposophie und Berichte aus den Zeitschriften «Luzifer» und «Lucifer–Gnosis» 1903-1908),* GA 34. This article series, in which Rudolf Steiner, beginning with the problem of the division of labor, formulates the "foundational social law" [Soziale Hauptgesetz] and demonstrates the necessity of separating work from income was also published separately. Available in English as *Anthroposophy and the Social Question,* Mercury Press, Spring Valley, NY.

Page 11, "Take … the Lenins, the Trotskys"
Leading personalities of the Bolshevist movement in Russia. For more on the perspectives that Rudolf Steiner offers here, see especially Lenin's book *Staat und Revolution* (Published in English as *The State and Revolution* by Penguin Classics 1993).

Page 11, "They do not trust themselves"
E. A. Karl Stockmeyer noted in his comments on this passage: "People today do not trust themselves to seek the beginnings of spiritual life in the soul." From: E. A. Karl Stockmeyer's handwritten notes to the lecture given on February 12, 1921, in the archive at Dornach, Switzerland.

Page 12, "Schopenhauer"
Arthur Schopenhauer – 1788-1860, philosopher. The literal quote that Steiner cites here is: "Thus it follows that it is easy to preach, but difficult to found morality." See the essay "On the Will in Nature." The twelve-volume edition of Schopenhauer's collected works published in 1894 included an introduction by Rudolf Steiner.

Page 13, "who wrote an article in *Die Tat* [*The Act*] …"
Ernst Michel – "Anthroposophy and Christianity," an article that appeared in *Die Tat*, a journal for the future of German culture, published by Eugen Diedrichs in Jena, in the February issue, 1921. Rudolf Steiner cites this article in his lecture on February 8, 1921, collected in "The Human Being in Relationship to the Cosmos 3: Humanity's Responsibility for World Evolution through Its Connection with the Planet Earth and the World of the Stars" [*Der Mensch in Zusammenhang mit dem Kosmos 3: Die Verantwortung des Menschen für die Weltentwickelung durch seinen geistigen Zusammenhang mit dem Erdplaneten und der Sternenwelt*, GA 203]. This volume has not yet been translated into English.

Page 14, "from the lectures I have given since April 1919."
In the following volumes of Rudolf Steiner's Collected Works: CWs 189-199 and CWs 329-334. See the list of Rudolf Steiner's Collected Works starting on p. 251.

Page 14, "as we started to form our threefold social organism movement"
In his book *Towards Social Renewal* (among others) Rudolf Steiner developed the idea of a threefolding of the social organism as an alternative to the existing unitary state. In the interest of spreading this idea, the "Association for the Threefold Social Organism" was formed on April 22, 1919. For more on the history of the movement for social threefolding, see the series *Beiträge zur Rudolf Steiner Gesamtausgabe* (previously *Nachrichten der Rudolf Steiner-Nachlassverwaltung* Vol. 24/25 and 27/29, 1969); also Walter Klugler's *Rudolf Steiner und die Anthroposophie* (published by DuMont-Dokumente in Cologne, 1978): chapter 3.

Page 16, "Karl Marx and Rodbertus"
Karl Marx – 1818-1883, founder of economic socialism and dialectical materialism.

Johann Karl Rodbertus – 1805-1875, national economist and politician; one of the main supporters of economic socialism in an idealistic-monarchial understanding of it (state socialism).

Page 16, "the socialist leader Paul Singer"
1844-1911, social democratic politician. It cannot be determined under what

circumstances Rudolf Steiner heard Paul Singer speak. Most likely, it was in Berlin around the turn of the century when Rudolf Steiner held a number of lectures as part of the labor movement and was active as a teacher at the *Arbeiterbildungsschule* (Worker Development School) in Berlin from 1899-1904.

Lecture 2

Page 18, "the kinds of statements found in *Towards Social Renewal*"
See notes to pp. 6 and 14.

Page 19, "the national economist Terhalle"
Fritz Terhalle – 1889-1962, national economist. See his manuscript *Free or Fixed Pricing? A report on the politics of pricing since the start of the World War* [*Freie oder gebundene Preisbildung? Ein Beitrag zu unserer Preispolitik seit Beginn des Weltkrieges*, Jena, 1920, p. 121, untranslated]. There, Terhalle cites the following passage from Ludwig Pohle's *The Present Crisis in the German National Economic Model, Reports on the Relationship Between Politics and National Economics* [*Die gegenwärtige Krisis in der Deutschen Volkswirtschaftslehre, Betrachtung über das Verhältnis zwischen Politik und nationalökonomischer Wissenschaft*, Leipzig, 1910, p. 114, also untranslated]: "They (the sanctions) should serve the purpose of satisfying public opinion, which has been agitated by the discovery of certain occurrences felt to be "grievances," insofar as the people can now see that orders against those grievances have been given by the government. Public opinion, which, after several penetrating remarks by G. Brandes has been directed far more by fantasy than by reason, does not ask and does not care to assess whether these corrective measures were truly intended to improve something material, or whether the introduced reform only offers the appearance of something actual and leaves everything essentially as it was."—To this, Terhalle remarks: "Someday in the future, an important task will indeed arise and will require that even the broadest strata of socieity acknowledge economic necessities; only then will these stragglers be brought into the realm of scientific thought."

Page 19, "Georg Brandes"
1842-1927, Danish literary critic. See also note above on Fritz Terhalle.

Page 20, "since April 1919"
The month in which *Towards Social Renewal* was published. See notes to pp. 6 and 14.

Page 22, "the Treaty of Nystad"
In the small Finnish town Nystad (Finnish: *Uusikaupunki*) on the Gulf of Bothnia, the Treaty of Nystad was signed between Sweden and Russia on September 10, 1721, ending the so-called Great Northern War. With the signing of this treaty, Sweden lost its status as a great world power, and Russia's access to the Baltic Sea was secured. From that point on, the Baltic Sea was dominated by the opposition between Britain and Russia.

Page 22, "the Treaty of Paris"
After the Treaty of Fontainebleau (1762), Great Britain and Portugal, along with

France and Spain, signed the Treaty of Paris on February 10, 1763. France gave over its North American territories (Nova Scotia, Canada, and the Louisiana territory east of the Mississippi) to Great Britain. Spain received the Louisiana territory west of the Mississippi in compensation for Florida, which was surrendered to Great Britain. France's territories in India remained in control of Great Britain (except for five emporia), which also maintained control of its African conquests (Senegambia) and was now the undisputed sea and colonial power of the world.

Page 23, "whether Russia should come to Constantinople, or not"
It is possible here that the stenographer did not literally or correctly take down Rudolf Steiner's words. For the purposes of clarification, several important historical incidents connected with the relationship between Russia and Constantinople are presented here: On May 29, 1453, Constantinople fell into the hands of the Ottomans. The Greek Orthodox Church continued to exist under Turkish rule. Politically, the leading role in the Orthodoxy went to the Grand Prince of Moscow, which had aspirations of being the "Third Rome." In the Treaty of Constantinople from 1700, Asov (at the mouth of the Don River) was given over to Russia and subsequently became a Russian base for defending the Black Sea. Russia's status as a world power, realized under Czar Peter the Great (1672-1725) brought it closer to the Western world and caused it to have an increasing influence on the political life of Central Europe.

Page 27, "Spengler and his book *The Decline of the West*"
Oswald Spengler – 1880-1936. Historian and philosopher. His book has been translated into English in two volumes: "Form and Actuality" and "Perspectives." An abridged version is available from Vintage, 2006.

Page 28, "'barbarism' (in Schiller's sense of the word)"
Steiner makes use of Friedrich Schiller's polarity of barbarism and savagery:
"But man can be at odds with himself in two ways: either as savage, when feeling predominates over principle; or as barbarian, when principle destroys feeling. The savage despises Civilization, and acknowledges Nature as his sovereign mistress. The barbarian derides and dishonours Nature, but more contemptible than the savage, as often as not continues to be the slave of his slave. The man of Culture makes a friend of Nature, and honours her freedom whilst curbing only her caprice."
— Friedrich Schiller, *On the Aesthetic Education of Man*, Fourth Letter, section 6, trans. by Wilkinson and Willoughby.

Page 31, "Spencer, Huxley, … or even Emerson, Whitman, and the others"
Herbert Spencer – 1820-1903, English philosopher. *System of Synthetic Philosophy* in 10 volumes, 1862-1896.

Thomas Henry Huxley – 1825-1895, English zoologist and philosopher. *Evidence as to Man's Place in Nature*, 1863.

Ralph Waldo Emerson – 1803-1882, American philosopher and author. *Representative Men*, 1850.

Walt Whitman – 1819-1892, American poet.

Page 31, "Austria, as I have already said, was the experimental country"
See Rudolf Steiner's articles about Austria in the Vienna journal, *Deutschen Wochenschrift,* Annual VI, 1888, found in the volume *Gesammelte Aufsätze zur Kultur- und Zeitgeschichte 1887-1901* (Collected Articles on Culture and History 1887-1901), GA 31 (not yet translated into English).

Page 32, "an abstract man such as Woodrow Wilson"
Woodrow Wilson (1856-1924): American President from 1912 to 1920.
See notes to pp. 38 and 185.

Lecture 3

Page 38, "a thick book that Wilson had written back in the 1890s"
Woodrow Wilson (1856-1924): *The State* was published in 1889.

Page 39, "In Paris ... I was able to give a lecture in German"
Rudolf Steiner spoke in Paris on May 25, 26, and 27, 1914. The first two lectures he gave — "Das Hereinwirken der geistigen Welt in unser Dasein" and "Die Geisteswissenschaft als Zusammenfassun von Wissenschaft, Intelligenz und hellsichtiger Forschung"— are both found in the collection *Wie erwirbt man sich Verständnis für die geistige Welt?* (GA 154, not yet translated into English); the lecture from May 27— "Der Fortschritt in der Erkenntnis des Christus. Das Fünfte Evangelium" can be found in CW 152, *Approaching the Mystery of Golgotha.* Steiner is probably referring here to the lecture given on May 26. The stenographer noted that at the start of that lecture Steiner apologized to the audience for speaking in German.

Page 40, "the Lunacharskys of the world"
Anatoly Lunacharsky – 1875-1933; from 1917 to 1929, he was the Soviet People's Commissar of Enlightenment; in 1930, he served at the President of the Moscow Academy of Art.

Page 40, "I read a statement saying that in the conflict with spiritual science"
"the spiritual sparks have been enflamed enough that actual sparks and flames might take hold of this building in Dornach."—the actual quote from *Der Leuchtturm* (*The Lighthouse*), edited by Karl Rohm (15th Annual, 4th issue, October, 1920): "Spiritual sparks, sizzling like lightning on the wooden mousetrap, are now present enough that Steiner would do well to act "conciliatory," so that one day a proper spark does not bring the glory of Dornach to an inglorious end."—See also the piece by Elsbeth Ebertin, "Ein Blick in die Zukunft" ("A Look into the Future"), Freiburg, 1921, p. 63.

Page 41, "our journal *The Threefold Social Organism*"
The weekly journal *Dreigliederung des sozialen Organismus* (*The Threefold Social Organism*) published by the League for the Threefold Social Order; its managing editor was Ernst Uehli. It appeared from July 1919 to June 1922. After that it was renamed *Anthroposophie, Wochenschrift für freies Geistesleben* (*Anthroposophy:*

A Weekly Journal for Free Spiritual Life). This publication was then merged with the journal *Die Drei* (*The Three*) in 1931 and published as a monthly journal. According to something that he said in his lecture from February 16, 1921 (also appearing in this present volume), Rudolf Steiner saw the need for *The Threefold Social Organism* journal to become a daily newspaper.

The articles written by Rudolf Steiner that appeared in the weekly *The Threefold Social Organism* can be found in GA 24. In English: *The Renewal of the Social Organism,* trans E. Bowen-Wedgewood and Ruth Mariott, revised by Frederick Amrine, Anthroposophic Press, Spring Valley, NY, 1985.

Page 43, "is congealed within that commodity'"
See Karl Max, *Capital,* Chapter 1.1: "The Commodity." There it reads: "All values, all commodities are only definite masses of congealed labor time."

Page 45, "described concretely in my book *Towards Spiritual Renewal*"
See Rudolf Steiner, *Towards Social Renewal,* GA 23, chapter 3: "Capitalism and Social Ideas."

Page 45, "Spencer"
Herbert Spencer – See note to p. 31.

Page 46, "Stammler"
Rudolf Stammler – 1856-1938; author of *Wirtschaft und Recht nach der materialistischen Gesichtsauffassung (Economics and Law from a Materialistic Perspective)*; Translator's note: Steiner does, in fact, make a pun on Stammler's name here: "Stammler [kann] nur so stammeln..."—"Stammler can only stutter something like..."

Page 47, "Cromwell"
Oliver Cromwell – 1599-1685, Lord Protectorate of England. In December 1648, the Presbyterian members of Parliament were locked out of Parliament on his orders.

Page 47, "Wilhelm von Humboldt"
Wilhelm von Humboldt – 1767-1835; German statesman. The essay in English, "The Limits of State Action" by Cambridge University Press.

Page 49, "Förster"
Friedrich Wilhelm Förster – 1869-1966; ethicist, evolutionary biologist, and pacifist.

Page 50, "on the battlefield of the *Berliner Tageblatt*"
Steiner is referring here to the report by Christian Bouchholtz entitled "Die abergläublische Berlin. Okkulte Volksschulen und spiritistische Laboratorien" ("Superstitious Berlin: Occult Folk School and Spiritualist Laboratories") that appeared in No. 39 on Tuesday, January 25, 1921, in the *Berliner Tageblatt.* By January 26, an excerpt of that article appeared in the English newspaper *The Daily Telegraph.*

Page 50, "in English newspapers"
See the previous note.

Lecture 4

Page 52, "Der Kommende Tag (The Coming Day)"
Corporation for the Development of Economic and Spiritual Value (Stuttgart 1920-1925). An attempt at forming an associative undertaking in the spirit of threefolding; Steiner was, until 1923, Chairman of the Board of Directors. This undertaking was one of roughly twenty such undertakings and cultural institutions at the time. As a result of the general economic crisis, the association was liquidated in 1925.

Page 61, "Wissel"
Rudolf Wissel –1869-1962; German Minister for Economics in 1919. He supported the idea of a nationalized collective economy. Wissel's life and political career continued for some time after this lecture was given. In 1933, with the rise of Nazism, Wissel was expelled from political life, but became active again after 1945. He continued to support the Social Democratic Party (SPD) and was one of those not in favor of a union of the SPD and the Communist Party.

Page 62, "ecumenical council in Constantinople in 869"
The Eighth Ecumenical Council under Pope Adrian II decreed against Photius that the human being has only *one* rational and cognitive soul (*unam animam rationabilem et intellectualem*), disallowing talk of a specifically spiritual aspect of the human being. From then on, the spirit was seen to be only an aspect of the soul.

See also the Catholic philosopher Otto Willemann—of whom Steiner thought quite highly—and his three volume work *Geschichte des Idealismus* [History of Idealism]—unfortunately not translated into English. In paragraph 54, he writes: "The violation committed by the Gnostics with their Pauline distinction between the pneumatic and the physical human being, insofar as they published this distinction as the expression of their total system of belief and declared this truth as the agent of the Christian imprisoned by the Church, was then decreed by the Church as the express denial of the trichotomy."

Page 62, "Herr Wundt"
Wilhelm Wundt – 1832-1920; philosopher and psychologist.

Page 65, "the monstrosities that people call peace treaties"
Following Brest-Litovsk (March 3, 1918) and Versailles (June 28, 1919), peace treaties were signed in Saint-Germain-en-Laye (September 10, 1919), Neuilly (November 27, 1919), Trianon (June 4, 1920), and Sèvres (August 10, 1920).

Page 65, "among the lectures that I have given here"
Rudolf Steiner is probably referring here to the public lecture given in Stuttgart on June 18, 1919, "Freedom for the spirit, Equality in rights, Brotherhood in economic life," in *Neugestaltung des sozialen Organismus* (GA 330, not yet translated).

Lecture 5

Page 72, "Max Dessoir"
Max Dessoir – 1867-1947, Professor of Philosophy in Berlin; editor of the *Zeitschrift für Ästehtik und allgemeine Kunstwissenschaft* [*Journal of aesthetics and general studies of art*]. In his text *Vom Jenseits der Seele. Die Gehimwissenschaften in kritischer Betrachtung* (Stuttgart, 1917; not translated), he deals with anthroposophy in a critical and polemical way. See also the following note.

Page 73, "I brought this up in my *Riddles of the Soul*"
In chapter two of *Riddles of the Soul* (CW 21), Steiner writes a lengthy critique of Max Dessoir (translated by William Lindeman, Mercury Press, Spring Valley, NY).

Page 73, "a letter from a friend"
The friend is Dr. Jakob Mühlethaler (1883-1972). He wrote to Rudolf Steiner on November 19, 1920: "The reason why I have come to write you in this particular moment is because I am currently studying your book *Riddles of the Soul* and have just come to the passage where you address Dessoir's strange thinking defect. I can further justify your critique with an event that I experienced firsthand. In the winter semester of 1904-1905, I heard a course by Dessoir on logic and the theory of knowledge. It happened during one lecture that "pretty Max" (he turned up every week in a different colored vest) suddenly stood stunned and silent in the midst of his freely delivered lecture. Unhappily, one student had a newspaper in front of him in that very moment; this was then claimed as the scapegoat, and so the Herr Professor asked for a few minutes to think and find his train of thought again. After several long, tortured moments, he finally found it..." (Rudolf Steiner Archive, Dornach, Switzerland).

Page 73, "Kuno Fischer"
Kuno Fischer – 1825-1907, philosopher. He served as a professor in Heidelberg and taught philosophical-aesthetic analysis of classical literature.

Page 74, "I... knew a chemist"
Steiner is probably talking here about Hugo von Glim (1831-1906); see the relevant passage in *Autobiography: Chapters in the Course of My Life 1861-1907* (CW 28).

Page 74, "Liebig"
Justus von Liebig – 1803-1873.

Page 74, "Gorup-Besanez"
Eugen von Gorup-Besanez – 1817-1878.

Page 77, "Hermann Helmholtz"
Hermann Helmholtz – 1821-1894. Steiner is referring here to the lecture "Goethe's Anticipation of Future Natural Scientific Ideas," which was given by physicist Helmholtz in 1892 at the General Assembly of the Goethe Society in Weimar.

Page 81, "a southern German city"
Here, Steiner is referring to the lecture given on November 21, 1905, in Colmar, with the title: "The Wisdom Teachings of Christianity in the Light of Theosophy." There is no extant copy of that lecture.

Lecture 6

Page 87, "An Outline of Esoteric Science"
Originally published 1910 as *Die Geheimwissenschaft im Umriss* (GA 13).

Page 88, "Adam Smith"
Adam Smith – 1723-1790; English philosopher and economist. He is known as the founder of "classical national economics," and was the first to give a conclusive account of the individualistic and liberal economic theories of the eighteenth century. His main work was: *An Inquiry into The Health And Wealth of Nations,* originally published in 1776.

Page 97, "Waldorf School"
Founded in 1919 in Stuttgart by Emil Molt, Director of the Waldorf-Astoria Cigarette Factory, and Rudolf Steiner, who led the school until his death in 1925. Waldorf education is now a worldwide educational movement based on the curriculum that Steiner developed.

Page 99, "Eisenach platform"
Presented in August 1869 at the founding of the Social Democratic Workers' Party by Wilhelm Liebknecht and August Bebel.

Page 99, "Gotha platform"
Began in May 1875 when this Workers' Party merged with the General German Workers' Union, founded by Ferdinand Lasalle in May 1863.

Page 99, "Erfurt platform"
Worked on by Karl Kautsky, this platform started in October 1891 after the reorganization of the Social Democratic Party of Germany as a branch of the Second Internationale, which was begun two years before.

Page 99, *"State and Revolution"*
Written by V. I. Lenin and published in Bern in 1918. There it reads: "The state will be able to wither away completely when society adopts the rule: 'From each according to his ability, to each according to his needs,' i.e., when people have become so accustomed to observing the fundamental rules of social relations and when their labor has become so productive that they will voluntarily work according to their ability. 'The narrow horizon of bourgeois law,' which compels one to calculate with the heartlessness of a Shylock whether one has not worked half an hour more than anybody else—this narrow horizon will then be left behind. There will then be no need for society, in distributing products, to regulate the quantity to be received by each; each will take freely 'according to his needs.'"

Lecture 7

Page 102, "even Bismarck is among them"
See Georg Brodnitz, *Bismarck's Views on National Economy (Bismarcks nationalökonomische Anschauungen),* published in Jena in 1902, p. 39: He (Bismarck) stands for both of the great arteries of our societal organism: agriculture and industry. They alone make up the productive section of the population, the rest of which,

apart from those who just "make their living clipping coupons," belong either to "the educated or uneducated classes of people living on their money, their honor, or their stipend" (Reichstag, February 10, 1885) or to "those who participate in trade, which is an upscale but nevertheless useless industry" (Reichstag, May 9, 1884).—Herein lies something decisively one-sided... "According to this school of thought, the man who tends to pigs is a productive member of society, and the one who tends to people an unproductive one. A Newton, Watt, or Kepler is not as productive as a donkey, a horse or an animal that drives the plow" (Friedrich List).

Page 108, "Waldorf School"
See note to p. 97.

Page 108, "eurythmy"
A form of movement art developed by Rudolf Steiner (beginning in 1912) in which speech and music are made "visible." See, for example, CW 277, "Eurythmy: The Revelation of the Speaking Soul," and CW 277a, "The Origin and Development of Eurythmy."

Page 108, "our college level courses"
The first course took place concurrent with the opening of the Goetheanum and ran from September 27 through October 16, 1920. Approximately 100 lectures and many art presentations took place during those days. Rudolf Steiner's lectures from that course are collected in *The Boundaries of Natural Science* (CW 322). The second anthroposophical college level course took place from between August 3 and 10, 1921, also in Dornach. At the center of this event, attended by over 600 people, were five lectures by Rudolf Steiner, which can be found in CW 76, "The Fructifying Effect of Anthroposophy on Specialized Fields."

Page 108, "Kommende Tag"
See note to p. 52.

Page 112, "the Medical Therapeutic Institute"
The Clinical Therapy Institute was founded by Dr. Ludwig Noll, Dr. Otto Palmer, Dr. Felix Peipers, and Dr. Friedrich Husemann after the first course for doctors given by Rudolf Steiner (Easter 1920). Until 1924, it was a division of the Kommende Tag, and from 1924-1935 was the private undertaking of Dr. Otto Palmer.

Page 113, *"Theosophy and Anthroposophy"*
Wilhelm Bruhn, *Theosophierende Anthroposophie* (Theosophizing Anthroposophy), published in Berlin in 1921.

Page 113, "the law teacher in Graz"
The identity of this law teacher has not been determined.

Page 114, "I publicly described the baseless lies of Frohnmeyer"
On December 3, 1920, in Basel, where Steiner spoke on "Anthroposophical spiritual science, its value for human beings, and its relationship to art and religion" (unpublished lecture). Johannes Frohnmeyer, in his brochure "The Theosophical

Movement: Its History and Form, and an Evaluation of the Same," had written the following: "A 9-meter-tall statue of the ideal man is presently being carved in Dornach: above with human features, below with animal-like characteristics." (In the second edition, this sentence was removed). Frohnmeyer had taken this fully inaccurate description without checking its accuracy from an article by Father Heinrich Nydecker-Roos "A Visit to the Anthroposophists in Dornach near Basel" in *Christian Tidings from Basel* published in 1920.

Page 114, "And this Someone said"
Professor Gerhard Heinzelmann of Basel, in his review of the text "The Agitation at the Goetheanum" (Dornach, 1920) in the *Evangelical Mission Magazine* (Basel, 1921).

Lecture 8

Page 117, "a minister of police named Giskra"
Karl Giskra (1820-1879) was from 1867 to 1870 the Austrian Minister of the Interior.

Page 117, "Count Hermann Keyserling"
Count Hermann Keyserling – 1880-1946; founder of the School of Wisdom in 1920 in Darmstadt.

Page 117, *"The Road to Perfection"*
Published in Darmstadt, 1920.

Page 118, *"Philosophy as Art"*
Published in Darmstadt, 1920.

Page 118, "in a public lecture"
In the lecture from November 16, 1920, "The truth of spiritual science and the practical life demands of the present: a defense of spiritual science against its opponents" (in *The Present Crisis and The Way to Healthy Thinking*, CW 335), Steiner corrected Keyserling's statement: "It is not true that I have sought out some sort of connection to Haeckel. Haeckel came out in me, in the kind of striving that I have undertaken, of his own accord." See also his description in *Autobiography: Chapters in the Course of My Life* (CW 28).

Page 118, "I rely heavily on Haeckel"
See Keyserling's book *Philosophy as Art*, in which he writes about Rudolf Steiner: "it ... is in any case symbolic for his being that his spiritual course originates, in some regards, in Haeckel."

Page 119, "the name Heinzelmann comes from"
Translator's note: there is a pun at work here. Steiner is referring both to Professor Heinzelmann, who was mentioned in an earlier lecture as that "someone" who spoke charitably toward Frohnmeyer, and the Heinzelmännchen (literally: "little Heinzelmann"), which is the name used in Cologne for mischievous poltergeists, or house spirits. So Steiner is comparing Dr. Boos's efforts to respond to this

recent attack to the machinations of a puck-like spirit and also another member of the Anthroposophical Society who has been vocal about other things in the past.

Page 119, "Dr. Boos"
Roman Boos–1889-1952, a lawyer, author of many books, and lecturer. He was an active participant in the movement for the threefold social organism, particularly in Switzerland.

Page 119, "Akashic Record"
Regarding the particular issue mentioned here, see the indications that Steiner wrote about the concept of the Akashic Record in his preface to *Cosmic Memory* (CW 11).

Page 119, "wholly new definition of conscious falsehood"
In one of his main articles against the Goetheanum and anthroposophy (in the *Catholic Sunday Paper*, supplement to No. 20 from May 16, 1920), Father Max Kully of Arlesheim, under the pseudonym "Spectator," had written about the "Akashic Record" (a term used by Rudolf Steiner) as a physical book, whereas it is actually a purely spiritual image of the proceedings of human evolution and the cosmos. Dr. Roman Boos had responded to this (in the daily paper for Birseck, *Birsig and Leimental*, on May 20, 1920). Kully then responded again in the *Catholic Sunday Paper* (No. 22, May 30, 1920) and insisted anew that he saw the Akashic Record as a physical book. Rudolf Steiner took a position on this back-and-forth in his lecture on June 5, 1920, in Dornach (printed in *The Agitation Against the Goetheanum*, published in Dornach in 1920). In a review of this brochure (appearing in *Evangelical Mission Magazine*, published in Basel in 1921, No. 65 Vol. 2), Professor Heinzelmann wrote the response mentioned here in the lecture.

Page 121, "This will soon exert such power ..."
All of the citations in this paragraph are taken from Hermann Keyserling's book *The Road to Perfection*, published in Darmstadt in 1920.

Page 125, "he did the following"
Again, Steiner quotes from *The Road to Perfection.*

Page 126, "Professor Rein in Jena"
He wrote in his article "Ethical Heresy" in *The Day* (November 23, 1920): "... These free people of Dr. Steiner are, however, already no longer people. They have already stepped into the world of angels on Earth. Anthroposophy has helped them achieve that. Must it not be an unspeakable boon, in the midst of the many confusions of Earthly life, to be placed in such surroundings?"

Page 127, "in that lecture"
See note to p. 118.

Page 128, "Oscar Hertwig"
Oscar Hertwig – 1849-1922. *The Origin of Organisms: A Refutation of Darwin's Theory of Chance*, published in Jena in 1916.

Page 128, "also published a book on social questions"
Against Ethical, Social, and Political Darwinism, published in Jena in 1918.

Page 129, "Lunacharsky"
See note to p. 40.

Lecture 9

Page 136, "the question of property is dealt with in *Towards Social Renewal*"
See *Towards Social Renewal* (CW 23), Chapter 3. (German edition originally published in 1919). See also Steiner's lecture from June 16, 1920, "The Consequences of Threefolding for Property," in CW 335.

Page 139, "Poincaré"
Poincaré – 1854-1912, French mathematician, physicist and astronomer.

Page 139, "Mach"
Ernst Mach – 1838-1916, professor of physics in Graz and Prague; professor of philosophy in Vienna.

Page 139, "Lujo Brentano"
Lujo Brentano – 1844-1962, professor of national economics. Particularly supported the labor unions and free trade.

Page 139, "the national economist Terhalle"
Fritz Terhalle – (1889-1962), national economist. In his book *Free or Bound Price Formation* (published in Jena in 1920) in section 11, "The success of the wartime fight over price gouging," Terhalle writes: "If you were to make an *overall judgment* about the success of the prosecution against price gouging, you could summarize it as follows: 1) *Most of the time, a false understanding of what should be striven for predominated among the most interested and relevant circles.* 2) *The uncertainty* produced *by this fact, as well as by the theoretical constructions* that necessarily fought against praxis, and finally by *the wide diversity of applicable case law threw all the business parties concerned into a totally undesirable confusion and agitation.* 3) *The fight against price gouging achieved absolutely nothing in some areas*, in particular as far as primary production is concerned, *and only a little bit in other areas, and often to an exaggerated extent*, as was the case in certain branches of the retail sector. 4) All of that *combined to the detriment of real business over and against the side of profiteering*." See also note to p. 19.

Lecture 10

Page 144, "*Bildung*"
This refers to the German tradition of self-cultivation that arose during the late 18th and early 19th century and is often associated with works by Friedrich Schiller (*On the Aesthetic Education of Man*) and Johann Wolfgang von Goethe (*Wilhelm Meister's Years of Apprenticeship*). English speakers may be indirectly familiar with

the term through its association with the *Bildungsroman*—the novel of development. *Huckleberry Finn* is often identified as an American *Bildungsroman.*

Page 146, "Charlemagne"
Charlemagne – 742-814, crowned Caesar by Pope Leo III in Rome in 800 C.E.

Page 148, "the little economic pamphlet"
Neither the title nor the author of this pamphlet has been determined.

Page 156, "look to Nietzsche"
The source of the aphorism that Steiner quotes cannot be determined. A formulation similar to the one mentioned here can be found among Nietzsche's writings from the 1880s: "*The period of clarity*: one grasps that Old and New are fundamental opposites: the old values born of the life that is dying out, the new of the life that is rising. One grasps that *all old ideals* are ones hostile to life (born out of *décadence* and defining that decadence, especially in the magnificent moral purge of Sundays). We *understand* the Old and have long lacked the strength for the New."

II

TRAINING COURSE FOR UPPER SILESIANS

Lecture 1

Page 159, "Association for the Threefold Social Organism"
See note to p. 14.

Page 159, "the League of Nations meeting in Geneva"
Took place between November 15 and December 18, 1920. The USA declined to join the League of Nations. Argentina withdrew. Austria and Bulgaria were taken in as members. It was decided that an international court be formed. See also Rudolf Steiner's lecture "The true foundation of a League of Nations in the economic, rights-political, and spiritual powers of the people," collected in CW 329, "Liberating the Human Being as Foundation for Social Reorganization."

Page 160, "around fifty individuals would gather here"
Emil Leinhas, a close associate of Rudolf Steiner's, reported that Steiner would make himself available to teach speakers if one hundred interested individuals could be found. Although only fifty people ended up applying, Steiner was prepared to administer such a course. See Emil Leinhas's book *Aus der Arbeit mit Rudolf Steiner* [*Working with Rudolf Steiner*], published in 1950 in Basel (not published in English).

Page 162, "Helfferich"
Helfferich – 1872-1924, became the director of the Bagdad Railway in 1906, then Director of the Deutsche Bank in 1908. From 1915 to 1917, first as Secretary of the Treasury and then as Secretary of the Interior and Deputy Chancellor, he

was responsible for financing the war and for all economic proceedings relating to it. On April 23, 1924, shortly before a significant victory for his party in the elections, he died in a train accident in Bellinzona. His written works include *The Genesis of the World War in the Light of the Announcement of the Entente* (Berlin, 1915) and *The Pre-History of the World War* (Berlin, 1919). There is no clear record of the speech that Steiner mentions here.

Page 165, "Götz von Berlichingen"
Götz von Berlichingen – 1480-1562, German knight who lost a hand at the Siege of Landshut and had it replaced by an iron one. For a time, he was the leader of the so-called "Black Company," a peasant uprising group.

Page 165, "Franz von Sickingen"
Franz von Sickingen – 1481-1523, leader of a band of Swabian and Rhenish knights. In that role, he incited several protests in the name of religious and political reform.

Page 165, "Ulrich von Hutten"
Ulrich von Hutten – 1488-1523, a humanist who allied himself with Franz von Sickingen in the interest of changing political relationships.

Page 168, "dividing Poland"
The first division happened in August 1772. Prussia received West Prussia (excluding Danzig and Thorn) as well as Warmia and the northern part of Greater Poland (roughly 34,900 square kilometers with approximately 356,000 residents). Russia annexed Polish Livonia and Byelorussia. Austria was given Lesser Poland south of the Vistula River; and Red Ruthenia, Volhynia, and Podolia were incorporated into the kingdom of Galicia and Volhynia. The second division of Poland took place in 1793, the third in 1795.

Page 169, "Slowacki"
Juliusz Slowacki – 1809-1849, from Kremenets (later lived in Paris) was a Polish poet; his epics and dramas of the Bar Confederation, which dealt with the first resistance against Russia, attempted to speak to a sense of Polish national identity.

Page 170, "Dunajewski"
Julian Dunajewski – 1822-1907, was a Professor of Political Science in Preßberg, Lviv, and Krakow. From 1880-1891 he was the Austrian Finance Minister. See also Steiner's mention of Dunajewski in his autobiography (CW 28); see also the first lecture in *Karmic Relationships, Volume Two* (CW 236).

Page 170, "Hausner"
Otto Hausner – 1827-1890, was born in Brody in Galicia and later lived in Lviv. He was a member of the Austrian Parliament. He sought to protect his Fatherland from the threat of Russia, both as a European and a Pole. Steiner describes Hausner's speaking style in his *Autobiography* (CW 28); see also the first lecture in *Karmic Relationships, Volume Two* (CW 236).

Page 170, "Wolski"
Ludwig Wolski was a Polish member of the Austrian Parliament, and connected politically with Otto Hausner.

Page 171, "what is called Polish Messianism"
This goes back to the manuscript by the greatest Polish poet Adam Mickiewicz (1798-1855) entitled *Books of the Polish Nation and the Polish Pilgrims*. There, Mickiewicz writes: "And just as bloody sacrifice ceased the world over with the resurrection of Christ, so too with the resurrection of the Polish people will all war cease in Christendom."

Page 172, "Dzieduszycki"
Count Wojciech Dzieduszycki – 1845-1909, was a philosopher and poet, and from 1879 to 1886 a member of the Vienna House of Representatives.

Page 172, "Rieger"
Franz Ladislaus Rieger – 1818-1903, was born in Semil and died in Prague; he was a member of the Austrian Parliament and a member of the Alt-Tscheche (Old Czech) Party.

Page 172, "Grégr"
Eduard Grégr – 1827-1907, born in Steyr and died in Prague; he was a member of the Austrian Parliament and a member of the Jung-Tscheche (Young Czech) party.

Page 172, "Herbst"
Eduard Herbst – 1820-1892, was Professor of Legal Philosophy and Constitutional Law in Lviv, and then later in Prague. From 1867-1870 he was Minister of Justice and leading politician in the liberal German Left within the Austrian Imperial Assembly.

Page 172, "Plener"
Ernst Edler von Plener – 1841-1923, was born in Eger and died in Vienna; he was the leader of the liberal Germans.

Page 172, "Carneri"
Batholomäus Ritter von Carneri – 1821-1909, was born in Trient and died in Marbug; he was a philosopher and author, and from 1870-1891 he was a member of the Austrian House of Representatives.

Lecture 2

Page 176, "a big loan of currency"
For more on this, see J. M. Keynes's book *The Economic Consequences of the Peace* (published in English in 1919, in German translation in 1920).

Page 178, "Keynes"
John Maynard Keynes – 1883-1946, was an English economist; professor at the University of Cambridge. During the war he worked in the English treasury. There, he worked from an influential post with questions connected to the financing of the war; he ultimately took part in the Paris Conferences as the British financial representative and as Deputy of the English Treasury Chancellor. On June 7, 1919, he stepped down from his post after he had recognized that fundamental changes to the conditions of peace were impossible.

Page 178, "Norman Angell"
Author of *The Treaties and Economic Chaos* (published in English in 1919 and in German in 1920).

Page 180, "Ludendorff"
Erich Ludendorff – 1865-1937, was Hindenburg's Chief of Staff during World War I, appointed to General Quarter Master in 1916 and let go in 1918 because of his desire to continue fighting the war. In his later years, he and his wife Mathilde founded the *Bund für Gotteserkenntnis* [Society for the Knowledge of God]. In his memoirs, *My Memories of the War 1914-1918* (published in 1919), Ludendorff writes about the political necessity of dispatching Lenin to Russia: "By sending Lenin to Russia, our government had taken on a particular responsibility for itself. Militarily speaking, the trip was justified; Russia had to fall. But our government had also to ensure that we did not fall along with it…"

Page 182, "Lenin"
See notes to p. 11 and 99.

Page 183, "in reaction to the translation of *Towards Social Renewal* into English"
See the article by H. Wilson Harris in the *Daily News* from September 16, 1920, entitled "How Capital Should Be Handled (A Book on that Topic Being Discussed in Europe)".

Page 183, "spring of 1920"
See note to p. 160.

Page 184, "a striving for unity, particularly since 1848"
For a brief period of time, various streams such as the constitutional-liberal, the radical-democratic, the socialist-revolutionary, and the national-idealistic all melded together, but they quickly divided again and thereby negated the force of the revolution. The end of the revolutionary movement came in 1849 with the reinstitution of pre-revolution order in Austria-Hungary and Prussia. The calls for unity and freedom remained unanswered.

Page 184, "Fichte"
Johann Gottlieb Fichte – 1762-1814, was a professor of philosophy in Jena, Erlangen, Königsberg, and Berlin. In the last (fourteenth) of his "Speech[es] to the German Nation," he said: "The good fortune has been given to you to found the kingdom of spirit and reason and thereby negate raw, brute force as the dominant strength of the world." In his thirteenth speech, he said about the dominance of the seas: "To Germans, the often discussed freedom of the waters is just as foreign; that is true whether one is talking about having this freedom or simply having the ability of taking it away from everyone else. Throughout the centuries, during all of the rivalries between other nations, the German has displayed little eagerness to take part in them in an extensive way, and he never will."

Page 185, "Thoughts during the Time of War"
Subtitled "for Germans and those who feel they do not have to hate them," published in 1915. Collected in the CW 24, "Essays Concerning the Threefold Division of the Social Organism and the Period 1915-1921."

Page 185, "Woodrow Wilson"
In his speech on Flag Day in Washington on June 14, 1912: "[The German people] did not originate, or desire, this hideous war, or wish that we should be drawn into it, [...] They themselves are in the grip of the same sinister power [...]" At a joint session of both houses of Congress on April 2, 1917, Wilson said: "We have no quarrel with the German people. We have no feeling toward them but one of sympathy and friendship. It was not upon their impulse that their government acted in entering this war. It was not with their previous knowledge or approval."

Page 186, "Helfferich"
See note to p. 162.

Page 186, "Erzberger"
Mathis Erzberger – 1875-1921, was a member of the Center Party, signer of the armistice treaty in October 1918, Finance Minister from 1919-1921; he was murdered by the Nationalists in 1921. He was an opponent and rival of Helfferich.

Page 186, "The Wilhelmine period"
Wilhelmine is a term for the period of German history, also known as the German Empire. The term refers to the period running from the proclamation of Wilhelm I as German Kaiser at Versailles in 1871 to the abdication of his grandson Wilhelm II in 1918.

Page 187, "Kühlmann"
Richard von Kühlmann – 1873-1948, was the German Secretary of State for Foreign Affairs from 1917-1918. Kühlmann was familiar with the text of the memorandum that Steiner wrote in the summer of 1917 in which he described the idea of the threefold social organism. See Steiner's text "Social Future," collected in CW 332, "The Federation for Threefolding and the Complete Social Reform: Culture Councils Freeing The Spiritual Life."

Page 187, "journal *The Threefold Social Organism*"
See note to p. 41.

Page 188, "someone was campaigning heavily for the establishment of an organized news service in Zurich"
This is probably referring to Oberst Haeften, a close colleague of Helmuth von Moltke. The German government planned to establish a central news service or press office in Zurich in the fall of 1916, so that the world community might be informed about the war and peacetime goals of the Central Powers.

Page 189, "In Switzerland, when the people were very near to a revolution"
Steiner is referring here to the General Strike of November 1918, led by the Social Democrats. In addition to the bourgeois circles and the troops that had been deployed by the government, it was notably the farmers who spoke out in fierce opposition to the strike because they had no need for disruption and revolution. See Schmid-Ammann's book *Die Wahrheit über den Generalstreik 1918 (The Truth about the General Strike in 1918)*, originally published in 1967.

Page 190, "*Towards Social Renewal*"
See Chapter 2: "The realistic attempts at answers to social questions and needs as demanded by life."

QUESTION-AND-ANSWER SESSION

Page 191, "*Bildung*"
See note to p.144.

Page 192, "*Gymnasium*"
This type of school provides advanced secondary education in some parts of Europe, comparable to English grammar schools or sixth-form colleges and U.S. college preparatory high schools. Historically the German *Gymnasium* also included in its overall accelerated curriculum post-secondary education at college level, and the degree that was awarded substituted for the bachelor's degree previously awarded by a college or university, so that universities in Germany exclusively became graduate schools.

Page 192, "*Realschule*"
The *Realschule* was an outgrowth of the rationalism and empiricism of the seventeenth and eighteenth centuries. While efforts were made to introduce more science into the classical schools generally, the *Realschule* offered a more scientific emphasis than the *Gymnasium*, with its emphasis on classics and humanities. In 1747, Johann Julius Hecker established at Berlin an "economical-mathematical" *(ökonomisch-mathematische) Realschule*, which may be regarded as the prototype of the *Realschule* of the twentieth century. The *Realschule* offered a six-year course, while the *Oberrealschule* had a nine-year course.

Page 192, "Leo Thun"
Leopold Graf von Thun und Hohenstein–1811-1888, was a leading Austrian statesman from the Thun and Hohenstein family. From 1849-1860, when he was Austrian Minister of Education, he carried out an educational reform and reorganized the *Gymnasiums* and *Hochschules*;* and during his time as minister he appointed many artists and teachers to the Vienna Hochschule who later achieved world renown. See Steiner's essay "The German Educational Being (in Austria) and Herr von Gautsch" in CW 31, "Collected Essays on Culture and Current Events 1887-1901."

* *Hochschule* is a German term for an institution of higher education, used particularly in relation to institutions in the German and Austrian educational systems. It translates literally as "high school," but it is not the same as what is called a high school in English-speaking countries. A *Hochschule* might be referred to in English as a university or college (or sometimes as a university college.

Page 192, "Herr von Gautsch"
Paul, Baron Gautsch of Frankenthurn, lived in Vienna from 1851-1918. He was an Austrian statesman; from 1885-1893 he was Minister for Culture and Education in the Taaffe Cabinet. See also note above.

Page 193, "in my book *The Riddle of the Human Being*"
CW 20. Published by Mercury Press, Spring Valley, NY, as *The Riddle of Man,* translated by William Lindeman.

Page 195, "in Switzerland, we had to go on the defensive "
In particular, the Swiss priest Max Kully of Arlesheim spoke polemically against Steiner and anthroposophy, and through his speeches and newspaper articles, a fully distorted picture of anthroposophy was presented to the public. Steiner and several members of the Anthroposophical Society responded both in newspaper articles and lectures.

Page 197, "Herr M. Bartsch"
Moritz Bartsch – 1869-1944, was a member of the Theosophical Society during the 1890s. He became a member of the Anthroposophical Society in 1908 and was an active participant in the work in Silesia. His son, Erhard Bartsch, was also a participant in the course.

Page 197, "the so-called *Wasserpolak*"
This was the name used for people living in Upper Silesia who spoke Silesian (a Polish dialect with many German and Czech elements). German equivalent is *Wasserpolnisch.*

Page 199, "Telegraph Union"
The Telegraph Union and the Wolff Telegraph Agency were the largest German national newspaper telegraph agencies. The Telegraph Union was founded in 1862.

Page 199, "Stinnes"
An industrial interest (dealt in mining, sea trade) founded by Hugo Stinnes (1870-1924).

Page 201, "Lamprecht"
Karl Lamprecht – 1856-1915, was a historian and professor in Bonn, Margurg and Leipzig. His major work was a twelve-volume German history, published in Freiburg. Judging by his extensive marginalia and underlining in the book, Rudolf Steiner worked extensively with Lamprecht's *Modern Science of History* (published 1905 in Freiburg). Among the works on the history of Poland in his library, Rudolf Steiner had a copy of the work *History of Political Ideas in Poland Since Its Division*, edited by W. Feldman and published in 1917.

Page 203, "Kommende Tag"
See note to page 52.

Page 204, "Herr Molt"
Emil Molt – 1876-1936, was Councilor of Commerce, an industrialist, and the director of the Waldorf-Astoria Cigarette Factory in Stuttgart. He took an active role in bringing about the movement for the threefold social organism, and to that end acted as founder of the Waldorf School in Stuttgart (1919). He was also the co-founder of the Kommende Tag Association in Stuttgart and the Futurum Association in Dornach.

Page 210, "We tried this to a large extent with the question of the workers' council"
In the Summer of 1919, Steiner held multiple lectures and led gatherings of workers from the industry councils in Stuttgart in an effort to prepare for the founding

of workers' councils. See CW 337a, "Social Ideas, Social Reality, Social Practice, Vol. 1: Question Evenings and Study Evenings of the Federation for the Threefold Social Organism in Stuttgart, 1919-1920."

Page 211, "the minister that the parody comics wrote up as "Ta-affe"
Count Eduard Taaffe – 1833-1895, was an Austrian statesman, appointed Minister of Education in 1867 and served as Minister President from 1879-1893. His federalist way of thinking led him to attempt a reconciliation of the nationalities. When he tried to eliminate the overwhelming number of demands from the German clerics, the Poles, and the Czechs (and all of the difficulties they caused) through a reform vote (October 1893), he was forced to step down. The mocking comics that Steiner refer to liken Taaffe to an ape ("Ta-affe" = "That ape").

Page 213, "Waldorf School"
See note to p. 59.

Page 214, "Hindenburg"
Paul von Hindenburg – 1847-1934, was a general in the German military, and from 1925-1934 President of the German Reich.

Page 214, "Spengler"
See note to p. 27.

RUDOLF STEINER'S COLLECTED WORKS

The German Edition of Rudolf Steiner's Collected Works (the Gesamtausgabe [GA] published by Rudolf Steiner Verlag, Dornach, Switzerland) presently runs to over 354 titles, organized either by type of work (written or spoken), chronology, audience (public or other), or subject (education, art, etc.). For ease of comparison, the Collected Works in English [CW] follows the German organization exactly. A complete listing of the CWs follows with literal translations of the German titles. Other than in the case of the books published in his lifetime, titles were rarely given by Rudolf Steiner himself, and were often provided by the editors of the German editions. The titles in English are not necessarily the same as the German; and, indeed, over the past seventy-five years have frequently been different, with the same book sometimes appearing under different titles.

For ease of identification and to avoid confusion, we suggest that readers looking for a title should do so by CW number. Because the work of creating the Collected Works of Rudolf Steiner is an ongoing process, with new titles being published every year, we have not indicated in this listing which books are presently available. To find out what titles in the Collected Works are currently in print, please check our website at www.steinerbooks.org, or write to SteinerBooks 610 Main Street, Great Barrington, MA 01230.

Written Work

CW 1	Goethe: Natural-Scientific Writings, Introduction, with Footnotes and Explanations in the text by Rudolf Steiner
CW 2	Outlines of an Epistemology of the Goethean World View, with Special Consideration of Schiller
CW 3	Truth and Science
CW 4	The Philosophy of Freedom
CW 4a	Documents to "The Philosophy of Freedom"
CW 5	Friedrich Nietzsche, A Fighter against His Own Time
CW 6	Goethe's Worldview
CW 6a	Now in CW 30
CW 7	Mysticism at the Dawn of Modern Spiritual Life and Its Relationship with Modern Worldviews
CW 8	Christianity as Mystical Fact and the Mysteries of Antiquity
CW 9	Theosophy: An Introduction into Supersensible World Knowledge and Human Purpose
CW 10	How Does One Attain Knowledge of Higher Worlds?
CW 11	From the Akasha-Chronicle
CW 12	Levels of Higher Knowledge
CW 13	Occult Science in Outline
CW 14	Four Mystery Dramas
CW 15	The Spiritual Guidance of the Individual and Humanity

CW 16	A Way to Human Self-Knowledge: Eight Meditations
CW 17	The Threshold of the Spiritual World. Aphoristic Comments
CW 18	The Riddles of Philosophy in Their History, Presented as an Outline
CW 19	Contained in CW 24
CW 20	The Riddles of the Human Being: Articulated and Unarticulated in the Thinking, Views and Opinions of a Series of German and Austrian Personalities
CW 21	The Riddles of the Soul
CW 22	Goethe's Spiritual Nature and Its Revelation in "Faust" and through the "Fairy Tale of the Snake and the Lily"
CW 23	The Central Points of the Social Question in the Necessities of Life in the Present and the Future
CW 24	Essays Concerning the Threefold Division of the Social Organism and the Period 1915-1921
CW 25	Cosmology, Religion and Philosophy
CW 26	Anthroposophical Leading Thoughts
CW 27	Fundamentals for Expansion of the Art of Healing according to Spiritual-Scientific Insights
CW 28	The Course of My Life
CW 29	Collected Essays on Dramaturgy, 1889-1900
CW 30	Methodical Foundations of Anthroposophy: Collected Essays on Philosophy, Natural Science, Aesthetics and Psychology, 1884-1901
CW 31	Collected Essays on Culture and Current Events, 1887-1901
CW 32	Collected Essays on Literature, 1884-1902
CW 33	Biographies and Biographical Sketches, 1894-1905
CW 34	Lucifer-Gnosis: Foundational Essays on Anthroposophy and Reports from the Periodicals "Lucifer" and "Lucifer-Gnosis," 1903-1908
CW 35	Philosophy and Anthroposophy: Collected Essays, 1904-1923
CW 36	The Goetheanum-Idea in the Middle of the Cultural Crisis of the Present: Collected Essays from the Periodical "Das Goetheanum," 1921-1925
CW 37	Now in CWs 260a and 251
CW 38	Letters, Vol. 1: 1881-1890
CW 39	Letters, Vol. 2: 1890-1925
CW 40	Truth-Wrought Words
CW 40a	Sayings, Poems and Mantras; Supplementary Volume
CW 42	Now in CWs 264-266
CW 43	Stage Adaptations
CW 44	On the Four Mystery Dramas. Sketches, Fragments and Paralipomena on the Four Mystery Dramas
CW 45	Anthroposophy: A Fragment from the Year 1910

Public Lectures

CW 51	On Philosophy, History and Literature
CW 52	Spiritual Teachings Concerning the Soul and Observation of the World
CW 53	The Origin and Goal of the Human Being
CW 54	The Riddles of the World and Anthroposophy
CW 55	Knowledge of the Supersensible in Our Times and Its Meaning for Life Today
CW 56	Knowledge of the Soul and of the Spirit
CW 57	Where and How Does One Find the Spirit?
CW 58	The Metamorphoses of the Soul Life. Paths of Soul Experiences: Part One
CW 59	The Metamorphoses of the Soul Life. Paths of Soul Experiences: Part Two
CW 60	The Answers of Spiritual Science to the Biggest Questions of Existence
CW 61	Human History in the Light of Spiritual Research
CW 62	Results of Spiritual Research
CW 63	Spiritual Science as a Treasure for Life
CW 64	Out of Destiny-Burdened Times
CW 65	Out of Central European Spiritual Life
CW 66	Spirit and Matter, Life and Death
CW 67	The Eternal in the Human Soul. Immortality and Freedom
CW 68	Public lectures in various cities, 1906-1918
CW 69	Public lectures in various cities, 1906-1918
CW 70	Public lectures in various cities, 1906-1918
CW 71	Public lectures in various cities, 1906-1918
CW 72	Freedom – Immortality – Social Life
CW 73	The Supplementing of the Modern Sciences through Anthroposophy
CW 73a	Specialized Fields of Knowledge and Anthroposophy
CW 74	The Philosophy of Thomas Aquinas
CW 75	Public lectures in various cities, 1906-1918
CW 76	The Fructifying Effect of Anthroposophy on Specialized Fields
CW 77a	The Task of Anthroposophy in Relation to Science and Life: The Darmstadt College Course
CW 77b	Art and Anthroposophy. The Goetheanum-Impulse
CW 78	Anthroposophy, Its Roots of Knowledge and Fruits for Life
CW 79	The Reality of the Higher Worlds
CW 80	Public lectures in various cities, 1922
CW 81	Renewal-Impulses for Culture and Science–Berlin College Course
CW 82	So that the Human Being Can Become a Complete Human Being
CW 83	Western and Eastern World-Contrast. Paths to Understanding It through Anthroposophy

CW 84	What Did the Goetheanum Intend and What Should Anthroposophy Do?

Lectures to the Members of the Anthroposophical Society

CW 88	Concerning the Astral World and Devachan
CW 89	Consciousness – Life – Form. Fundamental Principles of a Spiritual-Scientific Cosmology
CW 90	Participant Notes from the Lectures during the Years 1903-1905
CW 91	Participant Notes from the Lectures during the Years 1903-1905
CW 92	The Occult Truths of Ancient Myths and Sagas
CW 93	The Temple Legend and the Golden Legend
CW 93a	Fundamentals of Esotericism
CW 94	Cosmogony. Popular Occultism. The Gospel of John. The Theosophy in the Gospel of John
CW 95	At the Gates of Theosophy
CW 96	Origin-Impulses of Spiritual Science. Christian Esotericism in the Light of New Spirit-Knowledge
CW 97	The Christian Mystery
CW 98	Nature Beings and Spirit Beings – Their Effects in Our Visible World
CW 99	The Theosophy of the Rosicrucians
CW 100	Human Development and Christ-Knowledge
CW 101	Myths and Legends. Occult Signs and Symbols
CW 102	The Working into Human Beings by Spiritual Beings
CW 103	The Gospel of John
CW 104	The Apocalypse of John
CW 104a	From the Picture-Script of the Apocalypse of John
CW 105	Universe, Earth, the Human Being: Their Being and Development, as well as Their Reflection in the Connection between Egyptian Mythology and Modern Culture
CW 106	Egyptian Myths and Mysteries in Relation to the Active Spiritual Forces of the Present
CW 107	Spiritual-Scientific Knowledge of the Human Being
CW 108	Answering the Questions of Life and the World through Anthroposophy
CW 109	The Principle of Spiritual Economy in Connection with the Question of Reincarnation. An Aspect of the Spiritual Guidance of Humanity
CW 110	The Spiritual Hierarchies and Their Reflection in the Physical World. Zodiac, Planets and Cosmos
CW 111	Contained in CW 109
CW 112	The Gospel of John in Relation to the Three Other Gospels, Especially the Gospel of Luke

CW 113	The Orient in the Light of the Occident. The Children of Lucifer and the Brothers of Christ
CW 114	The Gospel of Luke
CW 115	Anthroposophy – Psychosophy – Pneumatosophy
CW 116	The Christ-Impulse and the Development of "I"- Consciousness
CW 117	The Deeper Secrets of the Development of Humanity in Light of the Gospels
CW 118	The Event of the Christ-Appearance in the Etheric World
CW 119	Macrocosm and Microcosm. The Large World and the Small World. Soul-Questions, Life-Questions, Spirit-Questions
CW 120	The Revelation of Karma
CW 121	The Mission of Individual Folk-Souls in Connection with Germanic-Nordic Mythology
CW 122	The Secrets of the Biblical Creation-Story. The Six-Day Work in the First Book of Moses
CW 123	The Gospel of Matthew
CW 124	Excursus in the Area of the Gospel of Mark
CW 125	Paths and Goals of the Spiritual Human Being. Life Questions in the Light of Spiritual Science
CW 126	Occult History. Esoteric Observations of the Karmic Relationships of Personalities and Events of World History
CW 127	The Mission of the New Spiritual Revelation. The Christ-Event as the Middle-Point of Earth Evolution
CW 128	An Occult Physiology
CW 129	Wonders of the World, Trials of the Soul, and Revelations of the Spirit
CW 130	Esoteric Christianity and the Spiritual Guidance of Humanity
CW 131	From Jesus to Christ
CW 132	Evolution from the View Point of the Truth
CW 133	The Earthly and the Cosmic Human Being
CW 134	The World of the Senses and the World of the Spirit
CW 135	Reincarnation and Karma and their Meaning for the Culture of the Present
CW 136	The Spiritual Beings in Celestial Bodies and the Realms of Nature
CW 137	The Human Being in the Light of Occultism, Theosophy and Philosophy
CW 138	On Initiation. On Eternity and the Passing Moment. On the Light of the Spirit and the Darkness of Life
CW 139	The Gospel of Mark
CW 140	Occult Investigation into the Life between Death and New Birth. The Living Interaction between Life and Death
CW 141	Life between Death and New Birth in Relationship to Cosmic Facts
CW 142	The Bhagavad Gita and the Letters of Paul

CW 143	Experiences of the Supersensible. Three Paths of the Soul to Christ
CW 144	The Mysteries of the East and of Christianity
CW 145	What Significance Does Occult Development of the Human Being Have for the Sheaths – Physical Body, Etheric Body, Astral Body, and Self?
CW 146	The Occult Foundations of the Bhagavad Gita
CW 147	The Secrets of the Threshold
CW 148	Out of Research in the Akasha: The Fifth Gospel
CW 149	Christ and the Spiritual World. Concerning the Search for the Holy Grail
CW 150	The World of the Spirit and Its Extension into Physical Existence; The Influence of the Dead in the World of the Living
CW 151	Human Thought and Cosmic Thought
CW 152	Preliminary Stages to the Mystery of Golgotha
CW 153	The Inner Being of the Human Being and Life Between Death and New Birth
CW 154	How does One Gain an Understanding of the Spiritual World? The Flowing in of Spiritual Impulses from out of the World of the Deceased
CW 155	Christ and the Human Soul. Concerning the Meaning of Life. Theosophical Morality. Anthroposophy and Christianity
CW 156	Occult Reading and Occult Hearing
CW 157	Human Destinies and the Destiny of Peoples
CW 157a	The Formation of Destiny and the Life after Death
CW 158	The Connection Between the Human Being and the Elemental World. Kalevala – Olaf Asteson – The Russian People – The World as the Result of the Influences of Equilibrium
CW 159	The Mystery of Death. The Nature and Significance of Middle Europe and the European Folk Spirits
CW 160	In CW 159
CW 161	Paths of Spiritual Knowledge and the Renewal of the Artistic Worldview
CW 162	Questions of Art and Life in Light of Spiritual Science
CW 163	Coincidence, Necessity and Providence. Imaginative Knowledge and the Processes after Death
CW 164	The Value of Thinking for a Knowledge That Satisfies the Human Being. The Relationship of Spiritual Science to Natural Science
CW 165	The Spiritual Unification of Humanity through the Christ-Impulse
CW 166	Necessity and Freedom in the Events of the World and in Human Action
CW 167	The Present and the Past in the Human Spirit
CW 168	The Connection between the Living and the Dead
CW 169	World-being and Selfhood

CW 170 The Riddle of the Human Being. The Spiritual Background of Human History. Cosmic and Human History, Vol. 1

CW 171 Inner Development-Impulses of Humanity. Goethe and the Crisis of the 19th Century. Cosmic and Human History, Vol. 2

CW 172 The Karma of the Vocation of the Human Being in Connection with Goethe's Life. Cosmic and Human History, Vol. 3

CW 173 Contemporary-Historical Considerations: The Karma of Untruthfulness, Part One. Cosmic and Human History, Vol. 4

CW 174 Contemporary-Historical Considerations: The Karma of Untruthfulness, Part Two. Cosmic and Human History, Vol. 5

CW 174a Middle Europe between East and West. Cosmic and Human History, Vol. 6

CW 174b The Spiritual Background of the First World War. Cosmic and Human History, Vol. 7

CW 175 Building Stones for an Understanding of the Mystery of Golgotha. Cosmic and Human Metamorphoses

CW 176 Truths of Evolution of the Individual and Humanity. The Karma of Materialism

CW 177 The Spiritual Background of the Outer World. The Fall of the Spirits of Darkness. Spiritual Beings and Their Effects, Vol. 1

CW 178 Individual Spiritual Beings and their Influence in the Soul of the Human Being. Spiritual Beings and their Effects, Vol. 2

CW 179 Spiritual Beings and Their Effects. Historical Necessity and Freedom. The Influences on Destiny from out of the World of the Dead. Spiritual Beings and Their Effects, Vol. 3

CW 180 Mystery Truths and Christmas Impulses. Ancient Myths and their Meaning. Spiritual Beings and Their Effects, Vol. 4

CW 181 Earthly Death and Cosmic Life. Anthroposophical Gifts for Life. Necessities of Consciousness for the Present and the Future.

CW 182 Death as Transformation of Life

CW 183 The Science of the Development of the Human Being

CW 184 The Polarity of Duration and Development in Human Life. The Cosmic Pre-History of Humanity

CW 185 Historical Symptomology

CW 185a Historical-Developmental Foundations for Forming a Social Judgment

CW 186 The Fundamental Social Demands of Our Time–In Changed Situations

CW 187 How Can Humanity Find the Christ Again? The Threefold Shadow-Existence of our Time and the New Christ-Light

CW 188 Goetheanism, a Transformation-Impulse and Resurrection-Thought. Science of the Human Being and Science of Sociology

CW 189 The Social Question as a Question of Consciousness. The Spiritual Background of the Social Question, Vol. 1

CW 190	Impulses of the Past and the Future in Social Occurrences. The Spiritual Background of the Social Question, Vol. 2
CW 191	Social Understanding from Spiritual-Scientific Cognition. The Spiritual Background of the Social Question, Vol. 3
CW 192	Spiritual-Scientific Treatment of Social and Pedagogical Questions
CW 193	The Inner Aspect of the Social Riddle. Luciferic Past and Ahrimanic Future
CW 194	The Mission of Michael. The Revelation of the Actual Mysteries of the Human Being
CW 195	Cosmic New Year and the New Year Idea
CW 196	Spiritual and Social Transformations in the Development of Humanity
CW 197	Polarities in the Development of Humanity: West and East Materialism and Mysticism Knowledge and Belief
CW 198	Healing Factors for the Social Organism
CW 199	Spiritual Science as Knowledge of the Foundational Impulses of Social Formation
CW 200	The New Spirituality and the Christ-Experience of the 20th Century
CW 201	The Correspondences Between Microcosm and Macrocosm. The Human Being – A Hieroglyph of the Universe. The Human Being in Relationship with the Cosmos: 1
CW 202	The Bridge between the World-Spirituality and the Physical Aspect of the Human Being. The Search for the New Isis, the Divine Sophia. The Human Being in Relationship with the Cosmos: 2
CW 203	The Responsibility of Human Beings for the Development of the World through their Spiritual Connection with the Planet Earth and the World of the Stars. The Human Being in Relationship with the Cosmos: 3
CW 204	Perspectives of the Development of Humanity. The Materialistic Knowledge-Impulse and the Task of Anthroposophy. The Human Being in Relationship with the Cosmos: 4
CW 205	Human Development, World-Soul, and World-Spirit. Part One: The Human Being as a Being of Body and Soul in Relationship to the World. The Human Being in Relationship with the Cosmos: 5
CW 206	Human Development, World-Soul, and World-Spirit. Part Two: The Human Being as a Spiritual Being in the Process of Historical Development. The Human Being in Relationship with the Cosmos: 6
CW 207	Anthroposophy as Cosmosophy. Part One: Characteristic Features of the Human Being in the Earthly and the Cosmic Realms. The Human Being in Relationship with the Cosmos: 7
CW 208	Anthroposophy as Cosmosophy. Part Two: The Forming of the Human Being as the Result of Cosmic Influence. The Human Being in Relationship with the Cosmos: 8

CW 209 Nordic and Central European Spiritual Impulses. The Festival of the Appearance of Christ. The Human Being in Relationship with the Cosmos: 9

CW 210 Old and New Methods of Initiation. Drama and Poetry in the Change of Consciousness in the Modern Age

CW 211 The Sun Mystery and the Mystery of Death and Resurrection. Exoteric and Esoteric Christianity

CW 212 Human Soul Life and Spiritual Striving in Connection with World and Earth Development

CW 213 Human Questions and World Answers

CW 214 The Mystery of the Trinity: The Human Being in Relationship with the Spiritual World in the Course of Time

CW 215 Philosophy, Cosmology, and Religion in Anthroposophy

CW 216 The Fundamental Impulses of the World-Historical Development of Humanity

CW 217 Spiritually Active Forces in the Coexistence of the Older and Younger Generations. Pedagogical Course for Youth

CW 217a Youth's Cognitive Task

CW 218 Spiritual Connections in the Forming of the Human Organism

CW 219 The Relationship of the World of the Stars to the Human Being, and of the Human Being to the World of the Stars. The Spiritual Communion of Humanity

CW 220 Living Knowledge of Nature. Intellectual Fall and Spiritual Redemption

CW 221 Earth-Knowing and Heaven-Insight

CW 222 The Imparting of Impulses to World-Historical Events through Spiritual Powers

CW 223 The Cycle of the Year as Breathing Process of the Earth and the Four Great Festival-Seasons. Anthroposophy and the Human Heart (Gemüt)

CW 224 The Human Soul and its Connection with Divine-Spiritual Individualities. The Internalization of the Festivals of the Year

CW 225 Three Perspectives of Anthroposophy. Cultural Phenomena observed from a Spiritual-Scientific Perspective

CW 226 Human Being, Human Destiny, and World Development

CW 227 Initiation-Knowledge

CW 228 Science of Initiation and Knowledge of the Stars. The Human Being in the Past, the Present, and the Future from the Viewpoint of the Development of Consciousness

CW 229 The Experiencing of the Course of the Year in Four Cosmic Imaginations

CW 230 The Human Being as Harmony of the Creative, Building, and Formative World-Word

CW 231 The Supersensible Human Being, Understood Anthroposophically
CW 232 The Forming of the Mysteries
CW 233 World History Illuminated by Anthroposophy and as the Foundation for Knowledge of the Human Spirit
CW 233a Mystery Sites of the Middle Ages: Rosicrucianism and the Modern Initiation-Principle. The Festival of Easter as Part of the History of the Mysteries of Humanity
CW 234 Anthroposophy. A Summary after 21 Years
CW 235 Esoteric Observations of Karmic Relationships in 6 Volumes, Vol. 1
CW 236 Esoteric Observations of Karmic Relationships in 6 Volumes, Vol. 2
CW 237 Esoteric Observations of Karmic Relationships in 6 Volumes, Vol. 3: The Karmic Relationships of the Anthroposophical Movement
CW 238 Esoteric Observations of Karmic Relationships in 6 Volumes, Vol. 4: The Spiritual Life of the Present in Relationship to the Anthroposophical Movement
CW 239 Esoteric Observations of Karmic Relationships in 6 Volumes, Vol. 5
CW 240 Esoteric Observations of Karmic Relationships in 6 Volumes, Vol. 6
CW 243 The Consciousness of the Initiate
CW 245 Instructions for an Esoteric Schooling
CW 250 The Building-Up of the Anthroposophical Society. From the Beginning to the Outbreak of the First World War
CW 251 The History of the Goetheanum Building-Association
CW 252 Life in the Anthroposophical Society from the First World War to the Burning of the First Goetheanum
CW 253 The Problems of Living Together in the Anthroposophical Society. On the Dornach Crisis of 1915. With Highlights on Swedenborg's Clairvoyance, the Views of Freudian Psychoanalysts, and the Concept of Love in Relation to Mysticism
CW 254 The Occult Movement in the 19th Century and Its Relationship to World Culture. Significant Points from the Exoteric Cultural Life around the Middle of the 19th Century
CW 255 Rudolf Steiner during the First World War
CW 255a Anthroposophy and the Reformation of Society. On the History of the Threefold Movement
CW 255b Anthroposophy and Its Opponents, 1919-1921
CW 256 How Can the Anthroposophical Movement Be Financed?
CW 256a Futurum, Inc. / International Laboratories, Inc.
CW 256b The Coming Day, Inc.
CW 257 Anthroposophical Community-Building
CW 258 The History of and Conditions for the Anthroposophical Movement in Relationship to the Anthroposophical Society. A Stimulus to Self-Contemplation
CW 259 The Year of Destiny 1923 in the History of the Anthroposophical

Society. From the Burning of the Goetheanum to the Christmas Conference
CW 260 The Christmas Conference for the Founding of the General Anthroposophical Society
CW 260a The Constitution of the General Anthroposophical Society and the School for Spiritual Science. The Rebuilding of the Goetheanum
CW 261 Our Dead. Addresses, Words of Remembrance, and Meditative Verses, 1906-1924
CW 262 Rudolf Steiner and Marie Steiner-von Sivers: Correspondence and Documents, 1901-1925
CW 263/1 Rudolf Steiner and Edith Maryon: Correspondence: Letters, Verses, Sketches, 1912-1924
CW 264 On the History and the Contents of the First Section of the Esoteric School from 1904 to 1914. Letters, Newsletters, Documents, Lectures
CW 265 On the History and from the Contents of the Ritual-Knowledge Section of the Esoteric School from 1904 to 1914. Documents, and Lectures from the Years 1906 to 1914, as Well as on New Approaches to Ritual-Knowledge Work in the Years 1921-1924
CW 266/1 From the Contents of the Esoteric Lessons. Volume 1: 1904-1909. Notes from Memory of Participants. Meditation texts from the notes of Rudolf Steiner
CW 266/2 From the Contents of the Esoteric Lessons. Volume 2: 1910-1912. Notes from Memory of Participants
CW 266/3 From the Contents of the Esoteric Lessons. Volume 3: 1913, 1914 and 1920-1923. Notes from Memory of Participants. Meditation texts from the notes of Rudolf Steiner
CW 267 Soul-Exercises: Vol. 1: Exercises with Word and Image Meditations for the Methodological Development of Higher Powers of Knowledge, 1904-1924
CW 268 Soul-Exercises: Vol. 2: Mantric Verses, 1903-1925
CW 269 Ritual Texts for the Celebration of the Free Christian Religious Instruction. The Collected Verses for Teachers and Students of the Waldorf School
CW 270 Esoteric Instructions for the First Class of the School for Spiritual Science at the Goetheanum 1924, 4 Volumes
CW 271 Art and Knowledge of Art. Foundations of a New Aesthetic
CW 272 Spiritual-Scientific Commentary on Goethe's "Faust" in Two Volumes. Vol. 1: Faust, the Striving Human Being
CW 273 Spiritual-Scientific Commentary on Goethe's "Faust" in Two Volumes. Vol. 2: The Faust-Problem
CW 274 Addresses for the Christmas Plays from the Old Folk Traditions
CW 275 Art in the Light of Mystery-Wisdom
CW 276 The Artistic in Its Mission in the World. The Genius of

	Language. The World of Self-Revealing Radiant Appearances – Anthroposophy and Art. Anthroposophy and Poetry
CW 277	Eurythmy. The Revelation of the Speaking Soul
CW 277a	The Origin and Development of Eurythmy
CW 278	Eurythmy as Visible Song
CW 279	Eurythmy as Visible Speech
CW 280	The Method and Nature of Speech Formation
CW 281	The Art of Recitation and Declamation
CW 282	Speech Formation and Dramatic Art
CW 283	The Nature of Things Musical and the Experience of Tone in the Human Being
CW 284/285	Images of Occult Seals and Pillars. The Munich Congress of Whitsun 1907 and Its Consequences
CW 286	Paths to a New Style of Architecture. "And the Building Becomes Human"
CW 287	The Building at Dornach as a Symbol of Historical Becoming and an Artistic Transformation Impulse
CW 288	Style-Forms in the Living Organic
CW 289	The Building-Idea of the Goetheanum: Lectures with Slides from the Years 1920-1921
CW 290	The Building-Idea of the Goetheanum: Lectures with Slides from the Years 1920-1921
CW 291	The Nature of Colors
CW 291a	Knowledge of Colors. Supplementary Volume to "The Nature of Colors"
CW 292	Art History as Image of Inner Spiritual Impulses
CW 293	General Knowledge of the Human Being as the Foundation of Pedagogy
CW 294	The Art of Education, Methodology and Didactics
CW 295	The Art of Education: Seminar Discussions and Lectures on Lesson Planning
CW 296	The Question of Education as a Social Question
CW 297	The Idea and Practice of the Waldorf School
CW 297a	Education for Life: Self-Education and the Practice of Pedagogy
CW 298	Rudolf Steiner in the Waldorf School
CW 299	Spiritual-Scientific Observations on Speech
CW 300a	Conferences with the Teachers of the Free Waldorf School in Stuttgart, 1919 to 1924, in 3 Volumes, Vol. 1
CW 300b	Conferences with the Teachers of the Free Waldorf School in Stuttgart, 1919 to 1924, in 3 Volumes, Vol. 2
CW 300c	Conferences with the Teachers of the Free Waldorf School in Stuttgart, 1919 to 1924, in 3 Volumes, Vol. 3
CW 301	The Renewal of Pedagogical-Didactical Art through Spiritual Science

CW 302 Knowledge of the Human Being and the Forming of Class Lessons
CW 302a Education and Teaching from a Knowledge of the Human Being
CW 303 The Healthy Development of the Human Being
CW 304 Methods of Education and Teaching Based on Anthroposophy
CW 304a Anthroposophical Knowledge of the Human Being and Pedagogy
CW 305 The Soul-Spiritual Foundational Forces of the Art of Education. Spiritual Values in Education and Social Life
CW 306 Pedagogical Praxis from the Viewpoint of a Spiritual-Scientific Knowledge of the Human Being. The Education of the Child and Young Human Beings
CW 307 The Spiritual Life of the Present and Education
CW 308 The Method of Teaching and the Life-Requirements for Teaching
CW 309 Anthroposophical Pedagogy and Its Prerequisites
CW 310 The Pedagogical Value of a Knowledge of the Human Being and the Cultural Value of Pedagogy
CW 311 The Art of Education from an Understanding of the Being of Humanity
CW 312 Spiritual Science and Medicine
CW 313 Spiritual-Scientific Viewpoints on Therapy
CW 314 Physiology and Therapy Based on Spiritual Science
CW 315 Curative Eurythmy
CW 316 Meditative Observations and Instructions for a Deepening of the Art of Healing
CW 317 The Curative Education Course
CW 318 The Working Together of Doctors and Pastors
CW 319 Anthroposophical Knowledge of the Human Being and Medicine
CW 320 Spiritual-Scientific Impulses for the Development of Physics 1: The First Natural-Scientific Course: Light, Color, Tone, Mass, Electricity, Magnetism
CW 321 Spiritual-Scientific Impulses for the Development of Physics 2: The Second Natural-Scientific Course: Warmth at the Border of Positive and Negative Materiality
CW 322 The Borders of the Knowledge of Nature
CW 323 The Relationship of the various Natural-Scientific Fields to Astronomy
CW 324 Nature Observation, Mathematics, and Scientific Experimentation and Results from the Viewpoint of Anthroposophy
CW 324a The Fourth Dimension in Mathematics and Reality
CW 325 Natural Science and the World-Historical Development of Humanity since Ancient Times
CW 326 The Moment of the Coming Into Being of Natural Science in World History and Its Development Since Then
CW 327 Spiritual-Scientific Foundations for Success in Farming. The Agricultural Course

CW 328	The Social Question
CW 329	The Liberation of the Human Being as the Foundation for a New Social Form
CW 330	The Renewal of the Social Organism
CW 331	Work-Council and Socialization
CW 332	The Alliance for Threefolding and the Total Reform of Society. The Council on Culture and the Liberation of the Spiritual Life
CW 332a	The Social Future
CW 333	Freedom of Thought and Social Forces
CW 334	From the Unified State to the Threefold Social Organism
CW 335	The Crisis of the Present and the Path to Healthy Thinking
CW 336	The Great Questions of the Times and Anthroposophical Spiritual Knowledge
CW 337a	Social Ideas, Social Reality, Social Practice, Vol. 1: Question-and-Answer Evenings and Study Evenings of the Alliance for the Threefold Social Organism in Stuttgart, 1919-1920
CW 337b	Social Ideas, Social Realities, Social Practice, Vol. 2: Discussion Evenings of the Swiss Alliance for the Threefold Social Organism
CW 338	How Does One Work on Behalf of the Impulse for the Threefold Social Organism?
CW 339	Anthroposophy, Threefold Social Organism, and the Art of Public Speaking
CW 340	The National-Economics Course. The Tasks of a New Science of Economics, Volume 1
CW 341	The National-Economics Seminar. The Tasks of a New Science of Economics, Volume 2
CW 342	Lectures and Courses on Christian Religious Work, Vol. 1: Anthroposophical Foundations for a Renewed Christian Religious Working
CW 343	Lectures and Courses on Christian Religious Work, Vol. 2: Spiritual Knowledge – Religious Feeling – Cultic Doing
CW 344	Lectures and Courses on Christian Religious Work, Vol. 3: Lectures at the Founding of the Christian Community
CW 345	Lectures and Courses on Christian Religious Work, Vol. 4: Concerning the Nature of the Working Word
CW 346	Lectures and Courses on Christian Religious Work, Vol. 5: The Apocalypse and the Work of the Priest
CW 347	The Knowledge of the Nature of the Human Being According to Body, Soul and Spirit. On Earlier Conditions of the Earth
CW 348	On Health and Illness. Foundations of a Spiritual-Scientific Doctrine of the Senses
CW 349	On the Life of the Human Being and of the Earth. On the Nature of Christianity

CW 350	Rhythms in the Cosmos and in the Human Being. How Does One Come To See the Spiritual World?
CW 351	The Human Being and the World. The Influence of the Spirit in Nature. On the Nature of Bees
CW 352	Nature and the Human Being Observed Spiritual-Scientifically
CW 353	The History of Humanity and the World-Views of the Folk Cultures
CW 354	The Creation of the World and the Human Being. Life on Earth and the Influence of the Stars

SIGNIFICANT EVENTS IN THE LIFE OF RUDOLF STEINER

1829: June 23: birth of Johann Steiner (1829-1910)—Rudolf Steiner's father—in Geras, Lower Austria.

1834: May 8: birth of Franciska Blie (1834-1918)—Rudolf Steiner's mother—in Horn, Lower Austria. "My father and mother were both children of the glorious Lower Austrian forest district north of the Danube."

1860: May 16: marriage of Johann Steiner and Franciska Blie.

1861: February 25: birth of *Rudolf Joseph Lorenz Steiner* in Kraljevec, Croatia, near the border with Hungary, where Johann Steiner works as a telegrapher for the South Austria Railroad. Rudolf Steiner is baptized two days later, February 27, the date usually given as his birthday.

1862: Summer: the family moves to Mödling, Lower Austria.

1863: The family moves to Pottschach, Lower Austria, near the Styrian border, where Johann Steiner becomes stationmaster. "The view stretched to the mountains...majestic peaks in the distance and the sweet charm of nature in the immediate surroundings."

1864: November 15: birth of Rudolf Steiner's sister, Leopoldine (d. November 1, 1927). She will become a seamstress and live with her parents for the rest of her life.

1866: July 28: birth of Rudolf Steiner's deaf-mute brother, Gustav (d. May 1, 1941).

1867: Rudolf Steiner enters the village school. Following a disagreement between his father and the schoolmaster, whose wife falsely accused the boy of causing a commotion, Rudolf Steiner is taken out of school and taught at home.

1868: A critical experience. Unknown to the family, an aunt dies in a distant town. Sitting in the station waiting room, Rudolf Steiner sees her "form," which speaks to him, asking for help. "Beginning with this experience, a new soul life began in the boy, one in which not only the outer trees and mountains spoke to him, but also the worlds that lay behind them. From this moment on, the boy began to live with the spirits of nature...."

1869: The family moves to the peaceful, rural village of Neudorfl, near Wiener-Neustadt in present-day Austria. Rudolf Steiner attends the village school. Because of the "unorthodoxy" of his writing and spelling, he has to do "extra lessons."

1870: Through a book lent to him by his tutor, he discovers geometry: "To grasp something purely in the spirit brought me inner happiness. I know that I first learned happiness through geometry." The same tutor allows him to draw, while other students still struggle with their reading and writing. "An artistic element" thus enters his education.

1871: Though his parents are not religious, Rudolf Steiner becomes a "church child," a favorite of the priest, who was "an exceptional character." "Up to the age of ten or eleven, among those I came to know, he was far and away the most significant." Among other things, he introduces Steiner to Copernican, heliocentric cosmology. As an altar boy, Rudolf Steiner serves at Masses, funerals, and Corpus Christi processions. At year's end, after an incident in which he escapes a thrashing, his father forbids him to go to church.

1872: Rudolf Steiner transfers to grammar school in Wiener-Neustadt, a five-mile walk from home, which must be done in all weathers.

1873-75: Through his teachers and on his own, Rudolf Steiner has many wonderful experiences with science and mathematics. Outside school, he teaches himself analytic geometry, trigonometry, differential equations, and calculus.

1876: Rudolf Steiner begins tutoring other students. He learns bookbinding from his father. He also teaches himself stenography.

1877: Rudolf Steiner discovers Kant's *Critique of Pure Reason*, which he reads and rereads. He also discovers and reads von Rotteck's *World History*.

1878: He studies extensively in contemporary psychology and philosophy.

1879: Rudolf Steiner graduates from high school with honors. His father is transferred to Inzersdorf, near Vienna. He uses his first visit to Vienna "to purchase a great number of philosophy books"—Kant, Fichte, Schelling, and Hegel, as well as numerous histories of philosophy. His aim: to find a path from the "I" to nature.

October 1879-1883: Rudolf Steiner attends the Technical College in Vienna—to study mathematics, chemistry, physics, mineralogy, botany, zoology, biology, geology, and mechanics—with a scholarship. He also attends lectures in history and literature, while avidly reading philosophy on his own. His two favorite professors are Karl Julius Schröer (German language and literature) and Edmund Reitlinger (physics). He also audits lectures by Robert Zimmerman on aesthetics and Franz Brentano on philosophy. During this year he begins his friendship with Moritz Zitter (1861-1921), who will help support him financially when he is in Berlin.

1880: Rudolf Steiner attends lectures on Schiller and Goethe by Karl Julius Schröer, who becomes his mentor. Also "through a remarkable combination of circumstances," he meets Felix Koguzki, a "herb gatherer" and healer, who could "see deeply into the secrets of nature." Rudolf Steiner will meet and study with this "emissary of the Master" throughout his time in Vienna.

1881: January: "... I didn't sleep a wink. I was busy with philosophical problems until about 12:30 a.m. Then, finally, I threw myself down on my couch. All my striving during the previous year had been to research whether the following statement by Schelling was true or not: *Within everyone dwells a secret, marvelous capacity to draw back from the stream of time—out of the self clothed in all that comes to us from outside—into our innermost being and there, in the immutable form of the Eternal, to look into ourselves.* I believe, and I am still quite certain of it, that I discovered this capacity in myself; I had long had an inkling of it. Now the whole of idealist philosophy stood before me in modified form. What's a sleepless night compared to that!"

Rudolf Steiner begins communicating with leading thinkers of the day, who send him books in return, which he reads eagerly.

July: "I am not one of those who dives into the day like an animal in human form. I pursue a quite specific goal, an idealistic aim—knowledge of the truth! This cannot be done offhandedly. It requires the greatest striving in the world, free of all egotism, and equally of all resignation."

August: Steiner puts down on paper for the first time thoughts for a "Philosophy of Freedom." "The striving for the absolute: this human yearning is freedom." He also seeks to outline a "peasant philosophy," describing what the worldview of a "peasant"—one who lives close to the earth and the old ways—really is.

1881-1882: Felix Koguzki, the herb gatherer, reveals himself to be the envoy of another, higher initiatory personality, who instructs Rudolf Steiner to penetrate Fichte's philosophy and to master modern scientific thinking as a preparation for right entry into the spirit. This "Master" also teaches him the double (evolutionary and involutionary) nature of time.

1882: Through the offices of Karl Julius Schröer, Rudolf Steiner is asked by Joseph Kurschner to edit Goethe's scientific works for the *Deutschen National-Literatur* edition. He writes "A Possible Critique of Atomistic Concepts" and sends it to Friedrich Theodore Vischer.

1883: Rudolf Steiner completes his college studies and begins work on the Goethe project.

1884: First volume of Goethe's *Scientific Writings* (CW 1) appears (March). He lectures on Goethe and Lessing, and Goethe's approach to science. In July, he enters the household of Ladislaus and Pauline Specht as tutor to the four Specht boys. He will live there until 1890. At this time, he meets Josef Breuer (1842-1925), the coauthor with Sigmund Freud of *Studies in Hysteria*, who is the Specht family doctor.

1885: While continuing to edit Goethe's writings, Rudolf Steiner reads deeply in contemporary philosophy (Edouard von Hartmann, Johannes Volkelt, and Richard Wahle, among others).

1886: May: Rudolf Steiner sends Kurschner the manuscript of *Outlines of Goethe's Theory of Knowledge* (CW 2), which appears in October, and which he sends out widely. He also meets the poet Marie Eugenie Delle Grazie and writes "Nature and Our Ideals" for her. He attends her salon, where he meets many priests, theologians, and philosophers, who will become his friends. Meanwhile, the director of the Goethe Archive in Weimar requests his collaboration with the *Sophien* edition of Goethe's works, particularly the writings on color.

1887: At the beginning of the year, Rudolf Steiner is very sick. As the year progresses and his health improves, he becomes increasingly "a man of letters," lecturing, writing essays, and taking part in Austrian cultural life. In August-September, the second volume of Goethe's *Scientific Writings* appears.

1888: January-July: Rudolf Steiner assumes editorship of the "German Weekly" (*Deutsche Wochenschrift*). He begins lecturing more intensively, giving, for example, a lecture titled "Goethe as Father of a New Aesthetics." He meets and becomes soul friends with Friedrich Eckstein (1861-1939), a vegetarian, philosopher of symbolism, alchemist, and musician, who will introduce him to various spiritual currents (including Theosophy) and with whom he will meditate and interpret esoteric and alchemical texts.

1889: Rudolf Steiner first reads Nietzsche (*Beyond Good and Evil*). He encounters Theosophy again and learns of Madame Blavatsky in the Theosophical circle around Marie Lang (1858-1934). Here he also meets well-known figures of Austrian life, as well as esoteric figures like the occultist Franz Hartman and Karl Leinigen-Billigen (translator of C.G. Harrison's *The Transcendental Universe.*) During this period, Steiner first reads A.P. Sinnett's *Esoteric Buddhism* and Mabel Collins's *Light on the Path.* He also begins traveling, visiting Budapest, Weimar, and Berlin (where he meets philosopher Edouard von Hartmann).

1890: Rudolf Steiner finishes volume 3 of Goethe's scientific writings. He begins his doctoral dissertation, which will become *Truth and Science* (CW 3). He also meets the poet and feminist Rosa Mayreder (1858-1938), with whom he can exchange his most intimate thoughts. In September, Rudolf Steiner moves to Weimar to work in the Goethe-Schiller Archive.

1891: Volume 3 of the Kurschner edition of Goethe appears. Meanwhile, Rudolf Steiner edits Goethe's studies in mineralogy and scientific writings for the *Sophien* edition. He meets Ludwig Laistner of the Cotta Publishing Company, who asks for a book on the basic question of metaphysics. From this will result, ultimately, *The Philosophy of Freedom* (CW 4), which will be published not by Cotta but by Emil Felber. In October, Rudolf Steiner takes the oral exam for a doctorate in philosophy, mathematics, and mechanics at Rostock University, receiving his doctorate on the twenty-sixth. In November, he gives his first lecture on Goethe's "Fairy Tale" in Vienna.

1892: Rudolf Steiner continues work at the Goethe-Schiller Archive and on his *Philosophy of Freedom. Truth and Science*, his doctoral dissertation, is published. Steiner undertakes to write introductions to books on Schopenhauer and Jean Paul for Cotta. At year's end, he finds lodging with Anna Eunike, née Schulz (1853-1911), a widow with four daughters and a son. He also develops a friendship with Otto Erich Hartleben (1864-1905) with whom he shares literary interests.

1893: Rudolf Steiner begins his habit of producing many reviews and articles. In March, he gives a lecture titled "Hypnotism, with Reference to Spiritism." In September, volume 4 of the Kurschner edition is completed. In November, *The Philosophy of Freedom* appears. This year, too, he meets John Henry Mackay (1864-1933), the anarchist, and Max Stirner, a scholar and biographer.

1894: Rudolf Steiner meets Elisabeth Förster Nietzsche, the philosopher's sister, and begins to read Nietzsche in earnest, beginning with the as yet unpublished *Antichrist*. He also meets Ernst Haeckel (1834-1919). In the fall, he begins to write *Nietzsche, A Fighter against His Time* (CW 5).

1895: May, *Nietzsche, A Fighter against His Time* appears.

1896: January 22: Rudolf Steiner sees Friedrich Nietzsche for the first and only time. Moves between the Nietzsche and the Goethe-Schiller Archives, where he completes his work before year's end. He falls out with Elisabeth Förster Nietzsche, thus ending his association with the Nietzsche Archive.

1897: Rudolf Steiner finishes the manuscript of *Goethe's Worldview* (CW 6). He moves to Berlin with Anna Eunike and begins editorship of the *Magazin fur Literatur*. From now on, Steiner will write countless reviews, literary and philosophical articles, and so on. He begins lecturing at the "Free Literary Society." In September, he attends the Zionist Congress in Basel. He sides with Dreyfus in the Dreyfus affair.

1898: Rudolf Steiner is very active as an editor in the political, artistic, and theatrical life of Berlin. He becomes friendly with John Henry Mackay and poet Ludwig Jacobowski (1868-1900). He joins Jacobowski's circle of writers, artists, and scientists—"The Coming Ones" (*Die Kommenden*)—and contributes lectures to the group until 1903. He also lectures at the "League for College Pedagogy." He writes an article for Goethe's sesquicentennial, "Goethe's Secret Revelation," on the "Fairy Tale of the Green Snake and the Beautiful Lily."

1898-99: "This was a trying time for my soul as I looked at Christianity.... I was able to progress only by contemplating, by means of spiritual perception, the evolution of Christianity .... Conscious knowledge of real Christianity began to dawn in me around the turn of the century. This seed continued to develop. My soul trial occurred shortly before the beginning of the twentieth century. It was decisive for my soul's development that I stood spiritually before the Mystery of Golgotha in a deep and solemn celebration of knowledge."

1899: Rudolf Steiner begins teaching and giving lectures and lecture cycles at the Workers' College, founded by Wilhelm Liebknecht (1826-1900). He will continue to do so until 1904. Writes: *Literature and Spiritual Life in the Nineteenth Century; Individualism in Philosophy*; *Haeckel and His Opponents; Poetry in the Present;* and begins what will become (fifteen years later) *The Riddles of Philosophy* (CW 18). He also meets many artists and writers, including Käthe Kollwitz, Stefan Zweig, and Rainer Maria Rilke. On October 31, he marries Anna Eunike.

1900: "I thought that the turn of the century must bring humanity a new light. It seemed to me that the separation of human thinking and willing from the spirit had peaked. A turn or reversal of direction in human evolution seemed to me a necessity." Rudolf Steiner finishes *World and Life Views in the Nineteenth Century* (the second part of what will become *The Riddles of Philosophy*) and dedicates it to Ernst Haeckel. It is published in March. He continues lecturing at *Die Kommenden*, whose leadership he assumes after the death of Jacobowski. Also, he gives the Gutenberg Jubilee lecture before 7,000 typesetters and printers. In September, Rudolf Steiner is invited by Count and Countess Brockdorff to lecture in the Theosophical Library. His first lecture is on Nietzsche. His second lecture is titled "Goethe's Secret Revelation." October 6, he begins a lecture cycle on the mystics that will become *Mystics after Modernism* (CW 7). November-December: "Marie von Sivers appears in the audience...." Also in November, Steiner gives his first lecture at the Giordano Bruno Bund (where he will continue to lecture until May, 1905). He speaks on Bruno and modern Rome, focusing on the importance of the philosophy of Thomas Aquinas as monism.

1901: In continual financial straits, Rudolf Steiner's early friends Moritz Zitter and Rosa Mayreder help support him. In October, he begins the lecture cycle *Christianity as Mystical Fact* (CW 8) at the Theosophical Library. In November, he gives his first "Theosophical lecture" on Goethe's "Fairy Tale" in Hamburg at the invitation of Wilhelm Hubbe-Schleiden. He also attends a gathering to celebrate the founding of the Theosophical Society at Count and Countess Brockdorff's. He gives a lecture cycle, "From Buddha to Christ," for the circle of the *Kommenden*. November 17, Marie von Sivers asks Rudolf Steiner if Theosophy needs a Western-Christian spiritual movement (to complement Theosophy's Eastern emphasis). "The question was posed. Now, following spiritual laws, I could begin to give an answer...." In December, Rudolf Steiner writes his first article for a Theosophical publication. At year's end, the Brockdorffs and possibly Wilhelm Hubbe-Schleiden ask Rudolf Steiner to join the Theosophical Society and undertake the leadership of the German section. Rudolf Steiner agrees, on the condition that Marie von Sivers (then in Italy) work with him.

1902: Beginning in January, Rudolf Steiner attends the opening of the Workers' School in Spandau with Rosa Luxemberg (1870-1919). January 17, Rudolf Steiner joins the Theosophical Society. In April, he is asked to become general secretary of the German Section of the Theosophical Society, and works on preparations for its founding. In July, he visits London for a Theosophical congress. He meets Bertram Keightly, G.R.S. Mead, A.P. Sinnett, and Annie Besant, among others. In September, *Christianity as Mystical Fact* appears. In October, Rudolf Steiner gives his first public lecture on Theosophy ("Monism and Theosophy") to about three hundred people at the Giordano Bruno Bund. On October 19-21, the German Section of the Theosophical Society has its first meeting; Rudolf Steiner is the general secretary, and Annie Besant attends. Steiner lectures on practical karma studies. On October 23, Annie Besant inducts Rudolf Steiner into the Esoteric School of the Theosophical Society. On October 25, Steiner begins a weekly series of lectures: "The Field of Theosophy." During this year, Rudolf Steiner also first meets Ita Wegman (1876-1943), who will become his close collaborator in his final years.

1903: Rudolf Steiner holds about 300 lectures and seminars. In May, the first issue of the periodical *Luzifer* appears. In June, Rudolf Steiner visits London for the first meeting of the Federation of the European Sections of the Theosophical Society, where he meets Colonel Olcott. He begins to write *Theosophy* (CW 9).

1904: Rudolf Steiner continues lecturing at the Workers' College and elsewhere (about 90 lectures), while lecturing intensively all over Germany among Theosophists (about a 140 lectures). In February, he meets Carl Unger (1878-1929), who will become a member of the board of the Anthroposophical Society (1913). In March, he meets Michael Bauer (1871-1929), a Christian mystic, who will also be on the board. In May, *Theosophy* appears, with the dedication: "To the spirit of Giordano Bruno." Rudolf Steiner and Marie von Sivers visit London for meetings with Annie Besant. June: Rudolf Steiner and Marie von Sivers attend the meeting of the Federation of European Sections of the Theosophical Society in Amsterdam. In July, Steiner begins the articles in *Luzifer-Gnosis* that will become *How to Know Higher Worlds* (CW 10) and *Cosmic Memory* (CW 11). In September, Annie Besant visits Germany. In December, Steiner lectures on Freemasonry. He mentions the High Grade Masonry derived from John Yarker and represented by Theodore Reuss and Karl Kellner as a blank slate "into which a good image could be placed."

1905: This year, Steiner ends his non-Theosophical lecturing activity. Supported by Marie von Sivers, his Theosophical lecturing—both in public and in the Theosophical Society—increases significantly: "The German Theosophical Movement is of exceptional importance." Steiner recommends reading, among others, Fichte, Jacob Boehme, and Angelus Silesius. He begins to introduce Christian themes into Theosophy. He also begins to work with doctors (Felix Peipers and Ludwig Noll). In July, he is in London for the Federation of European Sections, where he attends a lecture by Annie Besant: "I have seldom seen Mrs. Besant speak in so inward and heartfelt a manner...." "Through Mrs. Besant I have found the way to H.P. Blavatsky." September to October, he gives a course of thirty-one lectures for a small group of esoteric students. In October, the annual meeting of the German Section of the Theosophical Society, which still remains very small, takes place. Rudolf Steiner reports membership has risen from 121 to 377 members. In November, seeking to establish esoteric "continuity," Rudolf Steiner and Marie von Sivers participate in a "Memphis-Misraim" Masonic ceremony. They pay forty-five marks for membership. "Yesterday, you saw how little remains of former esoteric institutions." "We are dealing only with a 'framework'... for the present, nothing lies behind it. The occult powers have completely withdrawn."

1906: Expansion of Theosophical work. Rudolf Steiner gives about 245 lectures, only 44 of which take place in Berlin. Cycles are given in Paris, Leipzig,

Stuttgart, and Munich. Esoteric work also intensifies. Rudolf Steiner begins writing *An Outline of Esoteric Science* (CW 13). In January, Rudolf Steiner receives permission (a patent) from the Great Orient of the Scottish A & A Thirty-Three Degree Rite of the Order of the Ancient Freemasons of the Memphis-Misraim Rite to direct a chapter under the name "Mystica Aeterna." This will become the "Cognitive-Ritual Section" (also called "Misraim Service") of the Esoteric School. (See: *Freemasonry and Ritual Work: The Misraim Service* (CW 265). During this time, Steiner also meets Albert Schweitzer. In May, he is in Paris, where he visits Edouard Schuré. Many Russians attend his lectures (including Konstantin Balmont, Dimitri Mereszkovski, Zinaida Hippius, and Maximilian Woloshin). He attends the General Meeting of the European Federation of the Theosophical Society, at which Col. Olcott is present for the last time. He spends the year's end in Venice and Rome, where he writes and works on his translation of H.P. Blavatsky's *Key to Theosophy*.

1907: Further expansion of the German Theosophical Movement according to the Rosicrucian directive to "introduce spirit into the world"—in education, in social questions, in art, and in science. In February, Col. Olcott dies in Adyar. Before he dies, Olcott indicates that "the Masters" wish Annie Besant to succeed him: much politicking ensues. Rudolf Steiner supports Besant's candidacy. April-May: preparations for the Congress of the Federation of European Sections of the Theosophical Society—the great, watershed Whitsun "Munich Congress," attended by Annie Besant and others. Steiner decides to separate Eastern and Western (Christian-Rosicrucian) esoteric schools. He takes his esoteric school out of the Theosophical Society (Besant and Rudolf Steiner are "in harmony" on this). Steiner makes his first lecture tours to Austria and Hungary. That summer, he is in Italy. In September, he visits Edouard Schuré, who will write the introduction to the French edition of *Christianity as Mystical Fact* in Barr, Alsace. Rudolf Steiner writes the autobiographical statement known as the "Barr Document." In *Luzifer–Gnosis*, "The Education of the Child" appears.

1908: The movement grows (membership: 1,150). Lecturing expands. Steiner makes his first extended lecture tour to Holland and Scandinavia, as well as visits to Naples and Sicily. Themes: St. John's Gospel, the Apocalypse, Egypt, science, philosophy, and logic. *Luzifer-Gnosis* ceases publication. In Berlin, Marie von Sivers (with Johanna Mücke (1864-1949) forms the *Philosophisch-Theosophisch* (after 1915 *Philosophisch-Anthroposophisch*) *Verlag* to publish Steiner's work. Steiner gives lecture cycles titled *The Gospel of St. John* (CW 103) and *The Apocalypse* (104).

1909: *An Outline of Esoteric Science* appears. Lecturing and travel continues. Rudolf Steiner's spiritual research expands to include the polarity of Lucifer and Ahriman; the work of great individualities in history; the Maitreya Buddha and the Bodhisattvas; spiritual economy (CW 109); the work of the spiritual hierarchies in heaven and on earth (CW 110). He also deepens and intensifies his research into the Gospels, giving lectures on the Gospel of St. Luke (CW 114) with the first mention of two Jesus children. Meets and becomes friends with Christian Morgenstern (1871-1914). In April, he lays the foundation stone for the Malsch model—the building that will lead to the first Goetheanum. In May, the International Congress of the Federation of European Sections of the Theosophical Society takes place in Budapest. Rudolf Steiner receives the Subba Row medal for *How to Know Higher Worlds*. During this time, Charles W. Leadbeater discovers Jiddu Krishnamurti (1895-1986) and proclaims him the future "world teacher," the bearer of the Maitreya Buddha and the "reappearing Christ." In October, Steiner delivers seminal lectures on "anthroposophy," which he will try, unsuccessfully, to rework over the next years into the unfinished work, *Anthroposophy (A Fragment)* (CW 45).

1910: New themes: *The Reappearance of Christ in the Etheric* (CW 118); *The Fifth Gospel; The Mission of Folk Souls* (CW 121); *Occult History* (CW 126); the evolving development of etheric cognitive capacities. Rudolf Steiner continues his Gospel research with *The Gospel of St. Matthew* (CW 123). In January, his father dies. In April, he takes a month-long trip to Italy, including Rome, Monte Cassino, and Sicily. He also visits Scandinavia again. July-August, he writes the first mystery drama, *The Portal of Initiation* (CW 14). In November, he gives "psychosophy" lectures. In December, he submits "On the Psychological Foundations and Epistemological Framework of Theosophy" to the International Philosophical Congress in Bologna.

1911: The crisis in the Theosophical Society deepens. In January, "The Order of the Rising Sun," which will soon become "The Order of the Star in the East," is founded for the coming world teacher, Krishnamurti. At the same time, Marie von Sivers, Rudolf Steiner's coworker, falls ill. Fewer lectures are given, but important new ground is broken. In Prague, in March, Steiner meets Franz Kafka (1883-1924) and Hugo Bergmann (1883-1975). In April, he delivers his paper to the Philosophical Congress. He writes the second mystery drama, *The Soul's Probation* (CW 14). Also, while Marie von Sivers is convalescing, Rudolf Steiner begins work on *Calendar 1912/1913*, which will contain the "Calendar of the Soul" meditations. On March 19, Anna (Eunike) Steiner dies. In September, Rudolf Steiner visits Einsiedeln, birthplace of Paracelsus. In December, Friedrich Rittelmeyer, future founder of the Christian Community, meets Rudolf Steiner. The *Johannes-Bauverein*, the "building committee," which would lead to the first Goetheanum (first planned for Munich), is also founded, and a preliminary committee for the founding of an independent association is created that, in the following year, will become the Anthroposophical Society. Important lecture cycles include *Occult Physiology* (CW 128); *Wonders of the World* (CW 129); *From Jesus to Christ* (CW 131). Other themes: esoteric Christianity;

Christian Rosenkreutz; the spiritual guidance of humanity; the sense world and the world of the spirit.

1912: Despite the ongoing, now increasing crisis in the Theosophical Society, much is accomplished: *Calendar 1912/1913* is published; eurythmy is created; both the third mystery drama, *The Guardian of the Threshold* (CW 14) and *A Way of Self-Knowledge* (CW 16) are written. New (or renewed) themes included life between death and rebirth and karma and reincarnation. Other lecture cycles: *Spiritual Beings in the Heavenly Bodies and in the Kingdoms of Nature* (CW 136); *The Human Being in the Light of Occultism, Theosophy, and Philosophy* (CW 137); *The Gospel of St. Mark* (CW 139); and *The Bhagavad Gita and the Epistles of Paul* (CW 142). On May 8, Rudolf Steiner celebrates White Lotus Day, H.P. Blavatsky's death day, which he had faithfully observed for the past decade, for the last time. In August, Rudolf Steiner suggests the "independent association" be called the "Anthroposophical Society." In September, the first eurythmy course takes place. In October, Rudolf Steiner declines recognition of a Theosophical Society lodge dedicated to the Star of the East and decides to expel all Theosophical Society members belonging to the order. Also, with Marie von Sivers, he first visits Dornach, near Basel, Switzerland, and they stand on the hill where the Goetheanum will be built. In November, a Theosophical Society lodge is opened by direct mandate from Adyar (Annie Besant). In December, a meeting of the German section occurs at which it is decided that belonging to the Order of the Star of the East is incompatible with membership in the Theosophical Society. December 28: informal founding of the Anthroposophical Society in Berlin.

1913: Expulsion of the German section from the Theosophical Society. February 2-3: Foundation meeting of the Anthroposophical Society. Board members include: Marie von Sivers, Michael Bauer, and Carl Unger. September 20: Laying of the foundation stone for the *Johannes Bau* (Goetheanum) in Dornach. Building begins immediately. The third mystery drama, *The Soul's Awakening* (CW 14), is completed. Also: *The Threshold of the Spiritual World* (CW 147). Lecture cycles include: *The Bhagavad Gita and the Epistles of Paul* and *The Esoteric Meaning of the Bhagavad Gita* (CW 146), which the Russian philosopher Nikolai Berdyaev attends; *The Mysteries of the East and of Christianity* (CW 144); *The Effects of Esoteric Development* (CW 145); and *The Fifth Gospel* (CW 148). In May, Rudolf Steiner is in London and Paris, where anthroposophical work continues.

1914: Building continues on the *Johannes Bau* (Goetheanum) in Dornach, with artists and coworkers from seventeen nations. The general assembly of the Anthroposophical Society takes place. In May, Rudolf Steiner visits Paris, as well as Chartres Cathedral. June 28: assassination in Sarajevo ("Now the catastrophe has happened!"). August 1: War is declared. Rudolf Steiner returns to Germany from Dornach—he will travel back and forth. He writes the last chapter of *The Riddles of Philosophy*. Lecture cycles include: *Human and Cosmic Thought* (CW 151); *Inner Being of Humanity between Death and a New Birth* (CW 153); *Occult Reading and Occult Hearing* (CW 156). December 24: marriage of Rudolf Steiner and Marie von Sivers.

1915: Building continues. Life after death becomes a major theme, also art. Writes: *Thoughts during a Time of War* (CW 24). Lectures include: *The Secret of Death* (CW 159); *The Uniting of Humanity through the Christ Impulse* (CW 165).

1916: Rudolf Steiner begins work with Edith Maryon (1872-1924) on the sculpture "The Representative of Humanity" ("The Group"—Christ, Lucifer, and Ahriman). He also works with the alchemist Alexander von Bernus on the quarterly *Das Reich*. He writes *The Riddle of Humanity* (CW 20). Lectures include: *Necessity and Freedom in World History and Human Action* (CW 166); *Past and Present in the Human Spirit* (CW 167); *The Karma of Vocation* (CW 172); *The Karma of Untruthfulness* (CW 173).

1917: Russian Revolution. The U.S. enters the war. Building continues. Rudolf Steiner delineates the idea of the "threefold nature of the human being" (in a public lecture March 15) and the "threefold nature of the social organism" (hammered out in May-June with the help of Otto von Lerchenfeld and Ludwig Polzer-Hoditz in the form of two documents titled *Memoranda*, which were distributed in high places). August-September: Rudolf Steiner writes *The Riddles of the Soul* (CW 20). Also: commentary on "The Chemical Wedding of Christian Rosenkreutz" for Alexander Bernus (*Das Reich*). Lectures include: *The Karma of Materialism* (CW 176); *The Spiritual Background of the Outer World: The Fall of the Spirits of Darkness* (CW 177).

1918: March 18: peace treaty of Brest-Litovsk—"Now everything will truly enter chaos! What is needed is cultural renewal." June: Rudolf Steiner visits Karlstein (Grail) Castle outside Prague. Lecture cycle: *From Symptom to Reality in Modern History* (CW 185). In mid-November, Emil Molt, of the Waldorf-Astoria Cigarette Company, has the idea of founding a school for his workers' children.

1919: Focus on the threefold social organism: tireless travel, countless lectures, meetings, and publications. At the same time, a new public stage of Anthroposophy emerges as cultural renewal begins. The coming years will see initiatives in pedagogy, medicine, pharmacology, and agriculture. January 27: threefold meeting: " We must first of all, with the money we have, found free schools that can bring people what they need." February: first public eurythmy performance in Zurich. Also: "Appeal to the German People" (CW 24), circulated March 6 as a newspaper insert. In April, *Towards Social Renewal* (CW 23) appears—"perhaps the most widely read of all books on politics appearing since the war." Rudolf Steiner is asked to undertake the "direction and leadership" of the school founded by the Waldorf-Astoria Company. Rudolf Steiner begins to talk about the "renewal" of education. May 30: a building is selected and purchased for the future Waldorf School. August-September, Rudolf Steiner gives a lecture course for Waldorf teachers, *The Foundations of Human Experience (Study of Man)* (CW 293). September 7: Opening of the first Waldorf School. December (into January): first science course, the *Light Course* (CW 320).

1920: The Waldorf School flourishes. New threefold initiatives. Founding of limited companies *Der Kommende Tag* and *Futurum A.G.* to infuse spiritual values into the economic realm. Rudolf Steiner also focuses on the sciences. Lectures: *Introducing Anthroposophical Medicine* (CW 312); *The Warmth Course* (CW 321); *The Boundaries of Natural Science* (CW 322); *The Redemption of Thinking* (CW 74). February: Johannes Werner Klein—later a cofounder of the Christian Community—asks Rudolf Steiner about the possibility of a "religious renewal," a "Johannine church." In March, Rudolf Steiner gives the first course for doctors and medical students. In April, a divinity student asks Rudolf Steiner a second time about the possibility of religious renewal. September 27-October 16: anthroposophical "university course." December: lectures titled *The Search for the New Isis* (CW 202).

1921: Rudolf Steiner continues his intensive work on cultural renewal, including the uphill battle for the threefold social order. "University" arts, scientific, theological, and medical courses include: *The Astronomy Course* (CW 323); *Observation, Mathematics, and Scientific Experiment* (CW 324); the *Second Medical Course* (CW 313); *Color*. In June and September-October, Rudolf Steiner also gives the first two "priests' courses" (CW 342 and 343). The "youth movement" gains momentum. Magazines are founded: *Die Drei* (January), and—under the editorship of Albert Steffen (1884-1963)—the weekly, *Das Goetheanum* (August). In February-March, Rudolf Steiner takes his first trip outside Germany since the war (Holland). On April 7, Steiner receives a letter regarding "religious renewal," and May 22-23, he agrees to address the question in a practical way. In June, the Klinical-Therapeutic Institute opens in Arlesheim under the direction of Dr. Ita Wegman. In August, the Chemical-Pharmaceutical Laboratory opens in Arlesheim (Oskar Schmiedel and Ita Wegman are directors). The Clinical Therapeutic Institute is inaugurated in Stuttgart (Dr. Ludwig Noll is director); also the Research Laboratory in Dornach (Ehrenfried Pfeiffer and Gunther Wachsmuth are directors). In November-December, Rudolf Steiner visits Norway.

1922: The first half of the year involves very active public lecturing (thousands attend); in the second half, Rudolf Steiner begins to withdraw and turn toward the Society—"The Society is asleep." It is "too weak" to do what is asked of it. The businesses—*Der Kommende Tag* and *Futura A.G.*—fail. In January, with the help of an agent, Steiner undertakes a twelve-city German lecture tour, accompanied by eurythmy performances. In two weeks he speaks to more than 2,000 people. In April, he gives a "university course" in The Hague. He also visits England. In June, he is in Vienna for the East-West Congress. In August-September, he is back in England for the Oxford Conference on Education. Returning to Dornach, he gives the lectures *Philosophy, Cosmology, and Religion* (CW 215), and gives the third priests' course (CW 344). On September 16, The Christian Community is founded. In October-November, Steiner is in Holland and England. He also speaks to the youth: *The Youth Course* (CW 217). In December, Steiner gives lectures titled *The Origins of Natural Science* (CW 326), and *Humanity and the World of Stars: The Spiritual Communion of Humanity* (CW 219). December 31: Fire at the Goetheanum, which is destroyed.

1923: Despite the fire, Rudolf Steiner continues his work unabated. A very hard year. Internal dispersion, dissension, and apathy abound. There is conflict—between old and new visions—within the society. A wake-up call is needed, and Rudolf Steiner responds with renewed lecturing vitality. His focus: the spiritual context of human life; initiation science; the course of the year; and community building. As a foundation for an artistic school, he creates a series of pastel sketches. Lecture cycles: *The Anthroposophical Movement; Initiation Science* (CW 227) (in England at the Penmaenmawr Summer School); *The Four Seasons and the Archangels* (CW 229); *Harmony of the Creative Word* (CW 230); *The Supersensible Human* (CW 231), given in Holland for the founding of the Dutch society. On November 10, in response to the failed Hitler-Ludendorf putsch in Munich, Steiner closes his Berlin residence and moves the *Philosophisch-Anthroposophisch Verlag* (Press) to Dornach. On December 9, Steiner begins the serialization of his *Autobiography: The Course of My Life* (CW 28) in *Das Goetheanum*. It will continue to appear weekly, without a break, until his death. Late December-early January: Rudolf Steiner refounds the Anthroposophical Society (about 12,000 members internationally) and takes over its leadership. The new board members are: Marie Steiner, Ita Wegman, Albert Steffen, Elizabeth Vreede, and Guenther Wachsmuth. (See *The Christmas Meeting for the Founding of the General Anthroposophical Society* (CW 260). Accompanying lectures: *Mystery Knowledge and Mystery Centers* (CW 232); *World History in the Light of Anthroposophy* (CW 233). December 25: the Foundation Stone is laid (in the hearts of members) in the form of the "Foundation Stone Meditation."

1924: January 1: having founded the Anthroposophical Society and taken over its leadership, Rudolf Steiner has the task of "reforming" it. The process begins with a weekly newssheet ("What's Happening in the Anthroposophical Society") in which Rudolf Steiner's "Letters to Members" and "Anthroposophical Leading Thoughts" appear (CW 26). The next step is the creation of a new esoteric class, the "first class" of the "University of Spiritual Science" (which was to have been followed, had Rudolf Steiner lived longer, by two more advanced classes). Then comes a new language for Anthroposophy—practical, phenomenological, and direct; and Rudolf Steiner creates the model for the second Goetheanum. He begins the series of extensive "karma" lectures (CW 235-40); and finally, responding to needs, he creates two new initiatives: biodynamic agriculture and curative education. After the middle of the year, rumors begin to circulate regarding Steiner's health. Lectures: January-February, *Anthroposophy* (CW 234); February: *Tone Eurythmy* (CW 278); June: *The Agriculture Course* (CW 327); June-July: Speech [?] Eurythmy (CW 279); *Curative Education* (CW 317); August: (England, "Second International Summer School"), *Initiation Consciousness: True and False Paths in Spiritual Investigation* (CW 243); September: *Pastoral Medicine* (CW 318). On September 26, for the first time, Rudolf Steiner cancels a lecture. On September 28, he gives his last lecture. On September 29, he withdraws to his studio in the carpenter's shop; now he is definitively ill. Cared for by Ita Wegman, he continues working, however, and writing the weekly installments of his *Autobiography* and *Letters to the Members/Leading Thoughts* (CW 26).

1925: Rudolf Steiner, while continuing to work, continues to weaken. He finishes *Extending Practical Medicine* (CW 27) with Ita Wegman.
On March 30, around ten in the morning, Rudolf Steiner dies.

INDEX